Roman Private Law around 200 BC

ROMAN PRIVATE LAW

around 200 BC

ALAN WATSON

at the

EDINBURGH
University Press

© W. A. J. WATSON 1971
EDINBURGH UNIVERSITY PRESS
22 George Square, Edinburgh

ISBN 0 85224 189 5

North America
Aldine Publishing Company
529 South Wabash Avenue, Chicago

Printed in Great Britain by
R. & R. Clark Ltd, Edinburgh

Preface

Since 1960 my main scholarly aim has been the elucidation of private law in the last two centuries of the Roman Republic. Hence my particular pleasure when I was asked to write a book for the Edinburgh University Press and found the present subject was acceptable. Each chapter betrays dependence on earlier works of mine—indeed this book, so different in character and intention, could not have been written (at least, not by me) without these other studies. In the circumstances I hope my apparent indulgence in self-citation (and correction) will be forgiven. Limitless encouragement and continuous criticism since 1957—even before my first work on the Republic—make it right that this book should be dedicated with affection and gratitude to Professor A. M. Honoré and also to his wife, Martine.

A number of friends, scholars in ancient law, Roman history and anthropology, have read this book or parts of it and helped to make it what it is. My thanks are above all due to Mr Robin Seager and to Drs Bernard Jackson, Olivia Robinson and Ian Hamnett. A special debt is owed to Mr Archie Turnbull, Secretary to the Edinburgh University Press, who suggested many improvements in style and thought.

Alan Watson
Edinburgh, March, 1971

Contents

Abbreviations

Bruns	Bruns, *Fontes iuris romani antiqui*, 7th edit. by Gradenwitz (Tübingen, 1909).
Buckland, *Textbook*	Buckland, *A Textbook of Roman Law*, 3rd edit. revised by Stein (Cambridge, 1963).
Corbett, *Marriage*	Corbett, *The Roman Law of Marriage* (reprinted Oxford, 1969).
Daube, *Roman Law*	Daube, *Roman Law: Linguistic Social and Philosophical Aspects* (Edinburgh, 1969).
FIRA	*Fontes iuris romani anteiustiniani*, i, ii, iii (Florence, 1940–3).
Index Itp.	*Index Interpolationum quae in Iustiniani Digestis inesse dicuntur* i, ii, iii and *supplementum* (Weimar, 1929–35).
JRS	*Journal of Roman Studies.*
Kaser, RPR	Kaser, *Das römische Privatrecht*, i, ii (Munich, 1955, 1959).
Kaser, ZPR	Kaser, *Das römische Zivilprozessrecht* (Munich, 1966).
Lenel, *Edictum*	Lenel, *Das Edictum perpetuum*, 3rd edit. (Leipzig, 1927).
Marquardt, *Privatleben*	Marquardt, *Das Privatleben der Römer*, i, ii (reprinted, Darmstadt, 1964).
RE	*Paulys Real-Encyclopädie der classischen Alertumswissenschaft* (Stuttgart, 1873–).

RIDA   *Revue internationale des droits de l'antiquité.*

RISG   *Rivista italiana per le scienze giuridiche*

Rotondi, *Leges*   Rotondi, *Leges publicae populi romani* (reprinted, Hildesheim, 1966).

SDHI   *Studia et Documenta Historiae et Iuris.*

T.v.R.   *Tijdschrift voor Rechtsgeschiedenis.*

Watson, *Obligations*   Watson, *The Law of Obligations in the Later Roman Republic* (Oxford, 1965).

Watson, *Persons*   Watson, *The Law of Persons in the Later Roman Republic* (Oxford, 1967).

Watson, 'Praetor's Edict'   Watson 'The Development of the Praetor's Edict' in JRS lx (1970).

Watson, *Property*   Watson, *The Law of Property in the Later Roman Republic* (Oxford, 1968).

Watson, *Succession*   Watson, *The Law of Succession in the Later Roman Republic* (Oxford, 1971).

ZSS   *Zeitschrift der Savigny-Stiftung (römische Abteilung).*

for Tony and Martine Honoré

Introduction

The period encompassing twenty years on either side of 200 BC is one of the most remarkable in Roman history. It is not enough to call it transitional. It was, above all, decisive.

The second Punic war lasted from 218 to 202 BC, and ended in the complete destruction of Carthaginian military power. From then on, Rome was safe, and – more important still – soon knew she was and that she was supreme in the Mediterranean. The cost to Rome and to her allies, though, in terms of both money and men was great. Thus, the currency was drastically devalued more than once.[1] And whereas at the beginning of the war the census showed about 280,000 citizens eligible for military service, this had fallen by 209 to 237,000. The ravages of Hannibal's armies especially in the south and the prolonged absence of peasants on campaigns ruined much agricultural land and ensured Rome's dependence in the future on grain from Sicily and Africa, and brought about the drift of free citizens from the land. This drift from the land was also aided by the influx of wealth and slaves in the class of citizens willing and able to buy up the farms. But most of Rome's Italian allies had remained loyal and Italy could be thought of much more as a unit than had hitherto been the case.

Rome, partly because of fear of another invasion of Italy, turned her attention in 200 BC to Greece and eventually decisively defeated Philip v of Macedon in 198. In 196 she proclaimed the complete autonomy of the peoples who had been subject to Macedonia. The generosity with which the Romans treated the Greeks at this time is a sign that they were already impressed and influenced by

[1] Cf. e.g. Crawford, 'War and Finance', JRS liv (1964), pp. 29ff.

Greek culture and were ready to accept more. But the events of subsequent years precipitated further wars and conquests.

Political power was completely in the hands of the aristocracy who ruled, not by means of political parties or policies, but by the strength of family groups. Each candidate for public office could rely upon the support of his whole *gens* or failing that, of at least a sept of the *gens*. Dynastic marriages helped to secure support from other families, and personal obligations between powerful individuals strengthened ties between groups. The whole Roman system of patronage, of *patroni* and *clientes*, operated to maintain the *nobiles* in power and to stabilise society. Hence we shall see that the law of the period had a strong aristocratic bias.

But if the internal political scene appeared static this was not true of Roman intellectual life. It is probably right to regard Livius Andronicus' [284(?)–204(?) BC] translation of the *Odyssey* as the first Roman literary production. And it was followed by the comedies and tragedies of the same writer and of Gnaeus Naevius [270(?)–201(?) BC], the comedies of Plautus [255(?)–184 BC] and the works of various types by Ennius [239–169 BC]. Not much later came the elegant plays of Terence whose earliest work, the *Andria*, was first produced in 166 BC. On all of these writers the dominant influence was their Greek forerunners.

Greek philosophy and dialectical method were also making progress at Rome – as the very opposition to them by men like Cato the Censor shows.[1]

The law of the period demonstrates stability and aristocratic calm while showing distinct signs of intellectual fervour. No innovation in these forty years at first sight seems world-shattering. But the time did see statutes on private law which were to keep their importance for centuries to come: thus, the *lex Cincia de donis et muneribus* of 204, the *lex Laetoria* (or *Plaetoria*) *de circumscriptione adolescentium* of 193/192, the *lex Atilia de tutore dando* probably of 210, and very likely the *lex Furia testamentaria*. No other period of similar length in the Republic after the XII Tables produced so many. The *tripertita* of Sextus Aelius Paetus Catus, consul in 198, was a law book of a new type. He also was the first jurist known to us who did not hold a priestly office. The earliest

[1] Cf. e.g. Marrou, *A History of Education in Antiquity* (London, 1956), pp. 245ff.

version of the Aediles' edict on the sale of slaves in the market place either existed in our period or was issued very shortly thereafter. The earliest known praetorian edict dates from 213 BC,[1] and though it itself had little importance for the development of private law or the Edict there is evidence that before the end of the 3rd century BC edicts were substituting new measures of damages for the old civil law penalties. Yet several decades of the 2nd century BC had to run before the Edict was used to effect what in fact were changes in the substantive law.

The two centuries from 300 to 100 BC are, for modern scholars, the darkest period of Roman law. Before 300 relatively little of the Twelve Tables of 451/450 BC is likely to have been changed and we know to a great extent what that codification contained. After 100 BC we have the voluminous writings of Cicero which contain much information on legal matters; and a considerable number of citations of late Republican jurists appears in Justinian's Digest.

The period covered by this book, however, is much clearer than the decades on either side of it, thanks to the plays of Plautus. His comedies are studded with legal scenes, legal jokes and comic references to legal terms which enable us to judge the changes which had occurred in the law since the XII Tables.[2] Admittedly since he was no lawyer and his plays are adaptations of Greek originals one cannot rely upon his technical accuracy, especially in details. But his use of appropriate terminology can prove the existence of the legal institution in question; and when he employs an elaborate scene we can be reasonably sure his point was understandable by his not over-educated audience.

Light is shed on aspects of the law of contract by Cato's *de agri cultura*, and much striking legal detail is provided by Aulus Gellius, an antiquarian writing in the Empire. A few sober facts are given by Livy, but his lack of interest in all things legal makes him a particularly unhelpful source. A great deal, however, can be learnt from Cicero who on occasion tells us what effect behaviour had before recent innovations and sometimes records early legal

---

[1] Livy, 25.1.12. On this topic see Watson, 'Praetor's Edict'.

[2] For instance, as we will see, he jokes about *furtum manifestum, fiducia*, the *exceptio legis Laetoriae, in diem addictio*, makes puns about real security, has a complex scene enabling a rogue to sell a free woman as a slave without incurring a legal obligation, and another making a brothel-keeper a *fur manifestus*, and tells us a considerable amount about *arra* in sale, the forms of words used in divorce, capacity to marry, and *manumissio vindicta*.

discussion. More important still, what he says of law in his own time can often be used to elucidate the law of an earlier period.

Direct information in the legal sources is rather sparse. Two Digest texts seem to give an opinion of Sextus Aelius,[1] and five – plus one in Justinian's Institutes – refer to Cato, though it is not clear whether these relate to the consul of 195 or his son who died in 152 when *praetor designatus*. More significant for us are those legal texts which show the survival of provisions of the XII Tables even after 200 BC, and those which say something of other early statutes. And much can at times be deduced from the known views of jurists of a rather later period.

When all is said, it must freely be admitted that the sources for our knowledge of the law in the decades immediately around 200 BC are very scanty and indirect. Any modern account of Roman private law in the time of Plautus will, accordingly, suffer from three major historical defects. In the first place, the law will appear much simpler and more settled than it actually was[2] since only very rarely do we have information on an actual juristic discussion of the time and usually it is possible to trace the outline of an institution but not its detail. In the second place, the law will appear less archaic than it was. Our lack of information is likely to be greatest precisely where changes were later introduced, and some primitive and unsatisfactory rules will have disappeared without trace. Thirdly, the law will seem much more systematized than it was. Any account has to adopt some plan and fit rules within recognized categories. But such a degree of organization cannot have existed around 200 BC when the only general plan was that of the much earlier XII Tables, which was followed in Sextus Aelius' *tripertita*. The arrangement of the XII Tables cannot even be guessed at, and the fairly neat order in which fragments appear in modern editions is almost entirely due to the fancy of the editors. Moreover, in 200 BC technical terms did not exist for a great many legal concepts whose rules were then in being, and from this can be deduced that the law was far less abstract and less conceptualized than is often supposed.[3]

---

[1] D.19.1.38.1 (Celsus, *8 dig.*) and D.33.9.3.8 (Ulpian, *22 ad Sab.*), though the latter actually talks of Sextus Caecilius.
[2] But the law was very simple.
[3] See Daube, *Roman Law*, pp. 11ff.

CHAPTER I

The Sources of Law

The sources of law around 200 BC were *leges*, *plebiscita*, the opinions and interpretations of the jurists, the Edicts of the higher magistrates and custom.

LEGES AND PLEBISCITA

The law in 200 BC was firmly based on the XII Tables, the code[1] properly attributed to the mid fifth century BC.[2] The original nature, purpose and effect of the XII Tables do not here concern us, and need not be discussed. The law, indeed, in the intervening centuries had undergone considerable change, as a result of legislation[3] and juristic interpretation, and the extent to which the provisions of the XII Tables still operated will be seen in subsequent chapters.

The legislative bodies in our time were the *comitia centuriata*, the *comitia tributa* and the *concilium plebis*.[4]

The organization of the *comitia centuriata* was reformed sometime between 241 and 218 BC,[5] but unfortunately we are better informed of its earlier, than its altered, constitution. In the old form

[1] Not in the modern sense of a complete systematic treatment of the law.
[2] Cf. now above all, Wieacker, 'Die XII Tafeln in ihrem Jahrhundert', *Entretiens sur l'Antiquité classique xiii, Les Origines de la Republique romaine* (Fondation Hardt, Vandoeuvres-Geneva, 1967), pp. 293ff.
[3] Laws (including *plebiscita*) important for private law, subsequent to the XII Tables and before our period, are the *lex Canuleia* of 445 BC, *lex Poetilia Papiria* probably of 326 BC, *lex Aquilia* of 287 BC, *lex Apuleia* of uncertain date.
[4] The *comitia curiata* had long before lost all political power.
[5] Cf. e.g. Mommsen, *Römisches Staatsrecht*, iii, 3rd edit. (Leipzig, 1887), p. 270; Botsford, *The Roman Assemblies* (New York, 1909), pp. 211ff; Taylor, *Roman Voting Assemblies* (Ann Arbor, 1966), pp. 86f.

of the *comitia*, traditionally the work of Servius Tullius, the citizens were divided into five classes according to their wealth, and each class was subdivided into centuries. The richest class had 80 centuries, the second, third and fourth each had 20, and the fifth had 30. In addition, the cavalry (*equites*) had 18, artificers and buglers together had 4 and there was 1 century for all those citizens who had not the wealth qualification for membership of even the lowest class. The centuries were the voting units, and since the first class plus the *equites* had 98 centuries out of a total of 193, the balance of power was firmly with the rich. The voting, moreover, was in order of classes and continued only until a majority was achieved. After the reform it seems that there were still 193 centuries, 18 of which were *equites*, 170 of *pedites* (i.e. footsoldiers), and 5 of unarmed citizens. The *pedites* were classified within the 35 tribes in centuries of *iuniores* (i.e. men liable for military service, 17-45) and *seniores* (i.e. men on the reserve, 46-60) and in 5 classes dependent upon a property qualification. The first and wealthiest class now had only 40 centuries, so that with the *equites* they no longer constituted an absolute majority. The number of centuries in each of the other classes is not known, but it is clear that the balance of power was certainly not with the poor.[1]

In the *comitia tributa* organization and voting was by tribe. There were 35 tribes originally formed on a landholding territorial basis, though by this time every Roman citizen was a member of a tribe as a result of the reform of Appius Claudius in 312 BC and membership was a personal affair, sons normally being in the same tribe as their fathers.[2] The organization was also slanted to the benefit of the wealthy.

The *concilium plebis* was the assembly of the plebeians who were arranged since a *lex Publilia* of 417 BC in tribes. Patricians were excluded from this assembly. Originally it would seem *plebiscita* had not full legislative force but after the *lex Hortensia* of 287 BC they had the same effect as *leges* and were binding on plebeian and patrician alike.[3]

None of these assemblies met in permanent session but each was summoned by a magistrate for the particular piece of legisla-

---

[1] Cf. now Taylor, *Voting Assemblies*, pp. 85 ff.

[2] Cf. in general Mommsen, *Staatsrecht*, iii, pp. 322ff.

[3] Cf. in general Mommsen, *Staatsrecht*, iii, pp. 149ff.

tion which he wished to lay before it. Usually the presidents of the *comitia centuriata* were the consuls; the *comitia tributa* could be summoned only by a magistrate appointed by the whole people (i.e. not an officer of the plebs), normally by consul or praetor, and the *concilium plebis* could be called together only by a magistrate appointed by the plebs. The great bulk of legislation was purely political in character and, though it is not clear why, most of the private law statutes were the work of the *concilium plebis*.

The assembly could deal only with the bill put before it by the magistrate. There could be no discussion or amendment and the power of the assembly was limited to passing or rejecting the bill. By convention however, bills were first discussed by the senate. The senate consisted of 300 members who were chosen by the censors, but former consuls, praetors and curule aediles had a right to be chosen, and hence the senate was a stronghold of aristocratic privilege.[1]

The assemblies had another function important for the development of law, namely the election of magistrates. The *comitia centuriata* elected the consuls and praetors, the *comitia tributa* the aediles.

Jurists of a later age classified laws as *leges perfectae, minus quam perfectae* and *imperfectae*.[2] The first declared void the legal transaction which they prohibited; the second did not make the transaction void but imposed a penalty for infringement of the statute; and the third neither made the transaction void nor imposed a penalty. *Leges perfectae* are not known until much later.[3] Examples from our time[4] of a *lex minus quam perfecta* are the *lex Laetoria*[5] (or perhaps *Plaetoria*) and the *lex Furia testamentaria*[6]; of a *lex imperfecta*, the *lex Cincia*.[7]

---

[1] It was exceptional for a person who was not an ex-magistrate to be a member of the senate.
[2] *Epit. Ulp.*, 1.1f. For literature see the works cited by di Paola, '*leges perfectae*', *Synteleia Arangio-Ruiz*, ii (Naples, 1964), pp. 1075ff.
[3] There is considerable dispute (which does not concern us) but the general opinion is that the first recognizable *lex perfecta* is the *lex Aelia Sentia* of AD 4.
[4] Indeed, they are the standard examples.
[5] Cf. infra, p. 42.
[6] Cf. infra, p. 115.
[7] Cf. infra, pp. 73f.

THE JURISTS

Jurists were important in three ways for the development of the law.

To begin with, they were mainly responsible for the interpretation of statutes and other acts in the law; hence it was primarily the jurists who determined the effectiveness of legal acts. In the almost complete absence of texts giving the opinions of jurists for our period[1] we have to rely on indirect evidence for their attitude to problems of interpretation. But the indirect evidence is very strong since it shows both for the preceding period and the subsequent two centuries that the jurists had considerable freedom and could successfully give a very wide interpretation when this seemed desirable.[2]

Secondly, the jurists adapted existing forms of legal acts to meet new needs. No instance can actually be shown to have originated in this period, but the general importance of the jurists in this connection – especially perhaps in earlier centuries – is apparent from, for example, the adaptation of *mancipatio* for the will *per aes et libram*, for real security by *fiducia*, for marriage by *coemptio* and for adoption; and the use of both *vindicatio in libertatem* and enrolment on the *census* for manumission.

Thirdly the jurists made the law more systematic. This must have been the inevitable result of juristic discussion and argument, of giving opinions and of legal drafting. The writing of law books was still in its infancy – and so was systematization – but a great step forward was taken at this time. Around the beginning of the third century BC there had been published a collection of the forms of action (the *ius Flavianum*)[3] and, if Pomponius

[1] Cf. supra, p. 4.
[2] The best-known early instance is the deliberate misinterpretation of the XII Tables' provision, *si pater filium ter venum duit filius a patre liber esto*, as being restricted to sons and not extending to daughters and remoter descendants who were freed finally from *patriapotestas* by one sale : cf. for all, Daube, 'Texts and Interpretations in Roman and Jewish Law', *Jewish Journal of Sociology*, iii (1961), pp. 3ff at p. 5. For the approach to interpretation in the later Republic, see now Watson, *Limits of Juristic Decision in the Later Roman Republic* (University of Edinburgh, Inaugural lecture, No. 36), reprinted with modifications in *Aufstieg und Niedergang der römischen Welt* i; (Berlin, 1970); 'Narrow, Rigid and Literal Interpretation in the Later Roman Republic', *T.v.R.*, xxxvii (1969), pp. 351ff; cf. *Succession*, pp. 35ff.
[3] D.1.2.2.7 (Pomponius *sing. enchiridii*); Cicero, *de orat.*, 1.41.186; *ad Att.*, 6.18; Livy, 9.46.5.

is to be believed, a book *de usurpationibus* by Appius Claudius Caecus,[1] consul in 307 and 296. But Sextus Aelius Paetus Catus, consul in 198, not only issued a further collection of the forms of action (the *ius Aelianum*),[2] but published a book of a new kind, called the *tripertita*.[3] The work was so named because it gave the text of the XII Tables, the interpretation and the appropriate *legis actio*. The organization betrays the influence of Greek method, though Sextus Aelius himself used to say (quoting Ennius) that he liked to study philosophy, but only in moderation, for he did not altogether approve of it.[4]

Originally the persons interested in law who were in a position to aid its development were the members of the College of Pontiffs, since they had a monopoly of knowledge of the forms of action. This monopoly was broken by the beginning of the third century BC but the *pontifices* and *augures* remained important. Sextus Aelius Paetus Catus was the first jurist known to us who did not hold a priestly office but he was the son of a *pontifex* and the brother of an *augur*. The connection between priestly office and jurisprudence continued until at least 150 BC.[5] It should be stressed, though, that Roman priests of this type were not men who dedicated their whole lives to the service of the gods, but men who had reached high distinction in the State and whose priesthood was simply another important public office. Just as significant – and perhaps even more so – for legal development is the fact that until the end of the second century BC almost all the known jurists were of the senatorial aristocracy.[6]

But if the men whose opinions could develop the law were of the upper classes, the strong popular interest in law should not be overlooked. This is shown for our time especially by the plays of Plautus. It is not just that his plays, though primarily aimed at a popular audience, are full of legal information[7]; they are more

---

[1] D.1.2.2.36. The accuracy of Pomponius' statement has been much doubted : cf., recently (arguing for accuracy), Mayer-Maly, 'Roms älteste Juristenschrift', *Mnemosynon Bizoukides* (Thessalonike, 1960), pp. 221ff.
[2] D.1.2.2.7.
[3] D.1.2.2.38
[4] Cicero, *de re pub.*, 1.18.30.
[5] Cf. above all, Kunkel, *Herkunft und soziale Stellung der römischen Juristen*, 2nd edit. (Graz, Vienna, Cologne, 1967), pp. 45ff.
[6] Cf. above all, Kunkel, *Herkunft*, pp. 41ff; cf. pp. 50ff.
[7] Cf. supra, p. 3 n. 2.

particularly instructive for social attitudes. In the *Mostellaria*, 118ff, the rather drunk Philolaches says:

> nunc etiam volo
> dicere uti homines aedium esse similis arbitremini.
> primumdum parentes fabri liberum sunt:
> i fundamentum supstruont liberorum;
> extollunt, parant sedulo in firmitatem,
> et ut ⟨et⟩ in usum boni et in speciem
> poplo sint sibique, hau materiae reparcunt
> nec sumptus ibi surptui ducunt esse;
> expoliunt : docent litteras, iura, leges,
> sumptu suo et labore
> nituntur ut alii sibi esse illorum similis expetant.

Thus, fathers build up their children like houses, and spare nothing to make them useful and ornamental for the people and themselves. They polish them – teach them *litteras, iura, leges*. That is, Philolaches gives a knowledge of both juristic law and statutory law as the distinguishing mark of fine men, and he mentions no other kind of practical skill. There is nothing to suggest that Plautus is thinking only of the aristocracy. Elsewhere, Plautus represents it as a moral obligation to act for someone in court.[1]

Cause and effect cannot be separated. But it can be confidently asserted that the continuing interest of Rome's leading men in law and their attitude to legal development could not but be stimulated and influenced by the popular interest in law and the appearance in court of men of much less exalted station as unpaid and voluntary advocates.

EDICTA

In the first century BC the *Edictum* of the praetor was the most important instrument of legal development, and the right of Roman magistrates to issue edicts – proclamations informing the people of their orders and their intentions – existed from the earliest times

---

[1] *Cas.* 563ff; cf. for a slightly later period, Terence, *Eun.*, 335ff. According to Dionysius of Halicarnassus, 2.10, the duties assigned by Romulus to the patrician patrons were 'to interpret the laws for their *clientes*, bring law suits for them if they suffered injury, and to help them when they were bringing an action'.

Yet the evidence we have indicates that the Edict did not become significant for the development of private law until well after 200 BC. In our time, modifications of substantive law were not yet made by the Edict and changes were restricted to penalties and damages, and probably also to procedural matters.[1]

But the aediles, with their lesser jurisdiction over streets and market-places in Rome would seem to have introduced the first version of their edict controlling the sale of slaves around our time or a little thereafter.[2]

CUSTOM

Custom is often listed as a source of Roman law,[3] and no doubt early law and legal forms were based on custom. But in times for which records survive custom was not prominent. This cannot surprise in a society which gave such power of development to the jurists. They might reach their decision on the basis of what was customarily done, but in such cases the material source of law was juristic opinion, not custom.

Gaius, however, tells us of one rule of law which had its origin in custom sometime after the XII Tables. This is the use of the *legis actio per pignoris capionem* by a soldier to distrain for his pay, for money allocated for the purchase of his horse, and for money assigned for buying barley for the horse.[4]

The sources of law, in particular the nature and procedure of the *comitia* and the social background of the jurists, could lead us to suppose that the law and its operation would have a strong bias in favour of the upper classes of Roman society. Other factors point in the same direction. Thus, the judges were not professionally

---

[1] See on all this, Watson, 'Praetor's Edict'. The thesis of that article is fundamental to this book. The main arguments are : (1) The development by the praetor of the *bonae fidei actiones tutelae, empti, venditi, locati, conducti, pro socio* and *mandati* – of which the last is probably no earlier than 140 BC – without an edict, though the Edict would apparently have provided the simplest means of creation. (2) The absence from Plautus' plays of any evidence for an edict modifying the substantive law, though the *edictum generale* existed and changed the damages and penalties for *iniuria*. (3) Of the recorded opinions of the jurists, none before Rutilius (probably praetor around 118 BC) relates to the praetor's Edict. (4) The earliest recorded action formulated *in factum* is the *actio Serviana* (or a forerunner) which was known to Cato the Censor and it was introduced without an edict.

[2] Cf. infra, pp. 134f.

[3] Cf. Cicero, *top.*, 5.28.   [4] G.4.26, 27.

trained lawyers working for a salary but were private individuals who gave their services gratuitously and who were appointed by the agreement of the parties from a list (*album iudicum*) drawn up by the magistrates. Only senators were eligible to be on the list.[1] Again, the censors could exercise their powers to control what they considered immoral conduct[2] and whole areas of behaviour, for instance abuse of paternal power, were left to their discretion and were scarcely touched by rules of positive law. But censors were appointed only every five years and could not hold office for more than eighteen months[3] so it is most unlikely that a wrongful act committed in the previous three and a part years would receive their attention unless it was particularly scandalous and involved prominent persons.

The substance of the law does, in fact, reflect the control of the upper classes and shows what might be regarded as aristocratic attitudes not always referable in simple financial terms. To take a few examples. First, the important ceremonies of *confarreatio*[4] and *adrogatio*[5] were such that the institutions themselves were restricted to the rich and powerful. This fact is of especial importance with regard to *adrogatio* since there was no other way of adopting a person *sui iuris*. Secondly, the law of *tutela*[6] was concerned with the safeguarding of the pupil's property and no legal rules existed for the protection of the person of the pupil. Moreover no guarantee (*cautio*) for the protection of the property was taken from the *tutor* who was legally liable only for fraud. It would seem as if the law could afford to leave certain areas to the protection of purely moral sanctions.[7] Thirdly, there is the contrast between on the one hand the virtually total absence of any rule of law peculiar to the institution of slavery[8] and on the other the very particular nature of the *vindicatio in libertatem*.[9] It looks as if those responsible for developing the law were uninterested in slaves as human beings

---

[1] Until the time of the Gracchi : cf. e.g. Kaser, ZPR, p. 35.

[2] It is not appropriate here to go fully into this essentially extra-legal matter, but see e.g. Mommsen, *Staatsrecht*, ii, pp. 375; Suolahti, *The Roman Censors* (Helsinki, 1963), pp. 47ff.

[3] Cf. e.g. Mommsen, *Staatsrecht*, ii, pp. 349f.

[4] Cf. infra, p. 18.   [5] Cf. infra, pp. 30f.   [6] Cf. infra, pp. 35ff.

[7] It should not be thought because the law punishes only fraud that negligence was not regarded as reprehensible : cf. Daube, *Roman Law*, pp. 157ff : and specifically for *tutela*, Aulus Gellius, *N.A.*, 5.13.2, 4, 5.

[8] Cf. infra, pp. 43ff, especially at pp. 50f.   [9] Cf. infra, pp. 51f.

while regarding the citizenship and freedom of Romans as matters of extraordinary importance. Fourthly, the rights and corresponding duties of adjacent landowners were particularly well developed.[1] There is more to this than the mere protection of property (though that, of course, is more the concern of the well-to-do than the poor). It is a recognition of the social importance of harmony between wealthy and powerful neighbours.[2]

[1] Cf. infra, pp. 75ff.
[2] There were, of course, small indigent land-holders who would also benefit from the existence of the rules.

CHAPTER 2

Husband and Wife

BETROTHAL (SPONSALIA)

In early times in Latium, and also apparently in Rome,[1] one promise of marriage was taken from the person responsible for giving the bride, and another from the future bridegroom.[2] The promises each took the form of a contract of *sponsio*[3] and an action was given if a promise was broken without good reason.[4] At some point, probably a later stage of development, the *sponsio* given to the future bridegroom was expressed in alternatives; either a sum of money would be paid or the girl would be given in marriage.[5]

The actionability of *sponsalia* disappeared sometime before the beginning of the first century BC[6] and probably even before our period. Breach of promise of marriage was presumably actionable simply because the betrothal had the form of a *sponsio* which required for its validity a question (*spondesne?*) by the promissee followed by an answer using the same verb (*spondeo*) from the promissor. But in one of Plautus' plays there is a *spondeo* without a preceding *spondesne?*[7] so no action could arise yet the betrothal is

[1] For the general view of the original identity of the law of Latium and Rome see Watson, *Persons*, p. 12, and the authorities cited, n. 1.

[2] Aulus Gellius, *N.A.*, 4.4.1-4; Varro, *de ling. lat.*, 6.70-72.

[3] For this see infra, pp. 117ff.   [4] Aulus Gellius, *N.A.*, 4.4.2.

[5] Varro, *de ling. lat.*, 6.70; cf. Watson, *Persons*, pp. 12f; most recently against the idea that this is a later development, Kaser, *T.v.R.*, xxxvi (1968), p. 430.

[6] This appears clearly from the opinion of Servius recorded in Aulus Gellius, *N.A.*, 4.4.3 that this *ius sponsaliorum* was observed in Latium until citizenship was conferred by the *lex Iulia* of 90 BC. on the whole region. The unspecified action which Cato the Younger (born 95 BC) wished to bring when his engagement to Lepida was broken (Plutarch, *Cato minor*, 7.2) cannot have been on the *sponsio* because the dating is too late.

[7] *Tri.*, 569ff.

certainly regarded as complete.[1] The comic representation of a betrothal in Plautus must correspond to a form actually in use, and hence if the full form for an enforceable *sponsio* is not given the implication must be that *sponsalia* had ceased to be actionable.[2] Naturally, the original form of question and answer would continue to be employed long after *sponsalia* ceased to be actionable and it is not surprising that in four other places Plautus has *spondesne* (or *sponden*)?, *spondeo*.[3] The text which departs from the old form is more revealing than the four which keep to it.

If betrothal owed its original actionability to its form as *sponsio*, then the loss of the right to an action must be attributed to the emergence of an opinion that it was immoral to grant an action for breach of promise, since *sponsiones* in general continued to give rise to an action.

It must be observed, however, that Varro,[4] writing around 47 to 45 BC, was of the opinion that betrothal was actionable in our period. He says the promisor was bound 'for as you see it said in comedies "Do you promise your daughter as wife to my son?" '. And this he declares was thought to be praetorian law in respect of the statute[5] and the decision of the censors based on equity. The line of verse quoted by Varro is from a *fabula palliata*[6] though it cannot be more nearly identified, and the general tenor of the passage with its reference to comedies in the plural (*nam ut in com⟨o⟩ediis vides dici*) suggests that he is not thinking merely of those plays written before the time of Plautus, the most celebrated of all writers of *fabulae palliatae*. Moreover the first such comedies

---

[1] *Tri.*, 603ff.
[2] In the play the girl is betrothed by a brother who is not even her *tutor*. So he has no legal right to arrange his sister's marriage : see infra, p. 21. But one would not expect this to affect the form in which the *sponsalia* are cast : cf. Watson, *Persons*, pp. 14f. Nothing to our purpose can be argued from the *spondeo* without a preceding *spondesne?* in line 20 of the second ending of Terence's *Andria* since that ending is not by Terence and its dating is quite uncertain: cf. Skutsch, 'Der zweite Schluß der *Andria*', *Rheinisches Museum für Philologie*, c (1957), pp. 53ff at pp. 64ff.
[3] *Aul.*, 256; *Poen.*, 1157; *Tri.*, 1157, 1162f.
[4] *de ling. lat.*, 6.71.
[5] The meaning of this is obscure, but presumably the praetors gave an action on the XII Tables' clause on *sponsio* : cf. infra, pp. 117ff.
[6] Cf. Ribbeck, *Scaenicae Romanorum Poesis Fragmenta*, II, 2nd edit. (reprinted, Hildesheim, 1962), p. 114.

cannot be earlier than 240 B C.[1] Probably Varro's opinion should be discounted, firstly because he is not likely to have had enough acquaintance with the historical background to know exactly when the actionability disappeared,[2] secondly because a few lines later he even writes as if breach of promise was still actionable in his own day.[3]

By the time of Plautus, too, it was no longer always the practice for the promise to be exacted from the future bridegroom or someone acting on his account. In none of the passages in the plays where there is an actual betrothal scene is there such a promise, though one is represented as having been given off-stage in the *Cistellaria*.[4]

The *sponsio* is never given by the girl but always on her behalf by her father,[5] and failing him, her mother[6] or brother.[7] A mother never had legal power over her children, and in the *Curculio* and the *Trinummus* the brother was not the girl's *tutor*, so there seems no legal reason for these people to promise the girl in marriage. The explanation is social, not legal : it is improper for the girl to appear to be taking too prominent or interested a rôle in the plans for her marriage. Sometimes the promise will be exacted by the young man's father,[8] but often by the young man himself,[9] even when his father is alive.[10] And there is no indication that the young man takes the promise when he is *sui iuris*, his father when he is *alieni iuris*, though Kupiszewski thinks that this difference in behaviour does depend upon the bridegroom's *status familiae*.[11] This view is, I suggest, too legalistic. In a patriarchal society it is natural

---

[1] Cf. Duckworth, *The Nature of Roman Comedy* (Princeton, 1952), pp. 39f.
[2] But the text can be used as evidence that betrothal had once been actionable, and that the promise of marriage by *sponsio* was rather uncommon in Varro's day. [3] *de ling. lat.*, 6.72; cf. Watson, *Persons*, p. 13.
[4] 98ff : cf. Kupiszewski, '*Das Verlöbnis im altrömischen Recht*', z s s, lxxvii (1960), pp. 125ff at pp. 146ff. But another suggested instance (pp. 140ff) in *Tri.*, 1157ff is not relevant : cf. Watson, *Persons*, pp. 16f.
[5] *Aul.*, 218ff, 255f; *Poen.*, 1156f, 1278f; *Tri.*, 1157f, 1162f.
[6] *Ci.*, 98ff. (It is not said that the mother betrothed her daughter but she took a promise from the young man.) [7] *Cu.*, 671ff; *Tri.*, 569ff.
[8] Plautus, *Tri.*, 571; for a slightly later period, Terence, *And.*, 99ff, 592ff, 951ff.
[9] Plautus, *Aul*, 219, 255f; *Ci.*, 98f; *Poen.*, 1156f, 1278f; *Tri.*, 1157; cf. Terence, *And.*, 951f.
[10] Plautus, *Ci.*, 98f; *Tri.*, 1157f; cf. Terence, *And.*, 951f.
[11] 'Verlöbnis', p. 138.

for a father either to arrange his son's marriage or to let him take the initiative, though a daughter would not be allowed this freedom.

Though there is no direct evidence for the time, the betrothal could take place before the future bride and bridegroom reached the age of puberty.[1]

Probably at this time as later,[2] legal consequences followed from the betrothal.[3]

FORMS OF MARRIAGE

There were two forms of marriage. The older, marriage *cum manu*, put the wife into the power (*manus*) of her husband or of his *paterfamilias* if he had one. In the other form, marriage *sine manu*, the wife remained free of her husband's *manus* and continued under the *potestas* of her *paterfamilias*.[4] By the late third century BC marriage *sine manu* was certainly common,[5] but, though no statistical analysis is possible, it is likely that marriage *cum manu* was much more usual.[6]

Manus was acquired in one of three ways; by *confarreatio*, by *coemptio*, by *usus*.[7]

[1] Cf. for later law, D.23.1.14 (Modestinus, *4 diff.*); *P.S.*, 2.19.1.

[2] Cf. e.g. Gaudemet, 'L'originalité des fiançailles romaines', *Iura*, vi (1955), pp. 47ff at p.55.

[3] No details can be given, but a century later Servius said that the terms father-in-law, mother-in-law, son-in-law and daughter-in-law were acquired even by betrothal: D.38.10.8 (Pomponius, *1 enchiridii*).

[4] Volterra maintains that the legal institution of marriage and *conventio in manum* were independent, and that a distinction between *matrimonium cum manu* and *matrimonium sine manu* did not exist: most recently, 'La *conventio in manum* e il matrimonio romano', RISG, xii (1968), pp. 205ff; review of Watson, *Persons, Iura*, xix (1968), pp. 161ff at p. 163; cf. also, e.g., Villers, '*Manus* et Mariage', *Irish Jurist*, iv (1969), pp. 168ff. But the historically important fact is that sometimes a wife came under the power of her husband and sometimes did not. There was a technical term, *materfamilias*, for a wife *in manu*; Cicero, *top.*, 3.14.

[5] Cf. Corbett, *Marriage*, pp. 90f.

[6] This is deduced from (1) the underlying assumptions in Plautus, *Cas.*, 191ff; cf. Watson, *Persons*, pp. 29ff; (2) the fact that *manus* was acquired automatically by *usus* unless specific steps were taken to avoid it; Watson, *Persons*, pp. 19ff; infra, p. 18; and (3) the assumption in 186 BC that the freedwoman prostitute, Fecenia Hispala, might marry *cum manu*; Livy, 39.19.5 (otherwise husband could not grant her *optio tutoris* in his will).

[7] All three date at least as far back as the XII Tables : cf. G.1.111 and Aulus Gellius, *N.A.*, 3.2.13 for *usus*; Watson '*Usu, farre(o), coemptione*', SDHI, xxix (1963), pp. 337f.

Confarreatio was a religious ceremony involving a sacrifice of a spelt cake (*farreus panis*)[1] to *Iuppiter farreus*[2] in the presence of ten witnesses[3] and of the *pontifex maximus* and *flamen dialis*.[4] Ritual words were spoken[5] but it is uncertain whether by the bride or bridegroom or the officiating priests.[6] If not in law,[7] at least in practice the ceremony was confined to patricians.

Coemptio was the transfer *per aes et libram*[8] applied to marriage, and was an imaginary[9] sale of the woman to her husband. It was commonly used.[10]

When the woman was *sui iuris*, the authority of her *tutor* was needed both for *confarreatio* and *coemptio*.[11],[12]

By *usus*, *manus* was automatically acquired if the couple lived together as husband and wife for a year unless the wife absented herself in each year for three nights.[13],[14] No specific authority had to be given on behalf of the girl for the acquisition of *manus* – as distinct from consent to the marriage[15] – hence the *tutor*'s authority was not needed.[16] *Usus* ensured that marriage *cum manu* re-

---

[1] G.1.112; *Epit. Ulp.*, 9; Servius, *in Georg.*, 1.31.

[2] G.1.112. [3] G.1.112; *Epit. Ulp.*, 9.

[4] Servius, *in Georg.*, 1.31. [5] G.1.112.

[6] For other details of the ceremony – joined chairs, a sacrificed sheep, veiled heads – see also Servius, *in Aen.*, 4.103; 4.374. For modern accounts see above all, Corbett, *Marriage*, pp. 68ff : cf. Kaser, RPR, i, pp. 69f.
[7] A slight argument for a legal restriction may be drawn from Cicero, *pro Flacco*, 34.84 : cf. Watson, *Persons*, p. 24.

[8] For the details of the ceremony *per aes et libram* see infra, p. 61. For *coemptio*, see G.1.113; 1.123; Boethius, II *ad Ciceronis top.*, 3.14.
[9] Presumably a real sale in early times.

[10] Argued from its importance even in the first century B C : *Laudatio Turiae*, 14ff; Cicero, *pro Flacco*, 34.84. It could also be employed to enable a woman to escape from the obligations of the *sacra familiaria* : Cicero, *pro Murena*, 12.27; cf. probably, Plautus, *Ba.*, 976.

[11] Cicero, *pro Flacco*, 34.84.

[12] The question of who is to be regarded in a *coemptio* as the seller of a girl *sui iuris* is unreal in this period : cf. Watson, *Persons*, p. 24 and n. 6.
[13] G.1.110; Aulus Gellius, *N.A.*, 3.2.12f.

[14] It was thus originally akin to *usucapio* : cf. infra, pp. 62ff.

[15] Infra, p. 21.

[16] Though it became necessary by the time of Cicero : argued from *pro Flacco*, 34.84 : cf. Watson, *Persons*, p. 21. Against the contrary arguments of Kaser, *T.v.R.*, xxvi (1968), pp. 430f, see Watson, 'The Limits of Juristic Decision in the Later Roman Republic', *Aufstieg und Neidergang der römischen Welt*, i, (Berlin, 1970), n. 38. Also contra Watson, Volterra, *Iura*, pp. 164f.

mained by far the more common form since the wife had to take positive, and often inconvenient, action in each year to avoid *manus*.

Marriage *sine manu* needed no ceremony and no formalities though it was customary for the bride to be led into her husband's home.[1] It was legally possible for a marriage to take place even when the husband and wife were in different towns.[2]

REQUIREMENTS OF MARRIAGE

A Roman citizen could contract a valid civil law marriage with another Roman and with a Latin on whose city the right of *conubium* had been conferred.[3] Slaves were incapable of marriage.[4] The *lex Canuleia* of 445 BC[5] enacted that patricians and plebeians could intermarry. There was no legal barrier to marriage between a free born citizen and a freed person[6] though such a marriage was regarded as socially and morally objectionable,[7] as was apparently one between a free born citizen and a prostitute.[8] It was customary for a bride to be sought within the same *gens* as the bridegroom[9]

[1] For marriage customs see Marquardt, *Privatleben*, i, pp. 42ff.

[2] Later the *deductio in domum* became essential, at least where the parties were not present together, but this had not occurred by the middle of the first century BC : argued from D.23.2.6 (Ulpian, *35 ad Sab.*); Watson, *Persons*, pp. 26f.

[3] Which Latin cities these were cannot be determined : cf. Mommsen, *Römisches Staatsrecht*, iii (reprinted Darmstadt, 1963), pp. 623ff; Corbett, *Marriage*, pp. 25f. It is unlikely that at this time grants of *conubium* were made to individual Latins, or to peregrine towns or individuals. For *conubium* with peregrines see Mommsen, *Staatsrecht*, iii, p. 715 and n. 1.

[4] Plautus, *Cas.*, 67ff. But it was natural for slaves to use terms appropriate to marriage of their own cohabitation : Plautus, *Mil.*, 1007f.

[5] Livy, 4.1.2; Cicero, *de re pub.* 2.37.63; Florus, 1.17 (1.25).

[6] This appears from D.23.2.44pr (Paul, *1 ad legem Iuliam et Papiam*). Other texts relevant to the problem are Livy, 39.19.5; Dio, 54.16; 56.7; D.23.2.23 (Celsus, *30 dig.*); Cicero, *pro Sestio*, 52.110 : on the whole question see now Watson, *Persons*, pp. 32ff; followed by Treggiari, *Roman Freedmen during the late Republic* (Oxford, 1969), pp. 82ff.

[7] And probably punished by a censorian mark. On attitudes to such a marriage see Cicero, *pro Sestio*, 52.110; Livy, 39.19.5. The latter text is especially significant.

[8] One cannot be too specific because the well-deserving lady of 186 BC, Fecenia Hispala, to whom the right of marrying an *ingenuus* was given and marriage to whom was not to disgrace the husband, was both a freedwoman and a prostitute.

[9] Cf. Marquardt, *Privatleben*, i, p. 30.

and it even seems that some special permission was needed for a woman to marry outside her *gens*.[1, 2]

Ascendant and descendant could not make a valid marriage, but first cousins could from at least 190 BC.[3] The minimum age of a girl for marriage was twelve and the attainment of puberty was legally irrelevant.[4] It would seem that some marriages actually occurred before the girl was twelve – there was no penalty though the marriage was not valid until she reached that age – and consummation before puberty was socially acceptable.[5] For a boy, matters were different and capacity for marriage was determined by his reaching puberty – proved by physical examination – not by his age. The view taken by the Proculian school of jurists in the Empire that fourteen should be the accepted age of puberty for boys is unlikely yet to have been proposed or, at all events, to have achieved any popularity.[6] This difference of attitude in respect of boy and girl is very significant. For a girl, the attainment of puberty or the age of twelve had otherwise little importance whether cere-

[1] One of the privileges given by the *senatusconsultum* to Fecenia Hispala was *enuptio gentis*; Livy, 39.19.5. But no other text mentions *enuptio gentis* and its meaning cannot be further determined. Mommsen's interpretation ['Die römischen Eigennamen', *Römische Forschungen*, i (Berlin, 1864), pp. 1ff at p. 10; *Staatsrecht*, iii, p. 21, n. 1: followed by Marquardt, *Privatleben*, i, p. 30, n. 3; Kübler, RE, 7, 1186; cf. Kaser, 'Ehe und *conventio in manum*', *Iura*, i (1950), pp. 64ff at p. 101] can scarcely be maintained since it requires holding that *quasi ei vir testamento dedisset* relates also to *gentis enuptio*, which is most unlikely in view of the *item* in *tutoris optio item esset* which separates that privilege from those previously mentioned and ties it alone to *quasi etc.* Endogamy *within* a society is commonly associated with keeping marriages within the same rank.

[2] For some restrictions on marriage which are later see Watson, *Persons*, p. 38.

[3] Livy, 42.34.3. relates to 171 BC, but the marriage had been in existence for a considerable time. Cf. for the early first century BC, Cicero, *pro Cluentio*, 5.11; *Phil.*, 2.38.99; Plutarch, *Brutus*, 13.2; *Antonius*, 9.2. In early law marriage even of second cousins was forbidden : cf. fragment of Livy, 20 published in *Hermes*, iv (1870), p. 372.

[4] The implication of Plutarch, *Comparison of Lycurgus and Numa*, 4, is that the age requirement was basic from earliest times. Servius, *in Aen.*, 7.53, appears to think that both the attainment of years and puberty were required, but this is contrary to all other evidence.

[5] This is argued from evidence for later times : see above all, Hopkins, 'The Age of Roman Girls at Marriage', *Population Studies*, xviii (1965), pp. 309ff.

[6] Cf. e.g. G.1.196; *Epit. Ulp.*, 11.28; J.1.22pr.

monially, socially or legally.[1] But for a boy, reaching puberty meant the attainment of political rights, wearing a man's toga and, if he were *sui iuris*, release from tutelage and the right to make a will.

A widow was forbidden to remarry within ten months – the old Roman year – of the death of her husband. The purpose of this was to observe proper mourning, not as in some systems to avoid difficulties over determining the father of a child born to her after remarriage. Hence the relatively long period of waiting and the fact that the restriction applied only to widows and not to divorcées and others. If such a marriage was nonetheless contracted it was valid but penalties were imposed.[2]

The consent was needed of the *patresfamiliarum* of both the bridegroom and the bride.[3] So was that of the bridegroom whether he was *sui iuris* or in *patriapotestas* though it was socially proper for the man to obey his father's directions. If the bride was in *patriapotestas* her consent was legally irrelevant but it was necessary if she was *sui iuris*.[4] In the latter case her *tutor*'s consent was probably needed if the marriage was by *confarreatio* or by *coemptio* and hence created *manus*, but not otherwise, and *manus* could even be acquired by *usus* without the *tutor*'s consent.[5] In practice the girl would be advised on her marriage by her relatives and *tutor*.

EFFECTS OF MARRIAGE

The main consequence of a Roman marriage was that the children were legitimate and in the *patriapotestas* of the husband or of his *pater* if he had one.

---

[1] Though, in time, *tutela mulierum* would be very different from *tutela pupillarum*.

[2] What these would be in this period is uncertain. Numa is said to have enacted that the woman had to sacrifice a pregnant cow : Plutarch, *Numa*, 10.12. But this provision was presumably obsolete. Disabilities in formulary proceedings were imposed by the edicts, *Qui nisi pro certis personis ne postulent* and *Qui ne dent cognitorem* on the woman if *sui iuris*, and on her *paterfamilias*, on her new husband unless he married at the command of his *paterfamilias* and on a *paterfamilias* who allowed his son to marry such a woman (if they knew of the previous husband's death); cf. now Watson, *Persons*, pp. 41ff. But it is unlikely that these edicts, or rather, early forms of them, had yet come into being.

[3] Appears from sources for the Empire : e.g. D.23.2.2 (Paul, *35 ad ed.*)

[4] For all this see Watson, *loc. cit.* The deductions from the edicts *Qui nisi pro certis personis ne postulent* and *Qui ne dent cognitorem* hold whether or not the edicts are later. [5] For this see Watson, *Persons*, pp. 46f and pp. 21ff.

The husband's status was unaffected by marriage but continued bachelorhood and failure to procreate children was frowned upon. The censors asked a citizen if he were married and might impose a punishment if he were not[1]; they might also exact an oath that a marriage was for the purpose of procreating children.[2] Marriage was, moreover, a distinct advantage in obtaining public office and it should be remembered that to become a *flamen* of Jupiter, Mars and Romulus or the *rex sacrorum* one had to be born of parents married by *confarreatio* and be so married oneself.[3]

The effects on the wife's status depended on whether the marriage was *cum manu* or *sine manu*. In the former case she ceased to be a member of her old family and entered the agnatic family and *gens* of her husband, and even her cult duties were now those of her new group. Her legal position was the same as that of a descendant *in potestate*.[4] The term *materfamilias* was restricted to a wife *in manu*.[5] If the marriage was *sine manu*, the wife did not enter her husband's family, remained under the *potestas* of her *paterfamilias* if she had one, and if she were *sui iuris* retained her existing *tutor*. Her capacity to make contracts and own property was not affected by the marriage. Gifts up to any amount were permitted between husband and wife.[6]

It should not be too lightly assumed that in practice a wife *in manu* would be very subordinate to her husband. She might well retain control of the objects comprising her dowry[7] and, especially if her family was powerful, exert considerable pressure on her

---

[1] Cf. e.g. Valerius Maximus, 2.9.1 (403 BC); Plutarch, *Camillus*, 2.2; *Cato maior*, 16.1; Cicero, *de leg.*, 3.3.7; Festus, *s.v. Uxorium*.

[2] E.g. Aulus Gellius, *N.A.*, 4.3.2; 17.21.4 (around 230 BC). The censor Q. Metellus Macedonicus (of 131 BC) argued that all men should be compelled to marry in order to procreate children : Livy, *ep.* 59. Aulus Gellius, *N.A.*, 1.6.1, 2, records a speech of Q. Metellus Numidicus, censor in 102 BC, urging marriage, despite its discomforts, for that reason.

[3] G.1.112.   [4] Cf. infra, pp. 28f.

[5] Cicero, *top.*, 3.14; Aulus Gellius, *N.A.*, 18.6.9. Boethius II, *ad top. Cic.*, 3.14 claims the term *materfamilias* is used only of a wife married by *coemptio*.

[6] The *lex Cincia* of 204 BC forbade gifts above a certain (unknown) value except between specified classes which included spouses. But before the end of the Republic custom changed the law and gifts between husband and wife were prohibited : cf. Watson, *Property*, pp. 229f.

[7] Cf. Plautus, *Aul.*, 167ff; 498ff; *As.*, 84ff; 897f; Watson, *Persons*, pp. 28f. See also Aulus Gellius, *N.A.*, 17.6.1.

husband. Cato the Censor could say that the Romans ruled all other men but were ruled by their wives.[1] On the other hand we know also from Cato that a husband could punish an erring wife. 'When a husband divorces his wife', he is reported as saying, 'he judges her as a censor would, and has full authority if she has behaved shamefully or improperly : she is punished by a fine if she drank wine; she is condemned to death if she misbehaved with another man. . . . If you caught your wife in adultery, you could kill her with impunity without a trial; but if you should commit adultery or an improper act she would not dare to lay a finger on you, nor does the law permit it.'[2] We cannot tell whether this right to punish extended to wives not *in manu* but it seems that even in marriages *sine manu* a husband was entitled to kill an adulterer caught in the act in the matrimonial home.[3]

DIVORCE

A husband had the power to divorce his wife, and so had the husband's *paterfamilias* even when this was against the husband's wishes.[4] But to even matters up, a husband could divorce despite the opposition of his *pater*.[5] When the marriage was *cum manu* neither the wife nor her father could take the initiative for divorce.[6] When it was *sine manu*, the wife could if she were *sui iuris*[7] and if she were in *patriapotestas* her father could, even without her approval,[8] but probably she could not unless with his agreement,[9, 10]

Where the marriage was *cum manu* the divorce required a reverse ceremony to remove the *manus*; *diffarreatio*[11] in the case of *confarreatio*, *remancipatio*[12] in the case of *coemptio* and *usus*. No for-

---

[1] Plutarch, *Cato maior*, 7.2. [2] Aulus Gellius, *N.A.*, 10.23.4,5.
[3] Argued from Plautus, *Mil.*, 1164ff; 1276ff; 1394ff; cf. *Ba.*, 851ff; 917ff.
[4] This continued to be so until well into the Empire : cf. Corbett, *Marriage*, pp. 239ff.
[5] Cf. Terence, *Hec.*, 470ff, especially at 482ff, 493f, 501, 614ff, 654ff, 698ff. The father argues against his son's divorce but there is no suggestion he could legally stop it.
[6] Plautus, *Merc.*, 817ff.   [7] Plautus, *Mil.*, 1164ff.
[8] Cf. fragment from Ennius, *Cresphontes*, reproduced in *Rhet. ad Herenn.*, 2.24.38.
[9] This appears from Plautus, *Men.*, 720-830 and from fact that consent of *filiafamilias* to her marriage was not necessary.
[10] On all this see Watson, *Persons*, pp. 48ff.
[11] Festus, *s.v. Diffarreatio*; Plutarch, *Quaest. Rom.*, 50.
[12] Festus, *s.v. Remancipatam*; G.1.137a.

malities of any kind were needed for divorce where the marriage was *sine manu*, but certain words, like '*Res tuas tibi habeto*', were traditional for indicating repudiation and could be used by either husband or wife.[1]

No grounds were needed but a spouse who had misbehaved or was unjustifiably divorcing the other lost certain rights in respect of the dowry.[2] And a husband who too lightly divorced his wife or treated her cruelly might suffer punishment from the censors.[3]

Captivity of one spouse in the hands of an enemy automatically ended the marriage but long absence by itself did not.[4]

DOWRY (DOS)

Dowry was not necessary for a Roman marriage but it was customary, and it could be created in three ways. *Dotis promissio* was the promise by *stipulatio*[5] to give a dowry.[6] *Dotis datio* was the constitution of a dowry by actually giving it. *Dotis dictio* could be used only by the *paterfamilias* of the bride, the bride herself or a debtor of the bride[7] and it was unusual in appearance since it is the only Roman verbal form where the initiative is taken by the donor, not the recipient. The donor simply promised the dowry and no reply was even needed. The fundamental reason for this lies in the social fact that when a man formally asks a father for his daughter in marriage it would be graceless for him to specify then the sum required as dowry. Rather, the father when agreeing

---

[1] Plautus, *Am.*, 928; *Tri*, 266; cf. Cicero, *Phil.*, 2.28.69 : cf. Watson, *Persons*, pp. 53f. For the significance of the clause see Watson, 'The Divorce of Carvilius Ruga', *T.v.R.*, xxxiii (1965), pp. 38ff. '*I foras*' and '*Baete foras*' were also used : Plautus, *Cas.*, 210; Nonius Marcellus, 77. Söllner, *Zur Vorgeschichte und Funktion der Actio rei uxoriae* (Cologne, 1969), p. 66, n. 11, rightly calls attention to two fragments of Titinius' *Gemina*, nos. XI [from Nonius, 306.29] and XIII [from Nonius, 232.20] in Ribbeck, *Scaenicae Romanorum Poesis Fragmenta*, ii, 2nd edit. (reprinted, Hildesheim, 1962), p. 141. But pace Söllner, *Vorgeschichte*, p. 67 n. 16, these texts are in keeping with the view proposed by Watson, 'Carvilius Ruga'. [2] Cf. infra, p. 27.
[3] Valerius Maximus, 2.9.2 [relates to 307–306 BC : Livy, 9.43.25]; Dionysius Hal., 20.13(2); Cicero, *de re pub.*, 4.6.
[4] Argued from the first 150 lines of Plautus, *Stichus* : cf. Watson, *Persons*, pp. 55f. [5] Cf. infra, pp. 117ff.
[6] Plautus, *Aul.*, 255ff; *Tri*, 1156ff : cf. also *Poe.*, 1278.
[7] But not by a debtor of the *pater* : G.3.95a; *Epit. Gai.*, 2.9.3; *Epit. Ulp.*, 6.2. For this see above all Daube, '*Tres personae possunt dictione dotis obligari*', *Juridical Review*, li (1939), pp. 11ff.

to the marriage of his daughter would promise a certain amount as dowry. *Dotis dictio* was thus originally attached to betrothal, but it had become separated by about 170 BC at the latest.[1] How *dotis dictio* became actionable is a complete mystery. The most widely accepted view is that it was regarded as a *pactum adiectum* or *lex dicta in sponsione* to the *sponsalia*, and was actionable on that account so long as *sponsalia* were actionable, and that when betrothal ceased to give rise to an action the clause relating to the dowry continued to be enforceable.[2] Kaser, indeed, thinks that when the action on *sponsalia* disappeared, an independent *actio ex dotis dictione* emerged.[3] The difficulty for all such opinions is that *pacta adiecta* or *leges dictae* to stipulations did not give rise to an action for at least another three and a half centuries.[4] It seems more plausible to imagine that once the *pater* at the time of betrothal declared the amount of dowry, only a bad-mannered bridegroom would demand a formal stipulation, and that eventually the unilateral declaration was given legal force.[5, 6, 7]

Both *dotis dictio* and *dotis promissio* created a contractual right only, not a real right, and if no special arrangement was made a

[1] Terence, *Heaut.*, 937ff; *And.*, 950f : cf. Watson, *Persons*, pp. 62ff. *Heauton Timorumenos* was produced in 163 BC, and *Andria* in 166 : cf. Duckworth, *Roman Comedy*, p. 60.

[2] Cf. e.g. Bechmann, *Das Dotalrecht*, ii (Erlangen, 1867), pp. 88ff: Daube, '*Tres personae*', pp. 16ff; Kaser, 'Die Wirkung der *dotis dictio*', SDHI, xviii (1951), pp. 169ff at pp. 171ff; RPR, i, pp. 286ff.

[3] 'Wirkung', pp. 183ff; RPR, i, pp. 286ff; *T.v.R.*, xxxvi, p. 431 ; followed by Kupiszewski, 'Verlöbnis', p. 146. But there is no evidence for the action.

[4] Cf. e.g. Buckland, *Textbook*, p. 528; Girard, *Manuel élémentaire de droit romain*, 8th edit. by Senn (Paris, 1929), pp. 637f; Kaser, PRP, i, p. 407 n. 11.

[5] Cf. Watson, *Persons*, pp. 60ff. A suggestion made there (p. 61), that the action might have arisen under the *edictum de pactis* which had originally a wider scope than it had in classical law can be discounted, since the *edictum de pactis* cannot be so early : cf. Watson, 'Praetor's Edict'. In the social circles where *dotis dictio* might be prevalent, social pressures would usually be strong enough, before the introduction of an action, to ensure that the dowry was given.

[6] It should be noted that contrary to common belief no text in Plautus (or from a source relating to that period or earlier) actually shows *dotis dictio* : cf. Watson, *Persons*, pp. 58ff.

[7] Incidentally when a woman *sui iuris* entered *manus* all her property belonged to her husband, and would be treated as dowry : cf. Cicero, *top.*, 4.23.

dowry consisting of money had to be paid in three annual instalments.[1] Though on delivery the husband became the owner of the dowry, the risk thereafter of damage to or destruction of the things forming the dowry was on the wife unless the husband was fraudulent (or perhaps negligent).[2]

Dowry was classified as *recepticia, profecticia* and *adventicia*. It was *recepticia* when there was express agreement as to its fate when the marriage ended. Such agreements first became necessary when Spurius Carvilius Ruga divorced his wife for sterility around 230 BC.[3] Presumably the action was a *condictio* on the *stipulatio*.[4] Dowry given by a paternal ancestor of the bride was called *profecticia* and it differed from the other types in being recoverable when the marriage ended by the wife's death. This quality it retained only during the lifetime of the giver and the right did not pass to his heir even if the heir was himself an ascendant of the woman.[5] Any *dos* which was not *profecticia* was *adventicia*, and when there was no express arrangement as to its fate the wife could sue for its recovery on divorce or on the husband's death by the *actio rei uxoriae*. The origins of this action are not clear[6] – and it had several surprising features – but it too arose after the divorce of Carvilius Ruga.[7] It was unique in that if it was ascertained that the dowry or part of it ought to be returned[8] to the

---

[1] This appears from Polybius, *Hist.*, 32.13 (or 31.27) though there the terms of payment were more complex and, at least to some extent, arranged: cf. Cicero, *ad Att.*, 11.2.2; 11.4a; 11.23.3; 11.25.3; 12.8. There is no evidence for the Republic of the times of payment of dowry which did not consist of money.
[2] By the time of Servius the husband was liable for negligence: D.24.3.66pr (Javolenus, *6 ex post. Labeonis*). But that text does not show liability for negligence in the days of Publius Mucius: cf. Daube, 'Licinnia's Dowry', *Studi Biondi*, i (Milan, 1963), pp. 199ff. Most recently Daube thinks that Publius Mucius considered a husband was liable only for *dolus*: *Roman Law*, pp. 154f.   [3] Aulus Gellius, *N.A.*, 4.3.2.: cf. Watson, 'Carvilius Ruga'.
[4] Infra, p. 117.   [5] Cf. Corbett, *Marriage*, p. 184.
[6] Cf. most recently, Söllner, *Vorgeschichte*, pp. 1ff.
[7] Aulus Gellius, *N.A.*, 4.3.1. It is possible that it came into being only after our period.
[8] The basis of the obligation is not clear, though in Hadrian's Edict it is the *ius civile*. The suggestion has been made with some plausibility that its civil law character derives from the control of the censors over family morals: e.g. Monier, *Manuel élémentaire de droit romain*, i, 6th edit. (Paris, 1949), pp. 291f. The more common view is that it was originally praetorian: e.g. Kaser, 'Die Rechtsgrundlage der *actio rei uxoriae*', RIDA, ii (1949), pp. 511ff at pp. 542ff and the references he gives; RPR, i, p. 288.

plaintiff, the judge was to condemn the defendant to give back whatever part of it should be returned in accordance with equity : *quod eius melius aequius erit*.[1, 2] The amount of the condemnation, that is, could be reduced but not increased. This reduction might fairly occur if the husband had reasonably incurred expenses in connection with the dotal property,[3] or if the wife had committed adultery[4] or was guilty of some other fault such as drinking more wine than was necessary for health.[5] But a bad husband might have to return almost all the dowry even to an adulterous wife.[6] Likewise, part of the dowry could be held back on account of children[7] if the divorce was the fault of the wife, but not if it was the fault of the husband.[8]

A further peculiarity of the *actio rei uxoriae* was that the wife's *paterfamilias* who had given the dowry could not sue alone, but had to join the wife as co-plaintiff.[9]

RELATIONSHIP OTHER THAN CIVIL LAW MARRIAGE

By the first century BC at the latest[10] a marriage between a Roman and a person who had not *conubium* was termed *matrimonium non iustum* and was treated as valid though children born of the union were not in *patriapotestas*. We do not know if *matrimonium non iustum* had any recognition in our period.

When a free woman lived out of marriage with a man she was termed *concubina*, and this designation was not used of a slave woman, or of a free woman involved in a casual love affair.[11] No legal consequences flowed from the relationship.[12]

---

[1] Cicero, *top.*, 17.66; *de off.*, 3.15.61; Boethius, *in top. Cic.*, 17.65.
[2] On this see Watson, *Persons*, pp. 67f.
[3] Though there is no text for the Republic on *impensae*.
[4] Valerius Maximus, 8.2.3; Plutarch, *Marius*, 38. The case involved is from 100 BC : cf. now Watson, *Persons*, p. 69.
[5] Pliny, *Nat. Hist.*, 14 (13).90 (relates to very early second century BC); Aulus Gellius, *N.A.*, 10.23.3, 4, 5 : cf. Watson, *Persons*, pp. 69f; Söllner, *Vorgeschichte*, pp. 71ff. The deduction seems justified even if the actions in the texts are *actiones de moribus*.
[6] Valerius Maximus, 8.2.3; Plutarch, *Marius*, 38.
[7] In classical law, one sixth for each child with a maximum of one half.
[8] Cf. Cicero, *top.*, 4.19, 20; *ad Att.*, 11.23.2.
[9] Cf. e.g. D.24.3.66.2 (Javolenus, *6 ex post. Labeonis*) referring to the later first century BC.
[10] Cicero, *top.*, 4.20.   [11] On this see Watson, *Persons*, pp. 1ff.
[12] Argued from Cicero, *de orat.*, 1.40.183; cf. Watson, *Persons*, pp. 9f.

CHAPTER 3

Parent and Child

CONTENT AND CONSEQUENCES OF PATRIAPOTESTAS

The power of the male head of a family over his children and remoter descendants, *patriapotestas*, was typically Roman. It was theoretically complete and perpetual : it did not end by the attainment of any particular age by the person in *potestas* but continued so long as both the parties remained alive. And when a *paterfamilias* died, all his descendants who did not have a surviving male ancestor became *sui iuris*, and the males in their turn became *patresfamiliarum* even if they had no children. But those who had been in the *potestas* of their grandfather and whose father was still alive would now be in their father's *potestas*.

The *paterfamilias* could expose infants at birth (and this was apparently quite a common practice[1]), put his children of any age to death without cause (*ius vitae necisque*),[2] inflict any lesser punishment upon them, sell them into slavery *trans Tiberim*[3] or into *mancipium* at Rome.[4] He could also give his son[5] in noxal surrender[6] for any delict which the son had committed. His consent was needed for a son's marriage and was alone necessary for that of a daughter. The *pater* could divorce his son even against the latter's

---

[1] Cf. e.g. Plautus, *Cas.*, 41f; *Ci.* 124; Terence, *Heaut.*, 627.

[2] For the numerous instances of sons or daughters put to death by their fathers see the list by Sachers, RE, 22 *s.v. Potestas patria*, 1046ff at 1086f; as amended by Yaron, '*Vitae necisque potestas*', *T.v.R.*, xxx (1962), pp. 243ff at pp. 243f.

[3] Such children ceased to be Roman citizens and their citizenship did not revive by *postliminium* : Cicero, *de orat.*, 1.40.181, 182; *pro Caecina*, 34.98.

[4] In very early law it appears that there were restrictions on the father's rights. But these had disappeared long before our time : see Watson, *Persons*, pp. 98f.

[5] There is no evidence that the right of noxal surrender of daughters (cf. J.4.8.7) was still in existence.   [6] Cf. infra, p. 159.

wishes, and also his daughter provided in this case that the marriage was *sine manu*. If the daughter was married *cum manu* she would no longer be in the *potestas* of her father.

The sole check on the father's arbitrary use of his power lay in the censors who might take notice of excessive punishment and improper behaviour.[1] But not too much reliance could be placed on this since the censors might be just as arbitrary as a father. Thus, when a senator embraced his wife before the eyes of his daughter, Cato as censor expelled him from the senate.[2]

Only persons *sui iuris* could own property though it was common for a father to give his children, especially sons, a fund called the *peculium*[3] which they could administer as if it were their own. Technically it remained in the ownership of the father, and the privilege could be withdrawn. Moreover, even though a son was granted the right to administer the *peculium* this did not entitle him to use it to make a gift[4] or free a slave.[5] There were no legal restrictions on a *filiusfamilias*, as such, entering a contract, but any rights acquired under the contract – even that of sueing on it[6] – adhered to the *pater*, not the *filius*. On the other hand, the other contracting party acquired no rights of any kind against the *paterfamilias*,[7] not even against the *peculium*.[8]

The legal disabilities of a *filiusfamilias* were confined to private law, and no distinction existed in public law between those *sui iuris* and those *alieni iuris*. Nonetheless, as Daube has recently made clear,[9] a *filiusfamilias* was unlikely to be successful in public life if he did not have his father's support. He would not otherwise have the financial resources needed to meet the expenses of office – such as the games organized by the aediles and the praetors – and to secure further election.

ACQUISITION OF PATRIAPOTESTAS

A child born in a valid civil law marriage whether *cum manu* or *sine manu* was in the *patriapotestas* of the husband or his *pater-*

---

[1] Dionysius Hal., 20.13(2).   [2] Plutarch, *Cato maior*, 17.7.
[3] Plautus, *Cap.*, 982, 1013.   [4] Cf. Cicero, *de leg.*, 2.20.50.
[5] See now, e.g. Daube, *Roman Law*, pp. 75ff.
[6] Cf. e.g. D.44.1.14 (Alfenus Varus, *2 dig.*).
[7] The praetorian *actiones adiecticiae qualitatis* are a later invention : cf. Watson, 'Praetor's Edict'.
[8] On the question of actions against the penniless *filius familias* see infra, p. 165.   [9] Daube, *Roman Law*, pp. 84f.

familias. An illegitimate child was not in the *potestas* of his father nor, since *potestas* was patrilineal, in the *potestas* of his mother's *pater.*

It was the custom for the father to pick up the child (*tollere liberum*) which had been placed before him, thus showing his intention to rear it. But the custom had no legal significance.[1]

Patriapotestas could also be acquired by adoption of which there were two forms, *adrogatio* and *adoptio.*

Adrogatio was the adoption of a male who was *sui iuris* and so involved the extinction of a Roman family. Not surprisingly, therefore, it was very formal and required first a sacral then a public act. The first step was an enquiry by the pontiffs into the advisability of the adoption. We have considerable information on the matters which the pontiffs took into account[2] though we do not know how far the rules which they followed were strictly set down[3] or should properly be regarded as rules of law. But Cicero, addressing the *pontifices*, talks in this connection of the *ius adoptionis.*[4] The adopter, we are told, should be too old to pro-

---

[1] Though Volterra argued, I thought, that this act, not birth, created *patriapotestas* : e.g. 'Un osservazione in tema di *tollere liberos*', *Festschrift Schulz*, i (Weimar, 1951), pp. 388ff; 'Ancora in tema di *tollere liberos*', *Iura*, iii (1952), pp. 216f; followed by Gualandi, '*Tollere liberos*', RISG, vi (1952–3), pp. 413ff; Capogrossi Colognesi, *La struttura della proprietà e la formazione dei 'iura praediorum' nell'età repubblicana* (Milan, 1969), p. 225 : contra Watson, *Persons*, pp. 72ff; accepted by Crook, *Classical Review*, xix (1969), p. 90. D.40.4.29 (Scaevola, *23 dig.*) is conclusive. But Volterra now writes [Review of Watson, *Persons*, *Iura*, xix (1968), pp. 161ff at pp. 168f] that he has never claimed that for the acquisition of *patriapotestas* the act of *tollere liberum* was necessary. Gualandi unequivocally has ['*Tollere liberos*', p. 417], and it is difficult to see what else Volterra – who attributes precise legal significance to the act – can mean, for instance, when he says of *tollere liberos* 'sembra che avesse efficacia giuridica agli effetti dell'assunzione della *patria potestas* e che potesse essere compiuto soltanto da cittadini romani nei confronti dei figli nati dall'unione coniugale con una cittadina romana' : *Novissimo Digesto italiano*, vii (Turin, 1965), p. 309, *s.v. filiazione.*
[2] Primarily from the adoption of Clodius.
[3] It may be that there was a general tendency here towards rigidity : cf. Watson, *Persons*, pp. 82ff.
[4] *de domo sua*, 13.34. The point is not over strong since it is to Cicero's interest to persuade these pontiffs that the law had been breached when they permitted the *adrogatio* of Clodius. In general I incline to the view that the *pontifices* were not bound by any rules of law but to a large extent observed standard practices.

create children[1] but (when he was able) ought to have tried, that is, have been married[2]; he ought to have no children of his own, and not be much younger than the person to be adopted.[3] The pontiffs had to consider the reasons of both parties for the adoption, the interest of birth, rank and religion.[4]

If the pontiffs approved of the *adrogatio*, the adoption next went before the *comitia curiata* which, as in other instances involving religion, was summoned by the *pontifex maximus* and was called the *comitia calata*. The adoptee was asked, *auctorne es, ut in te P. Fonteius* (or whoever was the *adrogans*) *vitae necisque potestatem habeat ut in filio?*,[5] and the *adrogans* was also asked if he agreed to the adoption. A *rogatio*[6] was put to the people : *Velitis, iubeatis, uti L. Valerius L. Titio tam iure legeque filius siet, quam si ex eo patre matreque familias eius natus esset, utique ei vitae necisque in eum potestas siet, uti patri endo filio est. Haec ita, uti dixi, ita vos, Quirites, rogo.*[7] This part of the proceedings, therefore, was true legislation.[8] The proceedings probably also included a formal abjuring of the *sacra* of his *gens* (*detestatio sacrorum*) by the person being adrogated.[9] The *comitia* met only at Rome.

Women were not admitted to the *comitia* and hence only males could be adrogated. It is perhaps unlikely that *impuberes* could be

[1] Cicero, *de domo sua*, 13.34; Aulus Gellius, *N.A.*, 5.19.6.

[2] Cicero, *de domo sua*, 13.34. But in classical law a bachelor could adrogate [*Epit. Ulp.*, 8.6; D.1.7.30 (Paul, *1 reg.*)] and Terence, whose accuracy on such a point can scarcely be trusted, shows a bachelor adopting his nephew : *Adelphoe*, 47, 114.

[3] Cicero, *de domo sua*, 13.36. In early classical law it was disputed whether an older person could be adopted by a younger : G.1.106. Again the implication for our period is that there were no fixed rules of law but there were standard practices.

[4] Cicero, *de domo sua*, 13.34 : cf. Aulus Gellius, *N.A.*, 5.19.6.

[5] Cicero, *de domo sua*, 29.77.   [6] Cf. supra, pp. 5ff.

[7] Aulus Gellius, *N.A.*, 5.19.9.

[8] And was still so in Cicero's time though in practice the requirements were not strictly observed : argued from Cicero, *de domo sua*, 16.41; cf. Watson, *Persons*, pp. 85f.

[9] But *detestatio sacrorum*, which is mentioned only in two texts (Aulus Gellius, *N.A.*, 7.12.1 and 15.27.3), neither of which expressly refers to *adrogatio*, is very obscure : cf. above all, Kübler, RE, 1A, 165ff *s.v. Sacrorum detestatio*. In later times there was further a *iusiurandum* which was formulated by Quintus Mucius when he was *pontifex maximus* : Aulus Gellius, *N.A.*, 5.19.6. The context suggests this was concerned with protecting the property rights of the adoptee.

adrogated.[1] The formality of the whole proceedings was such that *adrogatio* must have been confined to the upper classes.

Adoptio was the adoption of a person *alieni iuris* and consequently was less formal. It was a juristic adaptation of the XII Tables' provision that if a father sold his son three times the son became free of the father's *potestas*.[2] The father transferred the son by *mancipatio*, the recipient manumitted him and the son fell back into *potestas*, the *mancipatio* and *manumissio* were performed again, a third *mancipatio* took place and this was either followed by a further manumission whereupon the adopter claimed before the praetor that the son was his and the true father put up no defence, or alternatively the son was not remancipated to the father but the adopter claimed him from the person to whom he had been mancipated. Only one *mancipatio* by the *paterfamilias* was needed where the person to be given in adoption was a daughter or grandchild.[3] The consent of the person being adopted was not necessary,[4] and he could be an *impubes*.

The main effect of adoption was that the person being adopted came into the *patriapotestas* of the adopter. Hence, all the obligations of the adoptee were extinguished.[5] But further, the adoptee ceased to be a member of his *gens*[6] and entered the *gens*[7] and *tribus*[8] of his adopter. A patrician adopted by a plebeian became a plebeian[6] (and vice versa); a freedman, *libertinus*, adopted by one

---

[1] The power that the possibility of *adrogatio impuberis* would give a *tutor* would be so great that it is probable that such *adrogationes* were allowed only after machinery was available for protecting an *impubes*. But G.1.102 shows that before the *epistula* of the Emperor Antoninus, the *adrogatio* of an *impubes* was possible at some periods, at others not.

[2] Cf. G.1.134-6.

[3] For the history of the juristic interpretation of the XII Tables' provision, see Daube, 'Texts and Interpretations in Roman and Jewish Law', *Jewish Journal of Sociology*, iii (1961), pp. 3ff at pp. 5ff.

[4] Cf. D.1.7.5 (Celsus, *27 dig.*) : Buckland, *Textbook*, p. 124.

[5] That is, there was *capitis deminutio*. Against the idea of, for instance, Kaser ['Zur Geschichte der *capitis deminutio*', *Iura*, iii (1952), pp. 48ff] that *adrogatio* and *conventio in manum* did not then result in *capitis deminutio* see Watson, *Persons*, pp. 87f : unconvinced, Kaser, *T.v.R.*, xxxvi, p. 431.

[6] Thus, the patrician, Clodius, on his *adrogatio* by a plebeian became a plebeian : Cicero, *de domo*, 13.35; 14.37, 38; Suetonius, *Divus Iulius*, 20.4; *Tiberius*, 2.4; Plutarch, *Cato minor*, 33; Dio, 38.12 : another instance, Cicero, *ad Att.*, 7.7.6.   [7] There is no direct textual proof.

[8] Aulus Gellius, *N.A.*, 5.19.15, 16. The speech in question was apparently made in 142 BC : cf. Watson, *Persons*, p. 89.

free born, *ingenuus*, became himself *ingenuus*.[1] This principle that the adoptee took the civil status in the State of his adopter was carried so far that if a slave was adopted or given in adoption by his master, the slave was tacitly manumitted and became *ingenuus*.[2]

EXTINCTION OF PATRIAPOTESTAS

Patriapotestas was ended by the death or *capitis deminutio*[3] of either the *pater* or the person *in potestate*. When a Roman had a son and grandchildren in his *potestas*, his death would make his son *sui iuris*, but the grandchildren would now be in the *potestas* of their father. *Adrogatio* of a *paterfamilias* who had children of his own would end his *potestas* but his children would be in the *potestas* of his adopter. *Patriapotestas* could also be extinguished, if the *pater* wished it, by *emancipatio* which had the same form as *adoptio* except that at the end no one claimed the son as his and the son became *sui iuris*.[4, 5] A man who became a *flamen dialis* or a woman who became a Vestal Virgin also went out of *patriapotestas*,[6] and so did a person who, authorized by his father, gave in his name as a member of a newly founded Latin colony.[7]

THE GENS

A little must be said about a unit larger than the Roman family, the *gens*. A *gens*, which might be either patrician or plebeian, was a group of several families which had the same name and asserted their descent from a common ancestor. The *gentes* had lost much

---

[1] Aulus Gellius, *N.A.*, 5.19.11-13. The law had changed by the time of Sabinus.

[2] Aulus Gellius, *N.A.*, 5.19.11-14; J.1.11.2. This was no longer the case in classical law : cf. Watson, *Persons*, pp. 90ff; Calonge, 'Problemas de la adopción de un esclavo', RIDA, xiv (1967), pp. 245ff.

[3] *Capitis deminutio maxima* was loss of liberty and citizenship, *media* was loss of citizenship, *minima* a change of family or family status : G.1.159-63. The classification is almost certainly later.

[4] Cf. Cicero, *de domo*, 14.37.

[5] The son would probably remain a member of his *gens* though this has been denied, for instance by Kaser, *Iura*, iii, pp. 79ff on the basis of Cicero, *top.*, 6.29. But see Watson, *Persons*, pp. 100f.

[6] G.1.130; Aulus Gellius, *N.A.*, 1.12.9 : cf. Buckland, *Textbook*, pp. 130f; Düll, 'Privatrechtsprobleme im Bereich der *virgo Vestalis*', ZSS, lxx (1953), pp. 380ff.

[7] G.1.131 : cf. Daube, 'Two early Patterns of Manumission', JRS, xxxvi (1946), pp. 57ff at pp. 68ff.

of their significance long before this time, little is known about their organization and it is by no means clear what was needed for membership. Thus, whether the *gens* included freedmen and other clients is disputed.[1] But certain private law rights of the gens remained important particularly those relating to *tutela*,[2] *cura*,[3] and intestate succession.[4, 5] However we do not know how these rights – for example, the division of an estate which came to a *gens* on intestacy – were exercised.

[1] See on all this, Kübler, RE, 7, 1176ff *s.v. Gens*; and now Treggiari, *Roman Freedman in the late Republic* (Oxford, 1969), pp. 81f.
[2] Infra, pp. 36, 40.
[3] Infra, p. 41.
[4] Infra, p. 99.
[5] For the strange *enuptio gentis* see supra. p. 20, and n. 1. The *gens* also had their own *sacra*.

CHAPTER 4

Guardianship

A person *sui iuris* might nonetheless not be treated as competent to look after his own affairs. Hence, persons under puberty and women of any age would have *tutores*, and lunatics and prodigals would have *curatores*.

TUTELA IMPUBERUM

A *tutor* could be appointed to an *impubes* in various ways. A *paterfamilias* might appoint a *tutor* or *tutores*[1] by will to his *sui heredes*, that is to those in his *potestas* who would become *sui iuris* on his death.[2] Such a *tutor testamentarius* could be appointed even to a child who was not born until after the testator's death.[3] The appointment had to be made in formal words : *L. Titium liberis meis tutorem do*; and perhaps : *Liberis meis Titius tutor esto*.[4] It took effect at the same time as the will. The person nominated could refuse the *tutela* or he could resign[5] but he could not transfer it to another.

When there was no *tutor testamentarius* the tutelage went under the law of the XII Tables[6] to all the nearest agnates (that is, relatives linked through males) in the same degree of relationship who were themselves *puberes*.[7] Because this *tutela legitima* was based

---

[1] Cf. Cicero, *ad fam.*, 13.61.
[2] Established by XII Tables : XII Tab., 5.3 : cf. 5.6; D.26.2.1pr (Gaius, 12 *ad ed. prov.*).
[3] Evidenced for a century later by D.50.17.73.1 (Quintus Mucius, *lib. sing. ὅρων*).
[4] Cf. G.1.149, who regards the latter formulation as less proper.
[5] Cf. Cicero, *ad Att.*, 6.1.4.
[6] 5.6.
[7] Cf. G.1.157; D.27.3.9.1 (Ulpian, 25 (35?) *ad ed.*); Watson, *Persons*, p. 118 n. 1.

on the agnatic tie, it ended automatically if either party suffered *capitis deminutio* even *minima*. Presumably by this time a patron was the *tutor legitimus* of an *impubes* whom he had manumitted.[1] When there were no agnates the *tutela* descended to the *gens*.[2] Those entitled to the *tutela legitima* could not refuse it, but they could not be compelled to act.[3]

Under the *lex Atilia*, probably of 210 BC,[4] the praetor and a majority of the tribunes of the plebs could appoint a *tutor* to someone who had none (*tutela a magistratu dativa*).[5] Finally, a temporary *tutor*, the *tutor praetorius*, might be appointed by the praetor to act for the pupil if there was to be a *legis actio* (and perhaps if there was to be a *iudicium legitimum*) between the pupil and his *tutor*.[6]

Although tutelage did not give the *tutores* any power over the person of the pupil[7] they would no doubt have an important say in any decision affecting him or her. Their function was to look after the pupil's property. To some extent at least, early *tutela* was thought of as being in the interest of those who would succeed to

---

[1] This was not itself expressly stated in the XII Tables but was a rule reached sometime during the Republic by the jurists from the provision that succession to freedmen and freedwomen went to the patron and his children : G.1.165. As a result of this provision and the rule derived from it, it was also possible for an *impubes* descendant of the patron to be a *tutor legitimus* : G.1.177-9; *Epit. Ulp.*, 11.20, 22; cf. Watson, *loc. cit.*

[2] And still could in the middle of the first century BC : argued from *Laudatio Turiae*, 18-24; Watson, *Persons*, pp. 121ff.

[3] It is not known whether the *tutela* could be transferred by *cessio in iure*.

[4] Cf. Rotondi, *Leges*, pp. 275f; Kaser, RPR, i, p. 302 and n. 2. It was certainly in existence by 184 BC : Livy, 39.9.7. Pace Watson, *Persons*, p. 123, Plautus, *Vid.*, 20ff is no evidence for this type of *tutela* : Crook, *Classical Review*, xix (1969), p. 90.

[5] G.1.185 : much later, probably near the end of the Republic, the *lex Iulia et Titia* allowed *praesides* in the provinces to appoint *tutores*.

[6] G.1.184; *Epit. Ulp.*, 11.24 : cf. Watson, *Persons*, pp. 128ff. The fact that the appointment of such a *tutor* was possible when there was to be a *legis actio*, but was doubtful for a *iudicium legitimum*, is proof that *tutela praetoria* is early.

[7] For this see Watson, *Persons*, pp. 102ff; followed by Crook, *loc. cit.* The contrary dominant view (see the references given by Watson, *Persons*, pp. 106ff) is primarily based on the mistaken view that *vis ac potestas* in Servius' definition of *tutela* [D. 26.1.1pr (Paul, *38 ad ed.*) : cf. J.1.13.1] is, at least, semi-technical and refers to a power similar to *patria potestas*. But Kaser now relies on 'the general historical experience' : *T.v.R.* xxxvi (1968), p. 431. Livy, 34.2.11 has no significance in this connection : cf. Watson, *Persons*, p. 110.

the estate if the ward died; hence in the case of male pupils it ended when the pupil reached puberty and could dispose of his property by will, marry and have children of his own; hence too *tutela legitima* went to all those (male *puberes*) who would become entitled to the estate if the pupil died; and hence the rather protected position of the *tutores legitimi*. But the interest of the pupil was of primary importance. Thus, Marcus Cato declared that the *maiores* held it more holy (*sanctius*) to defend pupils than not to deceive a *cliens*.[1] There is here a direct and significant reference to the provision of the XII Tables,[2] *Patronus si clienti fraudem fecerit, sacer esto*; so the duty to a pupil was regarded very seriously. And Sabinus said that for the old Romans the duty of *tutela* took precedence over all others.[3] Still it would appear that the duty of which Sabinus spoke was primarily a moral one[4] and a *tutor* was legally liable only if he acted fraudulently.[5]

On account of his pupil's affairs the *tutor* could sue and be sued by third parties in a *legis actio*[6] and in a formulary process.[7] When he made a contract on behalf of his ward, the contract was his, and so legally were the rights and duties under it.[8] Similarly, any property he acquired for the ward was legally his since one could not acquire ownership for another.[9] When the pupil ceased to be *infans*, that is, literally and legally, unable to speak,[10] he himself became competent to take part in a legal transaction, but the agreement could not be enforced against him unless he had entered it with the authority of his *tutor*.[11] Similarly when a debt was paid to a pupil without notification to the *tutor*, the debtor was not released

[1] Aulus Gellius, *N.A.*, 5.13.4.
[2] 8.21.
[3] Aulus Gellius, *N.A.*, 5.13.5; cf. Cicero, *de off.*, 1.25.85. On all this, see Watson, *Persons*, pp. 103ff.
[4] Cf. Watson, *Persons*, p.105, n.1.
[5] Also no *satisdatio* was required and the edict *De administratione tutoris* is much later : cf. Watson, *Persons*, p. 131.
[6] J.4.10pr. This is one of the exceptional cases where a *legis actio* was allowed on another's behalf.
[7] Cf. G.4.82.
[8] But it would, of course, be fraud not to let the pupil have the benefits.
[9] For the question of *possessio* see infra, p. 64, n.8.
[10] Cf. e.g. Varro, *de ling. lat.*, 6.52; D.27.8.1.15 (Ulpian, *36 ad ed.*); 40.5.30.1, 2 (Ulpian, *5 fideicom.*).
[11] Where the transaction was solely in the interest of the pupil, the *tutor*'s *auctoritas* was unnecessary : cf. Watson, *Persons*, p. 132.

D

and the pupil could sue again for payment.[1] Normally the *auctoritas* was shown by the *tutor*'s being asked by the other party if he assented and he declared his approval.[2] The *auctoritas* of all the *tutores* was needed if the *tutela* was *legitima*[3] but not if it was *testamentaria* when the *auctoritas* of one was sufficient.[4]

In practice the real administration of the estate would be in the hands of the *tutor*, and the pupil would enter a contract on his instructions. The *tutor* was expected to keep accounts of all transactions[5] though he was under no legal obligation to do so.

The *tutela* ended if the pupil reached puberty, if either the *tutor* or pupil died, and, in a *tutela legitima*, if either underwent *capitis deminutio*. If a *tutor* was *remotus* by an *accusatio suspecti tutoris* he ceased to be *tutor* when a replacement was appointed.[6] Mysteriously, the capture of a *tutor* by the enemy did not deprive him of the *tutela*.[7]

If a *tutor testamentarius* was suspected of fraud a charge, *crimen suspecti tutoris*,[8] could be brought by anyone for his removal, and if it was successful the *tutor* became *infamis*.[9] The action was extended so that it also applied to *tutores dativi*,[10] but not until many centuries later to *tutores legitimi*. Against fraudulent *tutores*

---

[1] The *actio de dolo* which would inhibit the pupil's action if he had not lost the money was not introduced until about 66 B C.

[2] Cf. D.26.8.3 (Paul, *8 ad Sab.*). But this was not a ritual dialogue : cf. Buckland, 'Ritual Acts and Words in Roman Law', *Festschrift Koschaker*, i (Weimar, 1939), pp. 16ff at pp. 23f. Contra, De Visscher, 'Une Correction au texte de Paul, D.26.8 *de auct.*, 3', SDHI, xix (1943), pp. 16ff; Solazzi, 'La forma della *tutoris auctoritas* e della *patris auctoritas*', *Iura*, ii (1951), pp. 133ff.

[3] Cf. Cicero, *pro Flacco*, 34.84 (refers to *tutela mulierum*); *Epit. Ulp.*, 11.26.

[4] *Epit. Ulp.*, 11.26. Only for *tutela legitima* and *tutela testamentaria* is there likely to have been plurality of tutors.

[5] Proved by the name, *actio rationibus distrahendis*.

[6] Cf. Sachers, RE, 7A, 1562.

[7] J.4.10pr. It is not clear whether a *captivus* continued to be *tutor* in all kinds of *tutela*. For the problems of private law arising from capture see *infra*, pp. 63f.

[8] Established by the XII Tables : D.26.10.1.2 (Ulpian, *35 ad ed.*).

[9] Cf. J.1.26.6; D.26.10.3.18 (Ulpian, *35 ad ed.*). In classical law the action also lay for negligence but in this case there was no *infamia*.

[10] Cf. Buckland, *Textbook*, p. 160 and n. 10.

legitimi[1] lay the old[2] *actio rationibus distrahendis* for double the value of the things embezzled. This remedy suffered from the great disadvantage that it could be brought only when the *tutela* came to an end,[3] and it is easy to imagine the ravages which could be wrought by an unscrupulous *tutor*, especially a rather elderly one who did not expect to live until the ward reached puberty. And the action did not lie against the heir of a *tutor*.[4] But already by this time had come into existence the much more satisfactory *actio tutelae* which seems to be the earliest of the *bonae fidei iudicia*[5] and which lay against *tutores* of all types. The *formula* ran : *Quod Numerius Negidius Auli Agerii tutelam gessit, quidquid ob eam rem Numerium Negidium Aulo Agerio dare facere oportet ex fide bona eius iudex Numerium Negidium Aulo Agerio condemna, si non paret absolve.* Condemnation of a *tutor* in the action resulted in his *infamia*[6]; hence the action was available only against a fraudulent *tutor*.[7]

It is entirely typical of the materialistic outlook of Roman law that detailed rules should emerge for looking after the pupil's property but that no legal rules at all should develop for guarding the pupil himself. Equally characteristic is *tutela mulierum*.

TUTELA MULIERUM

The early Romans wished all women *sui iuris*, even those of full age, to be under permanent tutelage,[8] the sole exception being the Vestal Virgins.[9] Even marriage *sine manu* did not end the *tutela* and

---

[1] And perhaps by this time against other *tutores* as well.
[2] Also established by the XII Tables : D.26.7.55.1 (Tryphoninus, *14 disp.*).
[3] Cf. D.27.3.1.24 (Ulpian *36 ad ed.*). But there have been suspicions of substantive interpolation : cf. *Index Itp.*
[4] D.27.3.1.23.
[5] Cf. Watson, *Persons*, pp. 140ff; Cicero, *de off.*, 3.17.70; *de nat. deor.*, 3.30.74; *pro Caecina*, 3.7; *pro Roscio com.*, 6.16; *top.*, 10.42.
[6] Cicero, *pro Caecina*, 3.7, 8; *pro Roscio com.*, 6.16.
[7] But the action could be brought against a negligent *tutor* as early as the beginning of the first century BC : D.33.1.7 (Pomponius, *8 ad Quintum Mucium*); cf. Watson, *Persons*, pp. 143f. The change is likely to have occurred after the introduction of the *actio mandati* which can scarcely be earlier than 140 BC. For *infamia* see Watson, 'Some Cases of Distortion by the Past in Classical Roman Law', *T.v.R.*, xxxi (1963), pp. 69ff at pp. 76ff.
[8] G.1.144.
[9] G.1.145.

the woman remained under the guardianship of her existing *tutores*.[1]

Tutores were appointed to women in the same way as to *impuberes*. Thus, the *paterfamilias* could appoint *tutores* by will to the adult women in his *potestas* and to his wife *in manu*. In this latter case the husband could leave to his wife the right to choose her own *tutor*.[2,3] Failing *tutela testamentaria* the nearest agnates above puberty became the *tutores legitimi*[4] and if there were no agnates the *tutela* went to the *gens*.[5] Freedwomen were under the *tutela legitima* of their patron,[6] or, if he had died, the patron's son even when he himself was under puberty and in *tutela*.[7, 8] As in the case of *tutela impuberum* there could be a *tutor dativus* by the *lex Atilia*[9] and a temporary *tutor praetorius*.[10]

The woman could herself administer her property and the *tutor*'s function was simply to interpose his *auctoritas* where it was considered necessary, that is, where the transaction could adversely affect the woman's property. The *tutor*'s consent was not needed for a marriage *sine manu*, but was for marriage *cum manu* (since all the woman's property would go to her husband) contracted by *confarreatio* or *coemptio*. *Manus* could be acquired by *usus* automatically without the intervention of the *tutor*.[11] The *tutor*'s consent was needed for the promise of a dowry.[12] Similarly the woman could not promise anything by stipulation[13] or transfer anything

---

[1] This appears from Cicero, *pro Flacco*, 34.84: cf. Watson, *Persons*, p. 147.

[2] Livy, 39.19.5 (relates to 186 BC). Plautus, *Truc.*, 859 is probably not relevant: cf. Watson, *Persons*, p. 148, n. 2.

[3] At least in classical law the choice could be exercised an unlimited number of times unless it was expressly restricted in the will: G.1.151ff.

[4] Cf. Livy, 34.2.11.

[5] Cf. *Laudatio Turiae*, 15, 21f.

[6] Cf. G.1.165, 179ff: supra, p. 36, n. 1.

[7] Cf. G.1.177ff.

[8] Transfer of *tutela legitima mulierum* by *in iure cessio* was probably allowed though all the evidence is for classical law: G.1.168-72; *Epit. Ulp.*, 11.6-8; *Schol. Sin.*, 48-51.

[9] Livy, 39.9.7.

[10] G.1.184.

[11] For all this see supra, p. 18.

[12] Cicero, *pro Caecina*, 25.73. Perhaps the consent of the *tutor* could not be unreasonably withheld: argued very indirectly from common sense and from the rather later D.32.43 (Celsus, *15 dig.*).

[13] Cicero, *pro Caecina*, 25.72.

by *mancipatio*,[1] or, it appears, manumit a slave[2] without the *tutor*'s consent. But if a debtor paid the woman without the authority of her *tutor*, the debt was nonetheless released.[3] With her *tutor*'s consent[4] a woman could make a will[5] *per aes et libram*[6] provided she had undergone *capitis deminutio*.[7] The reason for the requirement of *capitis deminutio* is obscure but probably it was thought proper that a woman should be allowed to make a will only where her heirs on intestacy would not be her natural blood relatives.[8]

CURATIO

Under a provision of the XII Tables[9] a lunatic was placed under the *curatio* of his nearest *agnati* and, failing *agnati*, of his *gens*. This control was over both the person and the property of the lunatic,[10] but it applied only to lunatics and did not extend to those who simply suffered from weakness of the mind.[11]

At least as old as the XII Tables[12] was the provision that a prodigal who wasted an inheritance which came to him on intestacy[13] be interdicted by a magistrate from dealing with his property and placed in the *curatio* of the agnates. The interdiction ran[14]: *Quando tibi bona paterna avitaque nequitia tua disperdis liberosque tuos ad*

---

[1] Cicero, *pro Flacco*, 34.84; *ad Att.*, 1.5.6 (cf. Watson, *Persons*, pp. 137f); *Vat. Fr.* 1 (cf. Hausmaninger, *Die Bona Fides des Ersitzungsbesitzers im klassischen römischen Recht* (Vienna, Munich, 1964), pp. 13ff).

[2] Cf. Cicero, *pro Caelio*, 29.68.

[3] Cicero, *top.*, 11.46.

[4] This emerges from G.2.112.

[5] Already by this time : Livy, 39.9.7.

[6] But not *comitiis calatis* – if that form was still in existence – since she had no standing before the *comitia*, nor *in procinctu* since she could not be a soldier.

[7] Cicero, *top.*, 4.18; G.1.115a.

[8] For the argument see Watson, *Persons*, pp. 152ff.

[9] *Si furiosus escit, agnatum gentiliumque in eo pecuniaque eius potestas esto* : *Rhet. ad Herenn.*, 1.13.23; cf. Cicero, *Tusc. disp.*, 3.5.11.

[10] *In eo pecuniaque eius potestas* : cf. Watson, *Persons*, p. 155 n. 2.

[11] Cicero, *Tusc. disp.*, 3.5.11. Also on *curatio furiosi* see Varro, *de re rust.*, 1.2.8.

[12] *Epit. Ulp.*, 12.2; D.27.10.1pr (Ulpian, *1 ad Sab.*); 27.10.13 (Gaius, *3 ad ed. prov.*); 28.1.18pr (Ulpian, *1 ad Sab.*). The rule is said originally to have been introduced by custom (*moribus*) : D.27.10.1pr : *P.S.*, 3.4a.7.

[13] *Epit. Ulp.*, 12.3; Cicero, *Cato maior de senec.*, 7.22. When *interdictio* was extended to those prodigals who inherited by will is unknown but is presumably after our period.

[14] *P.S.*, 3.4a.7.

egestatem perducis, ob eam rem tibi aere[1] *commercioque interdico.*
The prodigal thereafter could not, for instance, make a will,[2]
transfer by *mancipatio*,[3] or bind himself by *stipulatio*.[4] But he
could accept an inheritance[5] and bind another to him by *stipulatio*.[6, 7]

Not until a much later period did a young male *sui iuris* over
puberty have a *curator* to help in administering his property,[8] and
legally he was in no different position from a fully grown man.
The only special protection was introduced by the *lex Laetoria* (or
perhaps *Plaetoria*) of 193 or 192 B C,[9] which gave an *actio popularis*
(that is, an action which could be brought by anyone) for a fine[10]
against a person who cheated someone under twenty-five.[11] Condemnation in the action involved *infamia*.[12] The *lex* also provided
an *exceptio* for a person under twenty-five who was sued on a contract which he had fraudulently been persuaded to make.[13, 14]

---

[1] The text has *ea re*; but see Kaser, 'Vom Begriff des *commercium*', *Studi
Arangio-Ruiz*, ii (Naples, n.d.), pp. 131 at pp. 152ff.
[2] *Epit. Ulp.*, 20.13.
[3] *Epit. Ulp.*, 20.13.
[4] D.45.1.6. (Ulpian, *1 ad Sab.*).
[5] D.29.2.5.1 (Ulpian, *1 ad Sab.*).
[6] D.45.1.6.
[7] Also on *interdictio* see Valerius Maximus, 3.5.2 (refers to 91 B C).
[8] Cf. Watson, *Persons*, p. 157.
[9] Argued from Plautus, *Ps.*, 303f: cf. now Watson *loc. cit.*
[10] Cicero, *de nat. deor.*, 3.30.74.
[11] Plautus, *Ps.*, 303f.
[12] *Lex Iulia Municipalis*, 112.
[13] Plautus, *Ru.*, 1376ff: cf. supra, p. 7.
[14] The edict, *De minoribus viginti quinque annis* is later: cf. Watson,
'Praetor's Edict'.

CHAPTER 5

Slavery and its Concomitants

ENSLAVEMENT

The main causes of enslavement were birth to a slave mother and capture in war.

A child born to a slave mother was himself a slave[1] and the status of the father was irrelevant. There are indications that the early Romans thought that giving birth was an annual standard event for a slave woman,[2] and the implication is that slave-rearing was not regarded as unprofitable.

A person, whether combatant or civilian, taken prisoner during war also became a slave. Indeed anyone belonging to a people with whom the Romans did not have *hospitium* or a treaty of friendship could simply be seized as a slave at any time.[3] This was not the case where there was such a treaty, though even a Latin could become a slave if he were sold by his father to a Roman citizen.[4]

There was also a number of minor grounds of enslavement. A

---

[1] Cf. Plautus, *Cap.*, 628ff; *Am.*, 179.

[2] Slaves born in the household are called *vernae* and Festus says they have this name because spring is the most natural time for birth : *s.vv. Vernae*; cf. now, Watson, 'Morality, Slavery and the Jurists in the Later Roman Republic', *Tulane Law Review*, xlii (1968), pp. 289ff at p. 292 n.19.

[3] This appears from D.49.15.5.2 (Pomponius, *37 ad Quintum Mucium*). Plautus' *Poenulus* is no real help; cf. Watson, *Persons*, pp. 159ff : and the *Persa*, 501ff, 520ff in this respect does not give good law; Watson, *Persons*, pp. 164f.

[4] This appears from Livy, 41.9.11 in conjunction with 41.8.10 : cf. Watson, *Persons*, p. 165, which is not fully satisfactory since it ignores the latter text. The two texts together, showing dodges to evade a *senatusconsultum* of 177 BC, are evidence that a Latin could not sell himself into Roman slavery or that, too, would have been mentioned. Cicero, *de orat.*, 1.40.182, also shows that a person *ex populo foederato* could be a Roman slave but tells us nothing more specific.

free *fur manifestus*[1] was beaten and made over (*addictus*) to the person from whom he stole,[2] though whether this *addictio* at once made him a slave, or only when, after the passage of the due time, he was sold *trans Tiberim* is not clear.[3] Likewise a judgement debtor could in due course be sold *trans Tiberim*.[4] A person who did not have himself enrolled on the *census* could be sold by the State into slavery,[5] and so could someone who evaded military service.[6, 7] In all these cases the Roman became a foreign slave. *Cessio in iure*[8] was treated so rigorously that a free man transferred in this way actually did pass into the ownership of the recipient,[9] but no doubt his liberty could be claimed.[10, 11]

A child of free parents who was exposed but rescued and brought up as a slave remained free.[12]

SLAVERY

Slaves were *res mancipi* and as such were transferable in the appropriate ways and were fully owned by their masters. The master's rights to put to death and to inflict any lesser punishment on the slave were at law completely without restriction[13] and he

[1] Cf. infra, pp. 148f.

[2] Aulus Gellius, *N.A.*, 11.18.8. It is just possible that this was already obsolete: cf. infra, p. 149.

[3] G.3.189 says this was disputed by the *veteres*. Sextus Caecilius Africanus' *in servitutem tradit* does not make the position clearer: Aulus Gellius, *N.A.*, 20.1.7. It is possible that this form of enslavement was already obsolete: cf. infra, p. 149. [4] This also might already be obsolete.

[5] G.1.160; *Epit. Ulp.*, 11.11; Cicero, *pro Caecina*, 34.99; Dionysius Hal., 4.15.6. The point of not enrolling was to avoid paying tax and the rule became unimportant around 166 BC when citizens ceased to be taxed.

[6] Cicero, *pro Caecina*, 34.99.

[7] For all this see Buckland, *The Roman Law of Slavery* (Cambridge, 1908), pp. 401f. [8] Cf. infra, p. 62.

[9] This appears from D.40.12.23pr (Paul, *50 ad ed.*): cf. Watson, *Persons*, pp. 166ff.

[10] At least if he had been innocent of deception. There is no evidence for the existence in the Republic of the rule of classical law that a free man who allowed himself to be sold as a slave in order to share in the price could not claim his liberty. [11] For the procedure in a claim of liberty see infra., pp. 51f.

[12] Cf. for a later time, Suetonius, *de gramm.*, 21; Watson, *Persons*, pp. 171f. It is doubtful whether Plautus, *Cas.*, 41ff, 79ff and Terence, *Heaut.*, 627ff., can be accepted as independent evidence of this since Attic law was the same: cf. Harrison, *The Law of Athens, The Family and Property* (Oxford, 1968), p. 71.

[13] Cf. e.g. Terence, *An.*, 863; *Eu.*, 853; Watson, *Persons*, pp. 173ff.

could properly demand any service from the slave, no matter how dangerous. When a slave committed a delict the master could hand him over in noxal surrender to the injured party.[1] The slave could own no property and everything he had was his master's but it was common for the owner to let him have a fund called the *peculium* which the slave could treat as if it were his.[2] Technically the *peculium* belonged to the master who might take it away if the slave misbehaved, but in practice it seems that the master did not abuse his rights[3] and the slave was even permitted to use the *peculium* to buy his freedom.[4] It was thus an inducement to good behaviour and frugality. Even when a slave had complete power to administer his *peculium* he could not use it to make a gift.[5] When a slave made a contract, whether with his *peculium* or otherwise on behalf of his owner, the owner acquired all the rights under it and he alone could sue. The other contracting party had no action of any kind against the master[6] and a slave could not be sued, facts which had the effect ultimately of reducing the value of a slave for effecting commercial transactions. A legal restriction which also limited slaves' usefulness was that they could not transfer property by *mancipatio*[7] though they could receive for their owners by *mancipatio*.

Slaves had, fundamentally, no civil position. Thus, they could

---

[1] Cf. infra, p. 159.

[2] Cf. Plautus, *As.*, 539f (very significant : *etiam opilio qui pascit, mater, alienas ovis, aliquam habet peculiarem qui spem soletur suam*); *Cap.*, 1028; *Cas.*, 258; *Pe.*, 192; *Poen.*, 843; *Ps.*, 1188f (*quid 'domino'? quid somniatis? mea quidem haec habeo omnia, meo peculio empta*); *Ru.*, 112 (*peculiosum esse addecet servom et probum*); *Tri.*, 434.

[3] So far as I can discover there is no clear text, lay or legal, from any period showing a master taking back the *peculium* without some justification. But for some of the legal aspects see D.40.1.6 (Alfenus Varus, *4 dig.*); Watson, *Persons*, pp. 178f.

[4] Plautus, *Cap.*, 119ff; *Ru.*, 927ff; *Tri.*, 563f. These texts, though, will largely reflect Greek practice : cf. Watson, *Persons*, p. 199.

[5] It is not clear whether at this time the mere grant of *peculium* implied the slave's right to administer it, or whether an express *concessio administrationis* was needed : cf. Watson, *Persons*, p. 179ff.

[6] The *actiones adiecticiae qualitatis* are later : cf. Watson, 'Praetor's Edict'.

[7] See now Watson, *Property*, pp. 183f. It is difficult to see a theoretical reason for this, especially since the transferor says nothing, and presumably the origins of the rule lie in the practical consideration that *res mancipi* were the most important things and it was thought unwise to allow them to be transferred by a slave.

not legally marry,[1] their deliberate killing even by a person not their master was not murder,[2] they could not take part in litigation and even their capacity to act as witnesses in legal proceedings was very restricted.

During the period covered by this book the number of slaves at Rome was already considerable as a result of the Punic wars, the occupation of Sicily, Corsica and Sardinia, the campaigns in Spain, the defeat of the Gauls, and the Macedonian wars. The slaves came from a variety of backgrounds and their treatment varied greatly. It is, however, likely that there were not many educated slaves from Greece who were regarded as trustworthy[3] and given positions of responsibility, such as looking after the master's accounts, or running a business or practising medicine. But there were some. Cato the Elder, for instance, at the time when his son was young, had a slave, Chilo, who was a schoolteacher with a certain reputation and had successfully taught several children.[4] Cato also lent money to his slaves to buy other slaves who could be trained for a year and then resold.[5] In general the best treated slaves were those serving in the household who were in a good position both to gain the ear of their master and to win tips from visitors, and who therefore might often reasonably hope for manumission. On farms the overseers were slaves[6] and their life, though hard, was not unbearable. Worst of all was the lot of the farm labourers who were often ill-housed and ill-treated and who had little hope of manumission. But this group suffered much more in the following few

[1] Cf. Plautus, *Cas.*, 67ff. Of course, sexual relationships among slaves were common and frequently lasting. Indeed, they were often managed or arranged by the owner : Cato, *de agri cult.*, 143; Plautus, *Cas.*, 191ff : cf. Marquardt, *Privatleben*, i, pp. 176f.

[2] Not even perhaps during the late Republic, under the *lex Cornelia de sicariis* : cf. now, Watson, *Persons*, pp. 173f and the references given, p. 174 n. 1.

[3] This is a fundamental qualification. In a very few years the situation changed and many slaves were given positions of trust.

[4] Plutarch, *Cato maior*, 20.3, 4. As censor in 180 BC, Cato ordered that slaves who were younger than twenty years old and had been sold since the last census for more than 10,000 *asses* should be estimated at ten times their value and heavily taxed : Livy, 39.44.3. This is evidence of a growth in trade of luxury slaves but in itself no indication that slaves were yet used much for their business or (in a modern sense) professional skills.

[5] Plutarch, *Cato maior*, 21.7.

[6] Cf. Cato, *de agri cult.*, 5.

decades when the Roman victories brought in so many slaves –
150,000 Epirotes in 167 BC – that their market value will have
fallen.[1]

MANUMISSION

A slave could be freed in one of three ways : by enrolment on the
census (*censu*), by a claim of liberty (*vindicta*), by will (*testamento*).[2] All three ways not only gave the slave his freedom but
also made him a citizen, a privilege which was uncommonly
generous both for ancient and more modern times.

A slave was manumitted *censu* when he had himself inscribed,
at his master's command, on the *census* as a Roman citizen. The
censors took office once every five years and the *census* had to be
issued within eighteen months of taking office. It is not known
whether the slave became free as soon as he was inscribed on the
census or only when the *census* was published[3]; nor is it clear
whether the inclusion of the name on the list itself gave him
citizenship or was regarded simply as evidence of citizenship,
which could be rebutted in the event of error.[4] This act of manumission does not appear technically to be such but to be a recognition that the man entered on the list actually was a citizen : the
census had been given a new, a perverted, function. The legal rôle
of the master in this form of manumission was non-existent and
the act was very much that of the State,[5] so it is all the more striking that the social realities were legally recognized and that the
new citizen owed to his former master all the duties which a
freedman owed his patron.[6]

---

[1] The change within even a few years could be so dramatic that one must
hesitate to treat as full evidence for our period Cato's *de agri cultura* (usually
thought to be written about 160 BC) which represents chained gangs of
farm workers who were locked in each night as commonplace : 56, 57. But
Daube suggests a much earlier date for the *de agri cultura* : *Forms of Roman
Legislation* (Oxford, 1956), pp. 96f : contra, Watson, 'The Imperatives of
the Aedilician Edict', *T.v.R.* xxxviii (1970).
[2] Cf. Cicero, *top.*, 2.10.
[3] The law was not settled even as late as Cicero : *de orat.*, 1.40.183; cf.
Watson, *Persons*, pp. 185ff.
[4] The latter was the case in Cicero's time : *pro Archia*, 5.11. But it does
not follow this had always been so : for the arguments see Watson, *loc. cit.*,
and the authorities cited.
[5] Properly emphasized by Daube, 'Two Early Patterns of Manumission',
JRS, xxxvi (1946), pp. 57ff at pp. 60ff.   [6] Cf. infra, pp. 53ff.

Manumissio vindicta was at first a particular use of the *vindicatio in libertatem*.[1] The master who wished to free his slave appeared with him in front of a magistrate who had *imperium*, and another Roman citizen, the *adsertor libertatis*, present by arrangement claimed that the slave was free. The master put up no defence and the magistrate declared the slave a free man. This collusive process still retained its character in our period as a *cessio in iure*,[2] and even the formalities remained. Thus, in the normal *vindicatio* under the *legis actio* procedure the claimants touched the object under dispute with a rod[3] called *festuca*,[4] and we know from Plautus that the *adsertor libertatis* also touched the slave with a *festuca*.[5] This manumission, too, is an application of an institution existing for other purposes, and again in character it is apparently not the freeing of a slave. Nonetheless, the former owner had all the rights of a patron.[6]

Manumission by will (*testamento*) is at least as old as the XII Tables.[7] It was the sole form actually created for manumission and the only one which could be conditional. In practice it is likely also

---

[1] For the process of *vindicatio in libertatem* see infra, pp. 51f.

[2] As it did to a large extent even in the time of Cicero : argued from *ad Att.*, 7.2.8 : cf. above all, Arangio-Ruiz, 'Romanisti e latinisti', *Scritti Mancaleoni* (*Studi Sassaresi*, xvi), pp. 15ff at pp. 27ff; most recently, Watson, *Persons*, pp. 191f. An early relaxation which may perhaps go back to our period is that if a magistrate declared a slave free on a *dies nefastus* – a day on which he could not utter the words, *do, dico, addico* – the slave did obtain his freedom though under a bad omen : Varro, *de ling. lat.*, 6.30.

[3] G.4.16.

[4] There is a problem here in that the ordinary meaning of *festuca* is 'a straw' but no explanation is satisfactory and the puzzle need not detain us since it concerns an earlier period. But see on the point, Nisbet, 'The *festuca* and *alapa* of manumission', JRS, viii (1918), pp. 1ff : and, most recently, Tondo, *Aspetti simbolici e magici nella struttura giuridica della manumissio vindicta* (Milan, 1967), pp. 1ff.

[5] *Mil.*, 961 : cf. Boethius, *ad Ciceronis top.*, 2.10. In the Empire it was customary for the master to give the new freedman a slap (*alapa*) and to turn him round, and it must not be thought that this position represents a weakening of an earlier legal requirement. The *alapa* could have no proper place in a ceremony which was a fictitious *vindicatio in libertatem*. In fact there is no evidence at all for the slap in the Republic : cf. sources quoted by Nisbet, '*Festuca*', p. 6; and Watson, *Persons*, p. 193; Tondo, *Aspetti simbolici*, pp. 177f; Treggiari, *Roman Freedmen during the late Republic* (Oxford, 1969), p. 24.

[6] Also on *manumissio vindicta* see Plautus, *Pe.*, 483ff; Livy, 41.9.11 (refers to 177 BC).

[7] *Epit. Ulp.*, 2.4.

to have been the most common.[1] The usual form[2] was '*Stichus servus meus liber esto*' or '*Stichum servum meum liberum esse iubeo*' and though it is nowhere so stated it is extremely likely that a manumission *testamento* was void unless expressed in one or other of these formulations.[3] The *manumissor* had to be the full owner at civil law (*dominus ex iure Quiritium*) at the time the will was made as well as at the time of his death.[4] This rule probably came into existence for the *testamentum per aes et libram*[5] in which originally all the testator's property was transferred to the *familiae emptor* when the will was made.[6] If for some reason the will failed, so did the manumission.[7]

When the manumission by will was not made subject to a condition it was frequently accompanied by a legacy to the slave of his *peculium*.[8]

A slave ordered by a will to be free under a condition is designated a *statuliber* until the condition is fulfilled. This status is old and goes back at least as far as the XII Tables which enacted that a slave who under a term of a will was to gain his freedom on paying a certain sum to the heir, would, if he was sold by the heir, become free on paying the sum to the purchaser.[9] The provision, which shows that a *statuliber* could be sold, illustrates a fact which is otherwise not properly evidenced for the Republic, that the *statuliber* was still a slave and was dealt with as such,[10] though the right to

---

[1] Though Treggiari convincingly argues that this was not the case in the late Republic : *Freedmen*, pp. 27f.
[2] Cf. G.2.267; D.32.29.4 (Labeo, *2 post. a Iavoleno epit.*); 32.30.2 (*idem*); 35.1.40.3 (*idem*); 33.8.14 (Alfenus Varus, *5 dig.*); 40.4.48 (Papinian, *10 quaest*); 40.7.3.12 (Ulpian, *27 ad Sab.*); 40.7.14pr, 1 (Alfenus Varus, *4 dig.*); 40.7.29.1 (Pomponius, *18 ad Quintum Mucium*); 40.7.39pr, 1, 3, 4 (Iavolenus, *4 ex post. Labeonis*).
[3] This appears from the need for formal words in wills for *institutio*, *substitutio*, legacies and the appointment of *tutores*.
[4] This appears from D.40.4.35 (Paul, *50 ad ed.*); G.2.267; *Epit. Ulp.*, 1.23.
[5] Cf. infra, pp. 100ff.
[6] Cf. now Watson, *Persons*, p. 194 and n. 7.
[7] This emerges from D.40.7.29.1 (Pomponius, *18 ad Quintum Mucium*); cf. Watson, *Persons*, pp. 201ff.
[8] Cf. D.33.8.14.
[9] Cf. *Epit. Ulp.*, 2.4; D.40.7.29.1; D.40.7.25 (Modestinus, *9 diff.*): Kaser, *Das altrömische Ius* (Göttingen, 1949), pp. 160ff. Voci expresses doubt on the accuracy of the tradition; *Diritto ereditario romano*, i, 2nd edit. (Milan, 1967), p. 75. [10] Cf. Buckland, *Slavery*, pp. 286f.

freedom under the condition could not be taken from him. The XII Tables' provision was inevitably widened and in classical law the slave became free if, without fault on his part, the condition could not be fulfilled.[1] In the late Republic the provision was not so wide and the *statuliber* was free only if it was the heir who brought it about that the condition could not be fulfilled.[2] But for our period we can safely assume that the clause of the XII Tables was applied to alienations of all kinds by the heir, not just sale, and extended to conditions demanding services from the slave,[3] not merely (the more common) payments. Whether the heir's conduct was fraudulent or negligent or in this respect purely accidental would be irrelevant.[4, 5, 6]

Finally on the subject of manumission, a *lex Fabia* which was known to Cicero[7] and may date from 209 or 183 or even be much later[8] enacted among other things that if a master punished his slave for kidnapping the slave could not be manumitted within ten years.[9,10]

It is remarkable that slavery, an institution of such social importance, should involve so little law, and especially so little law which is peculiar to it. Enslavement by capture differs not at all from the seizure of foreigners' goods, acquisition of ownership of a child born to a slave mother is the same as the acquisition of

---

[1] Cf. D.40.7.3.10 (Ulpian, *27 ad Sab.*).

[2] This emerges primarily from the absence of any text showing wider interpretation : cf. now Watson, *Persons*, pp. 204.

[3] Cf. for a later period in the Republic, D.40.7.14.1 (Alfenus Varus, *4 dig.*); 40.7.39.1 (Javolenus, *4 ex post. Labeonis*).

[4] But it might be treated as relevant in some circumstances : cf. Watson, *Persons*, pp. 209ff on D.40.7.3.11 (Ulpian, *27 ad Sab.*).

[5] From at least the beginning of the first century BC it was disputed whether a slave who was the object of a legacy could be a *statuliber* : D.40.7.39pr; cf. Watson, *Persons*, pp. 203. But there is no evidence for juristic attitudes in our time.

[6] Not for a long time afterwards is there any sign of *favor libertatis*, the doctrine that an ambiguous clause is to be interpreted so as to favour freedom : cf. Watson, *Persons*, p. 217.

[7] *pro. Rab.*, 3.8.

[8] Cf. Rotondi, *Leges*, pp. 258f.

[9] D.40.1.12 (Paul *50 ad ed.*). This rule was later generalized by the *lex Aelia Sentia* of AD 4.

[10] Nothing more for the Roman law of manumission is to be learned from Plautus, *Men.*, 1145ff; *Mer.*, 152ff; *Mo.*, arg. 1; 167, 204, 971ff; *Ps.*, 419ff, 494ff; *Ep.*, 497, 509; *Po.*, 164. cf. Watson, *Persons*, pp. 198f.

ownership of the young of any animal. Hardly any private law flows from the state of slavery – even the *peculium* has no legal existence[1] – though a contract made by a slave could be enforced by his master, who could also surrender the slave on account of a delict he had committed. But here in contract and delict, the position of a slave was basically the same as that of *filiusfamilias*. Only manumission was special and even there two of the three forms were adaptations of machinery devised for other purposes.

LIBER HOMO BONA FIDE SERVIENS

Surprisingly often a free man served as a slave, usually, but not always, unaware of his true status. An action, the *vindicatio in libertatem*, was available at an early date to establish that he was free, and though he himself could not bring it, a third party, the *adsertor libertatis*, could.[2] This was one of the very rare cases where one person could sue on another's behalf in a *legis actio*.[3] This *adsertor libertatis* need not be a relative of the free man nor even be of the same nationality.[4] Moreover, at least certain persons such as a mother could bring the action even against the wishes of the supposed slave.[5] It is equally characteristic that the rule that no action could be brought twice did not apply and an unlimited number of *adsertores* could successively bring the action.[6] Until judgement was delivered the supposed slave was provisionally regarded as free[7] and so he could even sue and be sued.[8] The various individual characteristics of this action demonstrate very clearly the Roman determination that a free man should not be improperly held as a slave.

[1] Except in so far as the extent of a legacy of *peculium* might be the object of interpretation.
[2] E.g. in Plautus, *Poe.*, 905f, 963ff.
[3] G.4.82; J.4.10pr; cf. Franciosi, *Il processo di libertà in diritto romano* (Naples, 1961), pp. 150ff.
[4] Livy, 3.45.2 for very early times; Cicero, *de domo*, 29.78. In practice when the supposed slave was not a Roman, only someone of the same nationality would be able to prove the true facts : this is the explanation of Plautus, *Poe.*, 905ff, 110ff; *Per.*, 541ff; cf. Watson, *Persons*, p. 219.
[5] See for a later period, Suetonius, *de gramm.*, 27; D.40.12.1-6; cf. Franciosi, *Libertà*, pp. 154ff.
[6] Cicero, *de domo*, 29.78.
[7] Livy 3.44.5, 12 for very early times; D.40.12.24.1 (Paul, *51 ad ed.*) : cf. Watson, *Persons*, pp. 219f.
[8] Cf. D.40.12.24.1.

The action was taken before the *decemviri stlitibus iudicandis*,[1] though probably even by this time the case would be heard by *recuperatores* if one of the parties was not a Roman.[2] The action before the *decemviri* was a *legis actio sacramento in rem*,[3] and the oath involved another peculiarity of the action : no matter how great the man's value if he were a slave, the amount of the oath was set at 50 *asses*, though in other cases concerning matters worth 1,000 *asses* or more, the oath was for 500 *asses*.[4] The *adsertor libertatis* claimed : '*Hunc ego hominem ex iure Quiritium liberum esse aio*',[5] and the supposed owner, '*Hunc ego hominem ex iure Quiritium meum esse aio.*'

When a person previously thought to be a slave is established as free, the question arises as to how much of what he acquired for the supposed owner is to remain with this latter. The simplest and crudest answer is everything. In Roman classical law there was no question of compensating the supposed slave for his time and effort; the presumed *dominus* acquired through him *ex operis*, i.e. basically by his services hired to another, and *ex re*, i.e. by means of the property of the presumed master.[6] Thus, everything acquired by the efforts of the supposed slave belonged to his presumed owner. We can be sure that in this respect the law of our period was the same. Problems exist, though, in respect of an inheritance left to the supposed slave firstly because the testator's intention might be to benefit either the supposed slave or the master; secondly because it might be argued on the one hand that the acquisition of the inheritance was not the result of the slave's work, on the other that the acquisition did need a formal act of acceptance which even required the presumed owner's authoriza-

---

[1] Cicero, *de domo*, 29.78; *pro Caecina*, 33.97; cf. Franciosi, *Libertà*, pp. 15ff; Kaser, ZPR, pp. 4of.

[2] Arguments are : (1), already *recuperatores* heard some private law suits; Plautus, *Ba.*, 270; *Ru.*, 1281ff (though neither text concerns a *vindicatio in libertatem* : cf. Watson, *Persons*, pp. 218 n. 2); (2) it is certain that in 70 BC *recuperatores* heard such *vindicationes*; *lex Antonia de Termessibus* 36; Cicero, *pro Flacco*, 17.40.

[3] G.4.14; Cicero, *pro Caecina*, 33.96f; *de domo*, 29.78.

[4] G.4.14.

[5] This appears from Cicero, *pro Caecina*, 33.96f. For the argument see now Watson, *Persons*, pp. 22of. Where the supposed slave would not be a Roman citizen the claim would be rather different.

[6] For acquisition *ex operis* and *ex re* see Reggi, *Liber homo bona fide seviens* (Milan, 1958), pp. 365ff and the authorities he cites.

tion[1]; and thirdly because the *hereditas* might turn out to be *damnosa*.[2] There is no evidence for the state of the law here – the problem would not often have arisen – and one can say only that in the first century B C the basic answer to the problem was that the inheritance was the property of the supposed slave.[3]

FREEDMEN

The freedman, (*libertus*), having undergone *capitis deminutio* had no rights or liabilities under contracts which he had made while a slave.[4] But the rule *caput noxa sequitur* applied and he was liable for any delicts he had committed, even if he had acted under the orders of his master.[5] The legal disabilities of the freedman vis-à-vis *ingenui* all concern public law and are not relevant here[6] though it is worth observing that the *lex Terentia*, a plebiscite of 189 B C, enacted that the children of freedmen should be citizens *optimo iure*.[7]

But the social and legal bond between the patron and his *libertus* was very close. The freedman often continued to live in his patron's home,[8] and helped him with his affairs.[9] Indeed, he would frequently act as 'front man'[10] especially if his patron was a senator since senators could not engage in business. Legally, the *libertus* owed the patron a duty of *obsequium*, it was also customary for him to give a promise that he would perform a certain number of days'

---

[1] Similar, but easier, problems existed in respect of legacies and gifts, different ones in respect of contracts by the supposed slave which were yet unfulfilled.

[2] That is, the testator's debts might be greater than his assets : cf. infra, pp. 94f.

[3] Emerges from D.41.1.19 (Pomponius, *3 ad Sab.*); 28.5.60(59) (Celsus, *16 dig.*) : cf. Watson, *Persons*, p. 222ff.

[4] Later there was a partial exception and the *formula in factum depositi* lay against a freedman who was still in possession of the thing deposited : D.16.3.21.1 (Paul, *60 ad ed.*); see now Watson, *Persons*, p. 226f.

[5] D.44.7.20 (Alfenus, *2 dig.*) shows that in the time of Alfenus the freedman was liable for most wrongs but not for some minor delicts which he had committed as a slave under his master's orders. The relaxation is likely to be later than our period. For the significance of the form of the text see Watson, 'Morality', pp. 298f.   [6] But see Treggiari, *Freedmen*, pp. 37ff.

[7] Plutarch, *Flamininus*, 18.1; cf. Rotondi, *Leges*, p. 274; Berger, *Encyclopedic Dictionary of Roman Law* (Philadelphia, 1953), p. 560.

[8] Cf. e.g. D.9.3.5.1 (Ulpian, *23 ad ed.*); Watson, *Obligations*, pp. 267f.

[9] Important for the development of *procuratio*; cf. e.g. Watson, *Obligations*, pp. 193ff.   [10] E.g. Plutarch, *Cato maior*, 21.6.

E

work (*operae*) in each year for the patron, and when he died the patron had rights to his *bona*.

The legal extent of *obsequium* is not closely defined and it must be emphasised that many modern scholars[1] greatly exaggerate the patron's authority over his freedmen. There is in fact no evidence that the patron had a legal right of putting his freedmen to death, or could exercise *manus iniectio*.[2] It would indeed seem that the duty of *obsequium* was primarily a moral one though it was not totally without legal substance since the freedman could not bring an action against his patron without the praetor's consent.[3] And from early times there were restrictions on *clientes* (which would include freedmen) giving (or being compelled to give) evidence against their *patroni* and vice versa.[4]

We do not know if there was a penalty established by law for a breach of *obsequium* – if there was it was certainly not automatic reenslavement[5] as was the case in post-classical law – but often the master and the slave about to be manumitted would agree on a penalty. Frequently this was that the patron would become entitled under partnership to one half of the freedman's property.[6]

The right to *operae* was the result of an agreement between the

[1] E.g. Kaser, RPR, i, p. 256.

[2] That Julius Caesar and Augustus could have a freedman put to death or order him to commit suicide need be no indication of the legal rights of patrons: Suetonius, *Divus Iulius*, 48; *Augustus*, 67.2. Valerius Maximus tells us that P. Maenius killed a freedman, but not that he had a right to do so; 6.1.4. And in *inst. orat.*, 7.7.9, Quintilian, as often (cf. 7.7.10), is concerned with an imaginary rule. For the argument see Watson, *Persons*, pp. 227f.

[3] This appears from D.2.7.1.2 (Ulpian, *5 ad ed.*); cf now Watson, *Persons*, p. 227 and the works cited n.2. At least in later times a freedman who could not bring an action for others *nisi pro certis personis* could sue for his patron; cf. Lenel, *Edictum*, pp. 77ff.

[4] Dionysius Hal., 2.10.1; Plutarch, *Romulus*, 13.6; Aulus Gellius, *N.A.*, 5.13.4 (concerns Cato). It is difficult to determine the extent of the obligation in our period and how far it was legal: cf. Watson, *Persons*, pp. 104f, and p. 105 n. 1. See also on the whole topic of *obsequium*, Treggiari, *Freedmen*, pp. 68ff.

[5] This emerges from the common agreement that the patron was to get one half of the miscreant's goods; cf. Watson, *Persons*, p. 229; and from the fact that a slave who killed his master and was manumitted by will did become free : *Rhet. ad Herenn.*, 1.14.24.

[6] D.38.2.1 pr, 1, 2 (Ulpian, *42 ad ed.*); 38.1.36 (Ulpian, *11 ad legem Iuliam et Papiam*); 44.5.1.7 (Ulpian, *76 ad ed.*). Rutilius, praetor around 118 BC, issued an edict that the patron was to get no more than *operarum et societatis actio*, and in classical law a *societas libertatis causa* was void.

patron and the freedman cast in the form either of a stipulation or of a unilateral oath, *iusiurandum liberti*,[1] confirming a promise made while the freedman was still a slave. The slave's promise prior to manumission would have no effect at civil law so it, too, for greater security was cast in the form of an oath which had a religious sanction.[2] The *iusiurandum liberti* itself was the sole case in Roman law of an oath creating a civil law obligation.[3] An *opera* was a day's labour and it appears that there was no restriction on the number of *operae* which could be agreed upon.[4]

If a freedman died intestate without leaving a *suus heres* his *hereditas* went to the patron.[5] Any *suus heres*, even a wife *in manu* or an adopted son, excluded the patron,[6] but if the patron had died his rights to the *hereditas* passed to his son, grandson by a son, great-grandson by a grandson by a son,[7] his daughter, granddaughter by a son, great-granddaughter by a grandson by a son.[8] Much later, after 118 but before 74 BC, these provisions were greatly modified by the Praetor's Edict which also, for the first time, restricted the freedman's right to exclude the patron by will.[9,10] Incidentally, a freedwoman could have no *suus heres*, and the patron as *tutor mulieris* was in a position to hinder gratuitous alienations by her during her lifetime.[11] When the freedwoman had undergone a further *capitis deminutio* and could make a will she would need the authority of her *tutor*[12] who would normally still be her patron.

---

[1] Cf. e.g. Cicero, *ad Att.*, 7.2.8.

[2] Cf. D.40.12.44pr (Venuleius, *7 act.*) which, admittedly, refers to a much later period.   [3] G.3.96.

[4] In classical law the patron either had to feed the freedman or leave him enough time each day to earn his food; and he could not demand services which were dangerous, immoral or beneath the freedman's dignity : see the texts in D.38.1. But there is no indication of how developed the law was in our time.

[5] *XII Tab.*, 5.8; *Epit. Ulp.*, 29.1.

[6] G.3.40.

[7] G.3.45.

[8] G.3.46.

[9] Of course, in earlier times when the sole will was made *comitiis calatis* it might have been difficult in practice for the freedman to exclude his patron.

[10] For the edict or edicts, see now Watson, *Succession*, pp. 82, 185ff.

[11] Hence the grant by *senatusconsultum* in 186 to Fecenia Hispala of *datio deminutio* for her services : Livy, 39.19.5. A different significance is wrongly attributed to the grant by Watson, *Persons*, p. 234.

[12] Cf. supra, p. 41.

When the slave's freedom was purchased with money provided by a third party (and perhaps even with the *peculium*) the former master's rights as patron were restricted.[1]

POSTLIMINIUM

Though *postliminium* was very much concerned with slavery it scarcely fits within this chapter. It is a branch of law on its own. Fundamentally but not exclusively *postliminium* was the right by which a Roman who had lost his citizenship by capture and had become a foreign slave recovered his citizenship and various private rights by coming back within Roman territory. In the Empire this branch of law was highly complex and sophisticated, and the effect of *postliminium* varied from institution to institution.[2] But the concept is old and in our period the law was already well-developed though the details cannot always be seen.

Originally and at this time there was no distinction between *postliminium* in war and *postliminium* in peace.[3] The main concern of *postliminium* was citizenship, and the principal rule was that a Roman who had lost his citizenship reacquired it by his return[4] within the boundaries of the State,[5] but this did not apply to a person sold by his father or by the State or surrendered by the *pater patratus*.[6] It did apply, however, to those returning from slavery among *populi liberi, foederati* and *reges*[7] as well as from

[1] This was the case in classical law and it seems possible to imply it for our period from Plautus, *Pe.*, 838ff. For the argument see Watson, *Persons*, pp. 234f.

[2] For instance, marriage with two exceptions was dissolved by capture and did not revive; *tutela* was ended but revived though not retroactively; *patria potestas* was suspended, and if the *pater* returned with *postliminium* it was as if he had never been a prisoner.

[3] Emerges from Festus, *s.v. Post liminium*; Cicero, *pro Balbo*, 11-12. 28-30; *de orat.*, 1.40.181, 182 : cf. above all, Amirante, *Captivitas e postliminium* (Naples, 1950), pp. 9ff; Watson, *Persons*, pp. 237ff.

[4] Whether an intention to remain within Roman territory was necessary cannot be determined : cf. Watson, *Persons*, pp. 242ff.

[5] Festus, *s.v. Post liminium*; Cicero, *top.*, 8.37.

[6] Cicero, *de orat.*, 1.40.181; *top.*, 8.37; D.50.7.18(17) (Pomponius, *37 ad Quintum Mucium*); 49.15.4 (Modestinus, *3 reg.*); cf. Watson, *Persons*, pp. 244ff.

[7] For the relationship of these three groups of people with the Romans, see Mommsen, *Römisches Staatsrecht*, iii, 3rd edit. (reprinted, Darmstadt, 1963), pp. 645ff.

slavery *apud hostes*.[1] A person who had been a citizen of another State and then become a Roman, similarly by the rules of *postliminium*, lost his Roman citizenship[2] if he returned to his native territory. This occurred automatically, even if he had no intention of settling there.[3]

Not all the effects of *postliminium* on private law rights are known or can be guessed at.[4] But the captive's property was not divided, his rights of ownership were in suspense and reemerged when he returned. Similarly the rights of at least certain kinds of *tutor* were in suspense and also could reemerge.[5] The will of a person who died a captive was void[6] and hence when a former Roman died a foreign slave, his property would descend to his heirs on intestacy whether he had once made a will or not.

Postliminium also applied to certain things – slaves, ships,[7] pack-mules, horses accustomed to reins, probably also land[8] – in the sense that such things which had belonged to a Roman and then been seized by a foreigner reverted to their former Roman owner if they came back into Roman territory.[9] Clearly these are things considered particularly useful in war,[10] but for *postliminium* to apply to them it was not necessary for them to have been captured in battle.[11]

---

[1] Festus, *s.v. Post liminium*. Later the law changed. For the argument see Watson, *Persons*, pp. 249ff.

[2] No one could at the same time be a Roman and a citizen of another state : Cicero, *pro Balbo*, 11-12.28-30.

[3] This appears from Cicero, *pro Balbo*, 11.28; D.49.15.5.3. For the argument see Watson, *Persons*, pp. 240ff. The law was different in the first century B C.

[4] In view of the number of possible approaches : cf. supra, p. 56 n. 2.

[5] This appears from J.4.10pr; cf. Watson, *Persons*, pp. 252f.

[6] Hence the need for the Sullan *lex Cornelia de confirmandis testamentis*.

[7] Perhaps only merchant ships and warships : cf., for a later period, D.49.15.2pr (Marcellus, *39 dig.*); Watson, *Persons*, p. 254.

[8] Cf. for a much later period, D.49.15.20.1 (Pomponius, *36 ad Sab*); 7.4.26 (Paul, *1 ad Nerat.*).

[9] Festus, *s.v. Post liminium*; Cicero, *top.*, 8.36.

[10] The absence from the list of cattle – which are *res mancipi* – is especially significant.

[11] Cf. D.49.15.27 (Javolenus, *9 ex post. Labeonis*); 49.15.6 (Pomponius, *1 ex var. lect.*).

CHAPTER 6

Acquisition of Ownership

KINDS OF THINGS

The main division of things was into those which were under divine law (*res divini iuris*) and those under human law (*res humani iuris*).[1] Things under divine law, which we will look at first, were further divided into *res sacrae* and *res religiosae*, while *res sanctae*[2] were regarded as being somehow under divine law.[3]

Res sacrae were those things dedicated to the gods above, hence primarily temples though moveables were also consecrated.[4] They were outside human ownership and so could not be usucapted,[5] they could be used only in sacred ways,[6] and if they were stolen the wrong was not the private law delict of *furtum* but the crime of *sacrilegium*.[7] Consecration was by an act of the pontiffs with the consent of the people which was shown by a *lex* or *plebiscitum*.[8]

Res religiosae were things dedicated to the gods beneath and were nothing but graves. The grave became *res religiosa* by the act of a private individual provided first that the burial was his concern,[9] and secondly that he had the right to bury the body in that

[1] Cf. G.2.2. [2] Cf. G.2.3.
[3] For our period this emerges not so much from G.2.8 as from Festus, *s.v. Religiosus* : and Macrobius, *Sat.*, 3.3.5 : cf. infra, p. 59.
[4] Cf. Festus, *s.v. Religiosum*; Macrobius, *Sat.*, 3.3.2.
[5] Cicero, *de harusp. resp.*, 14.32.
[6] Arnobius, *adversus gentes*, 7.31.
[7] Cicero, *de inven.*, 1.8.11; 2.18.55; cf. Watson, *Obligations*, pp. 226f. For *sacrilegium* see Mommsen, *Römisches Strafrecht* (reprinted Graz, 1955), pp. 76off.
[8] Cicero, *ad Att.*, 4.2.3; *de domo sua*, 49.127, 128; 53.137. In general for *consecratio* see Cicero, *de domo sua; lex a vicanis Furfensibus templo dicta,* Bruns, no. 105, of 58 BC.
[9] Cf. G.2.6 : ...*si modo eius mortui funus ad nos pertineat.*

place, that is in general that he was the owner of the land.[1] Nothing illustrates better the Roman sense of propriety expressed in the field of law than these two qualifications. Nonetheless it was pontifical law which established what was necessary to make a grave a *locus religiosus*. The proper rites – sacrifice of a pig, casting of earth upon the human corpse[2] – were necessary preliminaries. The importance of all this for private law[3] is that *res religiosae* also could not be owned by human beings, and could not be usucapted. By a provision of the XII Tables the entrance court of a tomb (*forum*) and the place where the body was burned and then buried (*bustum*) were expressly excluded from *usucapio*.[4, 5]

It was possible for *res sacrae* and *res religiosae* to be returned to human use and ownership.[6]

Res sanctae were the walls round a city[7] and the city gates and were under the protection of the gods though they did not belong to them. They, too, were excluded from human ownership.

Res humani iuris were either *res publicae* or *res privatae*. *Res publicae* were things belonging to the State and theft of them was *peculatus*,[8] not *furtum*. Certain other things, such as the sea shore, tended to be called *res publicae*[9] not in the sense that they were

---

[1] Cf. D.10.3.6.6 (Ulpian, *19 ad ed.*). Hence when bodies were found buried in a public place, that place was not regarded as having been *res religiosa* : Cicero, *de leg.*, 2.23.58 (refers probably to early third century BC).

[2] Cicero, *de leg.*, 2.22.57 : cf. de Visscher, *Le droit des tombeaux romains* (Milan, 1963), p. 23.

[3] There were numerous other provisions which cannot be regarded as relevant for private law : for instance, a body was not to be burned or buried within the city, no new funeral pyre was to be made nearer than 60 feet to another's building without the owner's consent : Cicero, *de leg.*, 2.23.58; 2.24.61.   [4] Cicero, *de leg.*, 2.24.61.

[5] It should not be forgotten that each *gens* had its common burial place and the right of the *gentiles* to be buried there was taken very seriously : cf. Marquardt, *Privatleben*, ii, pp. 364ff. To bury in a grave the bodies of persons who were not members of the *gens* and who were outside the *sacra* was contrary to religious law – that is, it was not *fas* : Cicero, *de leg.*, 2.22.55. There were also *sepulchra familiaria* where the right to be buried descended to members of the family, and *sepulchra hereditaria* where the right descended to the heirs : cf. e.g. D.11.7.5 (Gaius, *19 ad ed. prov.*); de Visscher, *Tombeaux*, pp. 101f. The poor, of course, were buried in communal graves.

[6] Cf. Macrobius, *Sat.*, 3.3.4.   [7] Festus, *s.v. Religiosus*.

[8] *Rhet. ad Herenn.*, 1.12.22; cf. Watson, *Obligations*, pp. 226f.

[9] Cf. Cicero, *top.*, 7.32.

owned by the State, but that they could be owned by no individual and could be used by everyone. Presumably, too, it had long been recognized that though the banks of navigable rivers were owned by individuals, the public had the right to use them, for instance to tie up boats to trees growing there, just as they had the right to sail in the river.[1]

Res privatae, the real subject of this chapter, were things which could be owned by individuals.[2] Slaves, oxen, horses, mules, asses, land in Italy whether built on or not[3] and rustic servitudes[4] were called *res mancipi*, and ownership could not be transferred by simple *traditio*, physical delivery. It seems that animals which were commonly broken to draught or burden became *res mancipi* only when they actually were broken in.[5] All other things were *res nec mancipi*. The basis of the distinction between *res mancipi* and *res nec mancipi* lies in remote antiquity but it is at least clear that the former were those things considered important for agriculture – slaves, oxen, land and rustic servitudes – and warfare – horses, mules and asses.

[1] How far the theory of ownership of things such as air and river beds had been worked out is another matter, but not of great importance.

[2] It is not necessary to discuss the distinction between corporeals and incorporeals. The sole legal importance of the distinction is in the modes of transfer since incorporeals logically cannot be transferred by modes which require physical delivery. Still it should not occasion surprise – or necessarily lead to theories that the early Romans did not distinguish ownership from lesser real rights, or thought of incorporeals as having a physical existence – that servitudes could be usucapted and transferred by *mancipatio*. Servitude rights were obviously desirable and a practical approach might have been taken to the problems of their creation and transfer : cf. Watson, *Property*, pp. 92ff. For a criticism of the common opinion which makes early lawyers incapable of drawing simple distinctions see Daube, *Roman Law*, at e.g. pp. 163ff.   [3] Cf. G.1.120.

[4] Cf. G.2.14a, 17, 29; *Epit. Ulp.*, 19.1; *Vat. Fr.*, 45.

[5] In classical law, the Sabinians held these animals were *res mancipi* from birth, the Proculians from the time they were broken in (or if they could not be tamed, from the usual age of breaking in – an obvious later qualification) : G.2.15. The dominant modern view is that the Sabinian is the ancient opinion but the weakness of the argument has recently been shown by Nicosia, '*Animalia quae collo dorsove domantur*', *Iura*, xviii (1967), pp. 45ff. His own arguments in favour of the antiquity of the Proculian view are, admittedly, not very persuasive. To me the antiquity of the Proculian view is shown by the connection between *res mancipi* and the animals to which *postliminium* applied (cf. supra, p. 57), and we know from Cicero, *top.*, 8.36 that not all horses but only those broken to reins had *postliminium*.

Of the ways of acquiring ownership, three, *mancipatio*, *in iure cessio* and *usucapio* were confined to citizens and could not be used by peregrines.

Mancipatio[1] was a ceremony for transferring *res mancipi* and it required the presence of five witnesses and a person who held bronze scales, all of whom had to be Roman citizens of full age. The transferee grasped with his hand the thing to be mancipated (unless it were land which could be mancipated at a distance), held a piece of bronze in his other hand and declared : '*Hunc ego hominem*[2] *ex iure Quiritium meum esse aio isque mihi emptus esto hoc aere aeneaque libra*'. Then he struck the scales with the bronze and gave it to the transferor as a symbolic price. Originally, the bronze would be the real price and the appropriate amount would be weighed out on the scales.[3] The wording of the *mancipatio* was capable of considerable variation, otherwise it could not have been used for so many other purposes such as *adoptio*, *coemptio*, the *testamentum per aes et libram* and *fiducia*. Indeed, *mancipatio* is a very fine example of the jurists' skill in using limited technical equipment to achieve a number of ends. When the transaction involved a sale the purchase price was usually expressly stated in the *mancipatio*, since this enabled the *actio auctoritatis* to be brought if the buyer were evicted within one year of the *mancipatio*, or two years if land had been transferred.[4] The *actio auctoritatis* was inherent in the *mancipatio*,[5] could not be directly excluded by agreement of the parties,[6] and lay for double the price stated in the *mancipatio*. When for one reason or another the purchaser was willing that the seller's liability be excluded, this could be achieved by declaring that the *mancipatio* was made *uno nummo*, and the *actio* would then lie for two *nummi* only whatever the true price was. Since the *actio auctoritatis* was given only when there had been

[1] See G.1.119-22.

[2] Assuming the object to be transferred was a slave.

[3] That the symbolic stage had already been reached appears from Plautus, *Truc.*, 273f : cf. Watson, *Property*, p. 17.

[4] Cicero, *top.*, 4.23; *pro Caecina*, 19.54.

[5] This appears from Varro, *de re rust.*, 2.10.5; cf. *P.S.*, 2.17.1-3. Against the contrary argument drawn from Plautus, *Poe.*, 146; Cicero, *pro Murena* 2.3; *de off.*, 3.16.65, see Girard, *Mélanges de droit romain*, ii (Paris, 1923), pp. 18ff.

[6] This appears from Varro, *de re rust.*, 2.10.5; Plautus, *Curc.*, 494; *Pers.*, 525, 589.

actual eviction, it appears that the transferor in a *mancipatio*[1] was under no legal obligation to transfer ownership. Also inherent in a *mancipatio* was the *actio de modo agri* which was given when the acreage of land stated in the *mancipatio* was less than that transferred. In the ordinary case, where the acreage was merely overstated, condemnation would be assessed on a quantitative basis : the amount by which the stated acreage exceeded the actual acreage, expressed as a fraction of the stated acreage. But when the buyer was evicted from a part of the land, damages were assessed qualitatively : the value of that part.[2] If the transferor denied liability, condemnation was doubled.[3] Probably *satisdatio secundum mancipium* and *repromissio secundum mancipium* were also guarantees connected with *mancipatio* but their nature is unknown.[4]

When a *res nec mancipi* was delivered by *mancipatio* the *mancipatio* would operate as a *traditio*.[5]

In iure cessio was an adaptation of the procedure of *legis actio sacramento in rem*.[6] The transferor and the transferee appeared with the thing before the praetor, the transferee claimed the thing was his, the transferor made no counter-claim and the praetor made *addictio* of the thing to the transferee.[7] *In iure cessio* could be used whenever the *legis actio sacramento in rem* was appropriate and so could transfer both *res mancipi* and *res nec mancipi*, create servitudes and *ususfructus*, cede *tutela* and be used for adoption. It was, in fact, not widely used for transferring ownership since there were more convenient modes,[8] unless the thing was an incorporeal *res nec mancipi* when *in iure cessio* had to be used.

Usucapio was the acquisition of ownership by exercising the requisite control over a thing for a period of time, two years in the

---

[1] Cf. *formula Baetica*, Bruns no. 135; *mancipatio Pompeiana*, *FIRA*, iii, p. 192.
[2] Cf. D.21.2.45 (Alfenus, *4 dig. a Paulo epit.*); Watson, *Obligations*, p. 82.
[3] Cicero, *de off.*, 3.16.65; *P.S.*, 1.19.1. (though *P.S.*, 2.17.4 says only that the action was given for double). Cf. Kaser, RPR, i, p. 150.
[4] Cf. Cicero, *ad Att.*, 5.1.2; Watson, *Obligations*, p. 83 and the literature cited, n.4.　　[5] Cf. Watson, *Property*, pp. 18f.
[6] Cf. infra, pp. 69ff.
[7] Cf. G.2.24.
[8] Only two texts for the whole of the Republic concern its use to transfer ownership, and both are connected with abstract law, not actual instances: Varro, *de re rust.*, 2.10.4; Cicero, *top.*, 5.28.

case of land including buildings, one year for other things.[1, 2] Some things could not be usucapted: *res sacrae, res religiosae,* the entrance court of a tomb and the *bustum* as we have seen, also the five feet separating *fundi*[3] and stolen goods, though it may have been that only the thief could not usucapt.[4, 5] Likewise *res mancipi* belonging to a woman in the *tutela* of her agnates could not be usucapted unless they were delivered with the authority of her *tutores.*[6] But praedial servitudes – though perhaps only rustic servitudes[7] – could be usucapted although they were incorporeal[8] and this was also true of release from servitudes.[9] Stranger still perhaps, inheritances – abstract collections of heterogeneous things – could

---

[1] Cicero, *pro Caecina,* 19.54; *top.,* 4.23. These periods were established by the XII Tables.

[2] Few parts of Roman law underwent so many changes between the XII Tables and the end of the Republic.

[3] By the law of the XII Tables; Cicero, *de leg.,* 1.21.55.

[4] Also by the XII Tables: G.2.45, 49. The *lex Atinia* dates from the middle of the second century BC: Aulus Gellius, *N.A.,* 17.7.1, 2, 3 : cf. now, Watson, *Property,* pp. 24f and the authors cited. The exact scope of the XII Tables' provision is disputed but the two views which alone can fit the surviving evidence (cf. Watson, *Property,* pp. 26ff) are as in the text. The main modern proponent of the latter view is Daube, '*Furtum proprium* and *furtum improprium*', *Cambridge Law Journal,* vi (1936–8), pp. 217ff at pp. 231ff; the former is put forward very powerfully by Yaron, 'Reflections on *usucapio*', *T.v.R.,* xxv (1967), pp. 191ff at pp. 215ff.

[5] For a debtor to seize a thing he had transferred in *fiducia* was not *furtum* (cf. infra, pp. 86f) and he could usucapt even in classical law : G.2.59, 60, 61 : see now Watson, *Property,* pp. 41ff.

[6] G.2.47; a rule of the XII Tables. But it is sometimes suggested that this rule applied only where the woman transferred the thing without authority : cf. e.g. Kaser, RPR, i, p. 120. G.2.80 tells us that neither a woman nor a pupil *sine tutoris auctoritate* can alienate a *res mancipi* and it is sometimes thought from this that it may have been the case that there could be no *usucapio* of *res mancipi* belonging to such persons and which were transferred without the *tutor's* authority : cf. Kaser, *Eigentum und Besitz im älteren römischen Recht,* 2nd edit. (Cologne, Graz, 1956), pp. 98ff; zss, lxviii (1951), p. 148.

[7] There is no evidence of *usucapio* of urban servitudes. Cicero, *pro Caecina,* 26.74 shows that *usucapio* was available for all rustic servitudes, not just the original four; for the argument see Watson, *Property,* pp. 22ff.

[8] *Usucapio* of servitudes was later prohibited by the *lex Scribonia* of about 50 BC : see now, Watson, *loc. cit.*

[9] To which the (later) *lex Scribonia* did not apply : D.41.3.4.28(29) (Paul, *54 ad ed.*). Rustic servitudes could be lost by non-use, but there had to be positive *usucapio* (i.e. the servient tenement had to be in breach) of urban servitudes : D.8.2.7 (Pomponius, *26 ad Quintum Mucium*).

also be usucapted and the required time was one year even when the inheritance included land.[1] Neither a *hereditas* nor individual things forming part of a *hereditas*[2] could be stolen and they could be taken and usucapted by someone who knew he had no right.[3] A person who usucapted land also usucapted anything, including treasure, buried in the land.[4]

In classical law there could be *usucapio* only if the acquirer had begun his possession in good faith[5] and if there was a *iustus titulus*, that is, if the person had obtained control as a result of a legally recognised transaction such as sale or constitution of dowry which would lead to the transfer of ownership. Originally, however, there was no need either for *bona fides* or *iustus titulus* and, though there can be no certainty, it is likely that the general opinion is correct which puts the changeover after our period.[6]

For *usucapio* the acquirer had to exercise the proper degree of control over the thing. Yaron has convincingly argued that in early law what was needed was the actual, reasonable, suitable use of the thing.[7] This would mean, as he points out, that in a system which did not yet know the requirements of *bona fides* and *iustus titulus*, the true owner would have the chance of learning what was happening, and of taking steps to block the *usucapio*. This, I suggest, was still the position in 200 B C.[8,9]

---

[1] G.2.54. *Usucapio* of *hereditates* seems still to have existed in Cicero's time; *pro Flacco*, 34.85 and see also *ad Att.*, 1.5.6 : for the argument, Watson, *Property*, pp. 32ff. The mechanics of *usucapio hereditatis* are not known, but presumably the usucaptor made *cretio*.

[2] Not yet entered; hence this rule could not apply where there was a *heres necessarius* : G.2.58.

[3] G.2.55, 56. G.2.52 declares this rule about *usucapio* in connection with individual things of which the heir – who has accepted the *hereditas* – has not taken possession [and cf. D.47.4.1.15 (Ulpian, *38 ad ed.*)] but this continuance of the availability of *usucapio* after entry was not originally part of the general rule and has no place in Gaius' explanation of the origins of the rule, and did not exist in our time since *possessio* as a legal concept itself appears to be later : cf. infra, p. 64n. 8.

[4] The doctrine of *thesauri inventio* is much later : D.41.2.3.3 (Paul, *54 ed.*); for the argument see Watson, *Property*, pp. 55ff, 74.

[5] With some exceptions.

[6] Usually in the course of the second century B C : cf. now Watson, *Property*, pp. 31ff, 48ff.

[7] 'Reflections', pp. 209ff.

[8] That is, *possessio* was not yet a requirement. I believe – though the point is arguable – that the technical legal concept of *possessio* did not exist. *Possessio*

Usucapio could be stopped by *usurpatio*, a contrary act by the owner which could be either deprivation or the raising of an action.[1]

The remaining ways of acquiring ownership were available to all, Roman and peregrine alike.

Traditio was the mode[2] for voluntarily transferring corporeal *res nec mancipi* and it involved no formalities but only actual physical delivery of the thing.[3,4] Delivery would, of course, have to be accompanied by some intention to transfer and receive ownership, and ownership would not be acquired if, for instance, the thing was handed over and received under a contract of hire. But how far the position was theoretically regularized cannot be

---

as a technical legal concept could not appear before the introduction of possessory interdicts which probably occurred only after 200 BC. At least one interdict, however, with a clause about *vi, clam, precario* existed in 161 BC – Terence, *Eun.*, 319 – but as I have argued elsewhere ['Praetor's Edict'] the main development of the Edict is later than is generally imagined, and it will not do to push the introduction of interdicts too far into the past. Moreover interdicts will have existed for some little time before the technical concept of possession emerged from them. It should be noticed, too, that even if the *interdictum utrubi* did then exist, it contains no reference to *possessio* or *possidere*. And, despite a widespread opinion, there is no evidence for the *interdictum utrubi* in Plautus, *Sti.*, 696, 750 : for the argument, see Watson, *Property*, pp. 86f; followed by Villers, *Revue des Etudes Latines* xlvii (1969). I would now hold that the *interdictum uti possidetis* is also later. For the evidence for possession and possessory interdicts in the Republic see Watson, *Property*, pp. 81ff.

[9] Plautus, *Am.*, 375 and 845 have joking references to *usucapio* but neither line increases our knowledge : cf. Watson, *Property*, p. 60 n. 5.

[1] Cf. Cicero, *de orat.*, 3.28.110. The sufficiency of a recognized, formal, act of non-acquiescence in the *usucapio* such as the breaking of a twig, is probably a development after the switch from *usus* to *possessio* : cf. Yaron, '*De usurpationibus*', *Studi Grosso*, ii (Turin, 1968), pp. 553ff, especially at pp. 561f.

[2] The only one, apart from *in iure cessio*.

[3] It is likely, that the view – held in the first century BC, but later rejected – that it could be enough if the goods were precisely ascertained in the presence of the transferee who marked his acceptance of them though they remained under the control of the transferor was not yet in existence. See D.18.6.1.2 (Ulpian, *28 ad Sab.*); 18.6.15(14).1 (Paul, *3 epit. Alfeni*); 19.1.40 (Pomponius, *31 ad Quintum Mucium*); 41.2.51 (Javolenus, *5 ex post. Labeonis*); Watson, *Obligations*, pp. 59ff; *Property*, p. 62.

[4] For the special case of *traditio* following upon sale see infra, p. 132.

determined – problems would not be frequent in practice – nor can it be determined what happened in a case of mistake when, say, the owner delivered in the belief that there was a contract of hire, and the recipient took in the belief that there was a sale.

Occupatio was the acquisition of ownership of a thing which previously did not have an owner. Normally it involved actual seizure, such as picking up precious stones found on the sea shore, or landing a fish, but it was probably enough for a wild animal to be so wounded that it could be captured,[1] though if the hunter gave up the chase he ceased to be owner. Wild animals, it may be observed, did not belong to the owner of the land on which they occurred. Booty taken from the enemy also legally belonged by *occupatio* to the person who actually seized it,[2] but here the law was obscured by military practice. To avoid the possibility of a new attack by an apparently defeated enemy while the soldiers were busy looting, the Romans devised a system for collecting booty whereby particular soldiers – never more than half the force – were detailed to collect booty while the rest performed other assigned duties. The booty so collected was then sold and the money divided by the tribunes among all the soldiers including those who were absent from the battle because of illness or special service.[3] Though this could not affect the legal theory, in practice the individual soldier taking the booty could not become owner because he had not the intention of becoming owner. The general acquired great discretion in the distribution and inevitably dedicated part to the gods and gave part, especially captives, to the State.[4] It is not surprising that offences against the booty were regarded as *peculatus*.[5]

Accessio was the acquisition of a thing by its incorporation in something already owned by the acquirer. This could occur in

[1] This appears from D.41.1.5.1 (Gaius, *2 rer. cott.*) for the first century B C, but in the Empire actual capture was needed : cf. Watson, *Property*, pp. 62f. It is not illogical to think that the less stringent requirements for *occupatio* existed in our time whereas they did not for *traditio*. (cf. supra, p. 65 n. 3) The situation in respect of *occupatio* of wild animals is both more straightforward and a fruitful source of conflict.

[2] Cf. G.2.69; D.41.1.5.7 (Gaius, *2 rer. cot.*); 41.2.1.1 (Paul, *54 ad ed.*); 41.2.3.21 (*ibidem*); J.2.1.17.   [3] Polybius, *Hist.*, 10.16.

[4] For sale of captives by the State, see Plautus, *Cap.*, 110ff; Varro, *de re rust.*, 2.10.4.   [5] For all this see Watson, *Property*, pp. 63ff.

various ways. One group of situations involved accession to an immoveable. Thus, if part of a man's land collapsed on to his neighbour's, the latter acquired ownership as soon as the earth united with his own;[1] likewise a transplanted tree became the property of the owner of the land in which it was placed as soon as it put forth roots[2]; and seeds planted in another's land became his. Again, where the extent of land was determined – as was usually the case – by natural boundaries, soil which was imperceptibly deposited by the action of a river at once entered the ownership of the proprietor of the river bank[3]; but where a perceptible parcel of land was washed downstream and finally lodged against a bank, the owner of the bank did not become its owner until trees on it put forth roots on to his land.[4] *Accessio* of a moveable to a moveable could also occur where the two things became so united that they could not be separated. Ownership of both would go to the owner of the principal thing.[5]

When one person of his own accord made a new thing out of materials belonging to another, for instance a ship out of another's timber or wine from another's grapes, the resulting thing is likely to have belonged to the maker.[6] This was the Proculian view in classical law though the Sabinians held that the thing belonged to the owner of the materials.[7] The Proculian view is probably the older

[1] Cf. D.39.2.9.2 (Ulpian, *53 ad ed.*) which is direct evidence for the first century B C.
[2] Cf. D.6.1.5.3 (Ulpian, *16 ad ed.*) which is direct evidence for the first century B C. There might, of course, be an action for theft against the taker and planter if he had acted in bad faith.
[3] Cf. D.41.1.16 (Florentinus, *6 inst.*); 41.1.38.
[4] No direct evidence for the Republic.
[5] D.41.1.26pr (Paul, *14 ad Sab.*) is instructive. It is most unlikely that the law of *accessio* (especially for moveables) and *specificatio* had been worked out in any detail. The law on these topics had little practical value and its importance has been exaggerated because the theoretical institutional writers made a place for it, for completeness in the treatment of acquisition of ownership, in their works. It is not accidental that the first 16 fragments in the Digest title, 41.1, on the acquisition of ownership come from institutional works. No other Digest title begins in this way.
[6] D.41.1.26pr (Paul, *14 ad Sab.*) may show that this was the opinion of Servius in the first century B C. But see Watson, *Property*, p. 77.
[7] Cf. e.g. G.3.79; D.41.1.7.7 (Gaius, *2 rer. cott.*); J.2.1.25. See in general for *specificatio* – as this came to be called in the Middle Ages – Voci, *Modi di acquisto della proprietà* (Milan, 1952), pp. 239ff; Kaser, R P R, i, pp. 362f.

since it would obviously be difficult for the owner of the materials to bring a *vindicatio* in which he claimed that he was the owner of the new thing, ship or grapes. When two persons mixed things belonging to them together the resulting mixture was owned in common.[1]

It is appropriate to say something in this place about Roman legal terminology. The recent work of Daube has shown that technical legal terms were very slow to develop, perhaps especially with regard to the acquisition of property[2] but also in other fields.[3] Thus the ancient lawyers never spoke of *occupatio* though they used the verb *occupare*, nor of *thesauri inventio* but spoke of *thesaurum invenire*. Nor is the noun used for *satio, inaedificatio, commixtio* or *specificatio*. And it appears that the nouns *mancipatio, in iure cessio* and *traditio* are all later than the appropriate verbal forms, and none of them is likely to have existed in our period.[4] The conclusion is obvious; Roman law around 200 BC and very much later was not nearly so institutionalized as would appear from later commentaries.

Ownership could not be acquired through a representative unless he was in the *potestas* or ownership of the principal or was a *liber homo bona fide serviens*,[5] or a slave in whom the principal had a usufruct.[6] Probably, though, a patron acquired ownership of whatever his freedman took on his behalf.[7] The exception would be allowed because the *libertus* often continued to live in the house of his former master, was very dependent upon him and could in some sense be regarded as a member of the family. Complications arose when a slave had more than one master. Whatever he acquired belonged to his masters in the proportion of the share they

---

[1] All the evidence is for a much later time : e.g. D.41.1.7.8; J.2.1.27. The position was disputed where the mixing was not agreed to by both owners : D.41.1.7.9; J.2.1.28.

[2] *Roman Law*, pp. 13ff.

[3] E.g. in obligations : *Roman Law*, pp. 24ff.

[4] Daube, *Roman Law*, pp. 22f.

[5] Cf. supra, p. 52.

[6] Cf. infra, pp. 90ff.

[7] This at least was a view current in the time of Servius when the bond between patron and freedman was less close : D.34.2.4 (Paul *54 ad ed.*). In the early empire this acquisition was not permitted. For the general development see Watson, 'Acquisition of Ownership by *traditio* to an *extraneus*', SDHI, xxxiii (1967), pp. 189ff.

owned in him.[1] This was so even when he acquired through funds belonging to one master though in this case the funds would have to be accounted for in the *actio communi dividundo*.[2] But whatever he acquired expressly for one master went to that master[3] and so did anything acquired at the command of one master.[4] The law on acquisition through intermediaries demonstrates convincingly the relationship between acquisition of ownership and physical dominance.

The action for a claim of ownership was the *vindicatio*, the *legis actio sacramento in rem*. At the *in iure* stage,[5] the defendant and the plaintiff both appeared before the praetor, the defendant bringing with him the object of dispute[6] of which he had physical control. The defendant opened the proceedings by declaring he was owner : '*Hunc ego hominem ex iure Quiritium meum esse aio secundum suam causam. Sicut dixi, ecce tibi vindictam imposui.*' As he said this he placed his rod on the thing. The plaintiff then said and did exactly the same. The praetor then told them both to let go of the slave : *Mittite ambo hominem.* The defendant demanded that the plaintiff explain why he claimed : '*Postulo anne dicas qua ex causa vindicaveris.*' And the plaintiff declared he had acted properly : '*Ius feci, sicut vindictam imposui.*' The defendant maintained that the plaintiff had claimed wrongfully and so he challenged him in an oath, of 50 *asses* if the thing was worth less than 1,000 *asses*, of 500 if it was worth 1,000 or more : '*Quando tu iniuria vindicavisti, quingenario* (or *quinquagenario*) *sacramento te provoco.*' The plaintiff then issued a counter-challenge for that oath : '*Et ego te.*' Both then appealed to the witnesses : '*Testes estote.*'[7] The praetor

---

[1] Cf. e.g. G.3.167. The evidence is all much later but the proposition cannot be doubted.

[2] Cf. D.10.3.24 (Iulianus, *8 dig.*) = 41.1.45 (Gaius, *7 ad ed. prov.*). Again the evidence is for a much later period.

[3] Cf. e.g. G.3.167. Here too there is no direct evidence for the Republic.

[4] Cf. e.g. D.45.3.6 (Pomponius, *26 ad Sab.*) : on the text see now Watson, *Property*, p. 78. For acquisition through a common slave see in general Buckland, *The Roman Law of Slavery* (Cambridge, 1908), pp. 379ff; and see also Bretone, *Servus communis* (Naples, 1958), pp. 57ff.

[5] For procedure in general see infra, pp. 161ff.

[6] Or a symbolic part where the object could not conveniently be produced : e.g. a sheep for a flock; G.4.17.

[7] G.4.16. For this way of understanding the procedure see Watson, 'Towards a New Hypothesis of the *legis actio sacramento in rem*', RIDA, xiv

F

declared *vindiciae* in favour of one of the parties, that is, he gave
that one interim possession and ordered sureties to be given to the
other.[1] Presumably in the usual case, interim possession would be
given to the party who already had physical control but where this
was thought unsuitable, for instance where he had obtained the
thing by violence, the other would get control. This would have
considerable advantages in a system which did not yet have interdicts to establish who would appear as plaintiff, who as defendant.[2]
Thereafter the case went to the trial judge who decided which oath
had properly been given.[3]

The proceedings were modified where the object of dispute was
land which could not be brought into court. This time only one
party, the plaintiff, claimed ownership, and the defendant's initial
declaration has been allowed to drop. After the claim, the plaintiff
summoned the defendant to the land: '*Eum fundum, qui est in agro,
qui Sabinus vocatur, ego ex iure Quiritium meum esse aio. Inde ibi ego
te ex iure manum consertum voco.*' The *manum consertum*, like the
rods in the standard *vindicatio*, shows that originally a formalized
battle between the parties was envisaged. The defendant replied:
'*Unde tu me ex iure manum consertum vocasti, inde ibi ego te revoco*',
that is, he summoned the plaintiff back to the place where the proceedings were being heard. The praetor then formally directed the
parties and the neighbours who supported them the way to the

(1967), pp. 455ff, which, however, had a forerunner in Abġarowicz, *Essai
sur la preuve dans la rei vindicatio* (Paris, 1912). On the common view, the
plaintiff spoke first, the two parties were placed completely on equal terms –
but note that in fact on this view the defendant alone was (oddly) asked to
explain why he claimed – and that party won who had the better claim to the
thing even if he was obviously not the owner. On this last point the *legis
actio* would differ fundamentally from the classical *vindicatio* where the
defendant would keep the thing unless the plaintiff proved he actually was
the owner. This doctrine is the strongest support of the theory of 'relative
ownership' so stoutly maintained by Kaser [e.g. 'Der römische Eigentums-
begriff', *Rabels Zeitschrift* (1962), pp. 19ff at p. 20; 'The Concept of
Roman Ownership', *Tydskrif vir Hedendaagse Romeins-Hollandse Reg*
(1964), pp. 5ff at pp. 6ff] and others, but against which see Watson,
Property, pp. 91ff. [1] G.4.16.
[2] Cf. Watson, 'New Hypothesis', pp. 46of. Kaser thinks the fact that the
thing did not simply stay with the defendant is evidence that he was suspected of theft: ZPR, p. 73 n. 44. But Lévy-Bruhl considers the praetor always
gave interim possession to the person who had control when the action began:
e.g. *Recherches sur les actions de la loi* (Paris, 1960), pp. 178ff.
[3] For this part of the procedure see Kaser, ZPR, pp. 82ff.

land and back again : '*Suis utrisque superstitibus praesentibus istam viam dico; ite viam.*' Then : '*Redite viam.*' At the land in question[1] the *manum conserere* took place and the parties and their supporters returned to the praetor with a symbolic part for the object of dispute, a tile for a house, a clod of earth for a farm.[2] The defendant then asked the plaintiff – the only one who had expressly claimed ownership – to declare why he had vindicated : '*Quando te in iure conspicio (postulo?) anne tu dicas qua ex causa vindicaveris.* And so on.[3]

Whether the *formula*[4] of the *vindicatio* of classical law yet existed can only be a matter for conjecture. The opinion of most scholars is certainly that no *formula* for any civil law action existed before the *lex Aebutia* of about 140–120 BC.[5] But it would seem, contrary to this opinion, that the *formula* for the *condictio* existed around 200 BC,[6] and if this is so there is no *a priori* reason for thinking that the *formula* for *vindicatio* was later. But equally the availability of the *formula* for *condictio* is no argument for holding that the *formula* for *vindicatio* was also in existence. We know, however, that in 70 BC the *formula* of the *vindicatio*[7] and the *legis actio sacramento in rem*[8] were in use contemporaneously.

In all probability, though, the device of an action *per sponsionem* was already used[9] in some cases as a substitute for the *legis actio*

[1] Apparently in the most developed stage of the procedure, the parties did not actually go to the land in question. But this development is almost certainly after our time.

[2] Pace Kaser, ZPR, p. 70 n. 30, there is nothing in Varro, *de ling. lat.*, 6.64 which proves that the expression *manum conserere* was not confined to disputes over land.

[3] Cicero, *pro Murena*, 12.26; Aulus Gellius, *N.A.*, 20.10.1-10; Varro, *de ling. lat.*, 6.64; Festus, *s.v. Consere manu*; Probus, 4.4. For this way of seeing the procedure, see Watson, 'New Hypothesis', pp. 462ff. On the traditional view (cf., most recently, Kaser, ZPR, pp. 74f) it was the plaintiff who uttered the sole challenge, but this conflicts with the fact made obvious by Cicero that the sole claim (hence the only one which could be challenged) was by the plaintiff. [4] For procedure *per formulas* see infra, pp. 164f.

[5] See for all, Kaser, ZPR, pp. 109ff, especially p. 114. There is, of course, great diversity of opinion on the precise steps of the introduction of *formulae*. [6] Cf. infra, p. 127.

[7] Cicero, *in Verrem*, II, 2.12.31 : cf. Watson, *Property*, pp. 96f.

[8] Cicero, *pro Murena*, 12.26, of 63 BC: cf. Watson, *Property*, p. 96.

[9] It can be argued that the device is older than the *lex Silia* : de Zulueta, *The Institutes of Gaius*, ii (Oxford, 1953), p. 276. And the *lex Silia* probably dates from the third century BC : cf. Kaser, ZPR, p. 81 n. 4.

sacramento in rem. For this the person who did not have control of
the thing and who would be the plaintiff took a *sponsio* from the
other party in a form such as this : '*Si homo quo de agitur ex iure
Quiritium meus est, sestertios XXV nummos dare spondes?*'[1] The
other promised, an action – almost certainly a *legis actio per iudicis
postulationem*[2] – was then brought on the *sponsio*, and the plaintiff
won the action if he proved that the thing in dispute was owned by
him. In classical law the *sponsio* of 25 *sesterces* (unlike the 50 or
500 *asses* in the old *legis actio sacramento in rem*) was never
claimed, and the *sponsio* had the sole function of bringing the issue
to trial, and no counter-stipulation was taken.[3] Whether this was
always the case from the beginning cannot be determined but is of
little importance. The procedure was thus technically in the form
of an *actio in personam* but it was in practice given the effect of a real
action since the defendant gave the plaintiff a *stipulatio pro praede
litis vindiciarum*, that is a contractual guarantee for the disputed
thing and its profits.[4] As the name shows, the guarantee was in
place of the personal guarantors (*praedes*) who intervened in the
legis actio sacramento in rem on behalf of the party who was given
interim custody of the disputed thing.[5, 6]

A real action of very different character was the *actio communi
dividundo* which was brought when owners wished to divide property they owned in common.[7] It was introduced by a *lex Licinnia*
probably somewhat earlier than 200 B C,[8] and it authorised a *legis
actio per postulationem iudicis*.[9] The judge could condemn either
party to the action (or any of them, when there were more than

---

[1] G.4.93.
[2] The *legis actio sacramento in rem* and the *legis actio per condictionem* were
also theoretical possibilities from the start, but for the arguments in favour
of procedure *per iudicis postulationem* see now Levy, *Gesammelte Schriften*, i
(Cologne, Graz, 1963), pp. 92f; cf. also, e.g. Kiefner, z s s, lxxxi (1964),
p. 227 and the references he gives, n. 71; Kaser, z p r, p. 77.
[3] G.4.94.
[4] G.4.91, 94.
[5] Cf. supra, pp. 69f.
[6] For this procedure see de Zulueta, *Gaius*, ii, pp. 276f; Kaser, z p r, pp.
76f. It should be noted that in this procedure it is certain that one party
played the role of plaintiff, the other that of defendant.
[7] Unless they were joint heirs (or had entered a partnership by *legis actio*)
when the action would be the *actio familiae erciscundae*: infra, p. 97.
[8] See the references given by Kaser, r p r i, p. 124 n. 1.
[9] G.4.17a.

two co-owners) to give to the other (or others) whatever was proper. As was inevitable where the property might consist of one thing, or of things which could not be divided equally, the judge had very considerable discretion in arranging the division and the appropriate equalising payments. Any damage done to the property by one owner and any expense incurred by an owner would be taken into account when assessing the amount due to the other (or others).[1]

APPENDIX

Donatio

The positioning of the discussion of the law of gift in a systematic account of Roman law is notoriously difficult, but here not a matter of great importance since a major historical falsification of this book is oversystematization.[2]

Gift is, in itself, not a mode of acquiring property but is the cause of a valid delivery. The mere promise of a gift at this time was not legally effective in any way unless it were cast in a form such as *stipulatio* which itself supplied the elements needed for actionability.

The law was governed by the *lex Cincia de donis et muneribus* of 204 B C which was a plebiscite of the tribune M. Cincius Alimentus,[3] and of which Q. Fabius Maximus was *suasor*.[4] The *lex Cincia* had two provisions.

The first and less important forbade gifts to be made to advocates for pleading cases.[5] The background to this provision is plain. Traditionally from the earliest times of the city,[6] and in this period,[7] the moral duty to appear in court to plead cases for depen-

---

[1] Even if this was not an original feature of the action if would very quickly have emerged. Cf. the *formula* for the action as reconstructed by Lenel, *Edictum*, p. 211; D.10.3.26 (Alfenus Varus, *2 dig.*); Watson, *Property*, p. 124. For the *actio communi dividundo* in general see Buckland, *Textbook*, pp. 539ff.   [2] Cf. supra, p. 4.

[3] Cicero, *de orat.*, 2.71.286; cf. Livy, 29.20.11.   [4] Cicero, *de senec.*, 4.10.

[5] Cicero, *ad Att.*, 1.20.7; Tacitus, *Ann.*, 11.5; 13.42; 15.20 : cf. Archi, *La donazione* (Milan, 1960), pp. 16f.

[6] Cf. Dionysius Hal., *Hist.*, 2.9, 10.

[7] Cf. Plautus, *Cas.*, 563ff. For a slightly later period see Terence, *Eun.*, 335ff.

dents and friends was very strong. But the moral order was breaking down, and some persons were using their oratorical skill to make money. Even in this provision the *lex Cincia* reveals itself as a defender of traditional Roman moral standards.

The other provision forbade gifts above a particular – unknown – amount except between specified classes, namely, between cognates up to second cousin, between *adfines* (husband and wife, fiancé and fiancée, parents-in-law, children-in-law, step-parents and step-children), to patrons,[1] to any female cognate if the gift was intended as dowry, and by a *tutor* who was administering a ward's property to the ward.[2]

The *lex Cincia* was a *lex imperfecta*, that is it did not declare a prohibited gift void if it was nonetheless made – the gift, indeed, was valid at civil law – and it did not establish any penalty for a breach of the statute. The statute seems to have been effective, in fact, only where the gift was not complete and the donee had to claim it in a court of law when the donor could raise the *exceptio legis Cinciae*.[3]

This provision, too, had its basis in an attempt to preserve the traditional austere Roman morality, to restrict over-liberality on the one hand and greed on the other. Another motive was to hinder pressure put on socially inferior persons by powerful individuals to make forced donations,[4] and it is possible that the *lex Cincia* was further intended as protection against over-hasty gifts.[5, 6]

---

[1] This must have been the meaning of the provision recorded in *Vat. Fr.*, 307 (Paul, *71 ad ed.*) where the word *servus* must, as Paul declares, originally have had the sense of *libertus* : cf. Mommsen, *Römisches Staatsrecht*, iii, 3rd edit. (Leipzig, 1887), p. 428 and n. 1; *Gesammelte Schriften*, iii (Berlin, 1907), pp. 21f; Treggiari, *Roman Freedmen during the late Republic* (Oxford, 1969), p.p 265f. For the expression of doubt see Archi, *Donazione*, pp. 19ff.

[2] For all this see *Vat. Fr.*, 298-309 (Paul, *71 ad ed.*).

[3] The detailed rules of operation of the *lex Cincia* are at least to some extent the work of later jurists and praetors : cf. in general; Buckland, *Textbook*, pp. 254f; Kaser, RPR, i, p. 504.

[4] Cf. Livy, 34.4.9; Archi, *Donazione*, pp. 13ff, especially at p.22.

[5] Cf. Biondi, *Successione testamentaria e donazioni*, 2nd edit. (Milan, 1955), p. 634.

[6] Though gifts in contemplation of death were no doubt common it is unlikely that the specific rules of *donatio mortis causa* were already in existence though the technical concept appears to have been known by 79 BC : Valerius Maximus, 8.2.2 : for the situation involved see Watson, *Obligations*, pp. 32ff.

CHAPTER 7

Neighbours' Rights and Duties

The law concerning the relationship between adjoining proprietors was well developed even from the earliest times.

The XII Tables forbade the *usucapio* of land 5 feet wide round boundaries.[1] They further declared that there had to be an *ambitus* of 5 feet,[2] that is, that no-one could build nearer than $2\frac{1}{2}$ feet to the edge of his land; that when a tree overhung a neighbour's land the neighbour was entitled to have the offending branches cut off up to a height of 15 feet from the ground[3]; that an owner of land was allowed to gather acorns – valuable feed for pigs – which fell from his trees on to the neighbour's land.[4] The regulation of these provisions on *usucapio*, *ambitus* and other matters was by the *actio finium regundorum*[5] which also, and more importantly, was used for settling boundary disputes, whether in the city or country.[6] The action was heard by three *arbitri* and, like the *actio communi dividundo* and the *actio familiae erciscundae*, it had the strange characteristic that the arbiters could condemn either party to the action. Moreover, the powers of the *arbitri* were very wide and

---

[1] Cicero, *de leg.*, 1.21.55.

[2] Festus, *s.v. Ambitus*; Varro, *de ling. lat.*, 5.22; cf. Volusius Maecianus, *Assis distr.*, 46.

[3] D.43.27.1.8 (Ulpian *71 ad ed.*); 43.27.2 (Pomponius *34 ad Sab.*) : cf. Watson, *Property*, pp. 117ff.

[4] Pliny, *N.H.*, 16.5.15 : cf. Watson, *Property*, pp. 120f. The juristic interpretation of *glans* to mean fruits in general might already have occurred by our time.

[5] Cicero, *de leg.*, 1.21.55; D.10.1.13 (Gaius, *4 ad legem XII Tab.*); D.10.1.4.3 (Paul, *23 ad ed.*) : for the argument see Watson, *Property*, pp. 111ff.

[6] Later in the Republic restricted to the country; Cicero, *top.*, 4.23; 10.43; D.10.1.4.10 (Paul, *23 ad ed.*) : for the argument, especially from Cicero, *top.*, 4.24, see Watson, *Property*, pp. 114ff.

they could where necessary change existing boundaries, and even adjudge more to one party, directing him to pay monetary compensation to the other.[1]

Protection was provided against the threat of loss caused by a neighbour's defective property (*damnum infectum*). The law here is obscure since the remedy was at a later but unknown[2] time superseded by praetorian provisions which made the law fuller and more convenient,[3] though the implication of the Gaius' text which is the source of our knowledge is that the old law was fundamentally similar to that of the praetor. There was certainly a *legis actio*[4] which seems to have been *per pignoris capionem*,[5] and apparently, a *cautio*.[6] So the protection might be envisaged thus : a person who feared that property on neighbouring land might cause him injury could ask for a guarantee (*cautio*) against financial loss. If the neighbour refused to give it, he could seize goods belonging to the neighbour as security against the injury feared.

The remedy for *damnum infectum* is very significant because the Romans did not otherwise grant an action for injury caused by inanimate objects. The mechanism involved means that the injury had to be foreseeable and the danger had to be pointed out in a formal manner to the owner. It thus shows the very considerable legal sophistication of the early jurists.

It seems reasonable to hazard the guess that the *cautio* could be taken against a fault in a building or other thing due, for instance, to natural wear and tear, and against a fault in the workmanship in making and repairing.[7] Also the guarantee could be demanded

---

[1] Cf. D.10.1.2.1 (Ulpian, *19 ad ed.*); 10.1.3 (Gaius, *7 ad ed. prov.*).
[2] Hence it is not possible to hold with safety that the older references are to the earlier procedure.
[3] G.4.31.
[4] G.4.31.
[5] The matter is very much disputed – Kaser, for instance recently excluding the *legis actio per pignoris capionem* as a possibility : ZPR, p. 25 n.13 – but see for the argument, Watson, *Property*, pp. 128ff; also Lévy-Bruhl, *Recherches sur les actions de la loi* (Paris, 1960), p. 327. For this *legis actio* see infra, p. 164.
[6] Appears from D.43.8.5 (Paul, *16 ad Sab.*) : for the argument, see Watson, *Property*, pp. 131ff.
[7] Cf. e.g. Pliny, *N.H.*, 36.2.5, 6; Cicero, *in Verr.*, II, 1.56.146; *top.*, 4.22; D.8.5.17.2 (Alfenus, *2 dig.*); 39.2.24.4, 5, 12 (Ulpian, *81 ad ed.*); 39.2.43pr (Alfenus, *2 dig.*); though they may all concern the edictal provisions: for the argument, Watson, *Property*, pp. 139ff.

from the person responsible for the thing even if he were not the owner,[1] and it could be demanded in respect of work done on public property.[2] More difficult to estimate is whether the *cautio* might be given for danger from moveables and things on the move[3] and whether the neighbour, having given the *cautio*, was automatically liable for injury emanating from the thing, even if it was not due to the *vitium*, the fault guarded against.[4]

We have more information, however, on another action from the XII Tables,[5] the *actio aquae pluviae arcendae*. This action was given if work had been done on a neighbouring estate, from which rain water might now injure the plaintiff's land, and if it was proper for the proprietor of that estate to protect the plaintiff from the water.[6]

Aqua pluvia, rain water, presumably included any water which might be dangerously swelled by heavy rain but it is likely that already by this time efforts were being made both to have a narrow interpretation, that only rain water unmixed with other water was *aqua pluvia*,[7] and also to have a wide interpretation, that, for instance, springs arising on the neighbouring land which were polluted by *opus factum* were *aqua pluvia*.[8] In the last century of the Republic there was greater diversity of opinion among the jurists on the scope of the *actio aquae pluviae arcendae* than on any other action and it is reasonable to think that the action was also causing controversy around 200 BC. At least, there were no new political,

---

[1] Thus, it could be from the person in right of the servitude of *aquae ductus* : D.43.8.5; cf. Watson, *Property*, pp. 131ff. See also Cicero *in Verr.*, II, 1.56.146; Pliny, *N.H.*, 36.2.5, 6, though these may relate to the Edict.

[2] D.43.8.5.

[3] It was by 58 BC : Pliny, *N.H.*, 36.2.5, 6 : cf. Watson, *Property*, pp. 139ff. But this might have been under the Edict.

[4] Later in the Republic the action was available only if the injury was the result of the *vitium* : D.39.2.24.4, 5; cf. now Watson, *Property*, pp. 149ff.

[5] D.40.7.21pr (Pomponius, 7 ex *Plautio*).

[6] Cf. Lenel's reconstruction of the (rather later) *formula* : *Si paret opus factum esse in agro Capenate, unde aqua pluvia agro Auli Agerii nocet, quam ob rem Numerium Negidium eam aquam Aulo Agerio arcere oportet, si ea res arbitrio iudicis non restituetur etc.* : *Edictum*, p. 375.

[7] This is unlikely at any time to have been more than a minority view; Cicero, *top.*, 9.38; D.39.3.1pr (Ulpian, *53 ad ed.*) : cf. Watson, *Property*, pp. 156f.

[8] Cf. D.39.3.3pr, 1 (Ulpian, *53 ad ed.*).

social or agrarian factors which might here create problems peculiar to the late Republic.

Not all *aqua pluvia* permitted the bringing of the action, but only where there was *opus factum*.[1] Generally this would be where new work was done but problems might also exist where earlier work of men – whether the authors were known or not – fell into disrepair. How much discussion there was on this cannot now be discovered, but it is safe to assume that it was widely held that when an *opus*, such as a ditch, on lower ground had previously enabled water to flow freely from higher ground for some time, and the disrepair of the *opus* subsequently threatened to cause flooding of the higher ground, then the proprietor of the higher ground had the *actio aquae pluviae arcendae*. Later texts strongly imply that the lower ground was subject to the higher ground, almost as if it were under a servitude to accept the water from higher ground.[2] This idea may have been even more prominent in our time. But the action was probably given to let the plaintiff clean out the ditch, not to make the defendant put it into a safe condition, or pay damages.[3, 4]

Not every *opus* which caused danger from rain water gave rise to the action. Exceptions were made for particular agricultural processes, and here too there was scope for the inevitable disputes. Some will have held that any ploughing for cultivation would not count as *opus factum* for the action,[5] while others will have taken the narrower view that only ploughing for a grain crop and not the deeper ploughing needed for vines and olives should be so treated.[6] Scope for dispute might also exist where ploughing a field in one direction would endanger a neighbour, though the danger could be avoided if the furrows pointed in a different direction.[7] Likewise

---

[1] Cf. for the principle, Cicero, *top.*, 9.39.

[2] Cf. D.39.3.2.1, 4, 6 (Paul, *49 ad ed.*); 39.3.11.6 (*idem*) : Watson, *Property*, pp. 161ff. But for the variety of opinions which could be held cf. D.39.3.2.5 : Watson, *Property*, pp. 167ff.

[3] Cf. D.39.3.2.1,6; 39.3.11.6; but see 39.3.2.4 (and also 39.3.2.1). The condemnation, if the action went so far, would always be in money.

[4] It had probably not yet been argued that the action should be given even where there was no man-made *opus*. But this opinion was held at least by Namusa in the first century BC : D.39.3.2.6.

[5] As later Quintus Mucius : D.39.3.1.3 (Ulpian, *53 ad ed.*).

[6] As later, Trebatius : D.39.3.1.3.

[7] Cf. D.39.3.24pr (Alfenus, *4 dig. a Paulo epit.*).

problems might arise where one proprietor dug ditches for the reasonable agricultural purpose of draining surplus water from his land[1]; or changed the cultivation of fields.[2]

The action was available whether the threatened ground was in the town or the country.[3] But it lay only for immission of water and could not be brought when the complaint was that the neighbour had reduced or stopped the flow of water on to one's land.[4] In fact in the climatic conditions then prevailing in Italy over-abundance of water was often a greater problem than scarcity.

From a legal point of view servitudes are probably the most significant real rights over neighbouring land. They gave the owner for the time being of the dominant land a right over the servient land to act in certain specific ways or to prevent the owner of the servient land acting in certain ways. Servitudes were attached to the land, not to its owner as an individual, and so were not affected by any change of ownership. To be accepted as a servitude a right had to fall within a recognized category, but there was no closed list of servitudes; each new situation when it arose was discussed by the jurists who decided whether a servitude right could exist in the circumstances.[5] *Iter, actus, via* and *aquae ductus* were the first to be recognized and were ancient, and *aquae haustus* was early associated with them.[6] Also already recognized[7] were *lumen*,[8] *prospectus*,[9] *cloaca*,[10] *aquam immittere*,[11] *servitus proiciendi protegendive*,[12] *stillicidium*,[13] *flumen*,[14] *pecoris ad aquam appellendi*,[15] and

---

[1] Cf. D.39.3.1.4, 5; 39.3. 24.1, 2.
[2] Cf. D.39.3.3.2 (Ulpian, *53 ad ed.*) : see also D.39.3.1.6.
[3] But later it was restricted to the country perhaps on the analogy of the *actio finium regundorum*: D.39.3.1.17; Cicero, *top.*, 4.23; 10.43 : cf. Watson, *Property*, pp. 172ff. [4] Cf. D.39.3.1.21.
[5] Cf. Watson, *Property*, pp. 176ff. [6] Cf. Cicero, *pro Caecina*, 26.74.
[7] Though the evidence in all cases is for a rather later time, and the point in some instances is arguable.
[8] Cf. D.8.2.16 (Paul, *2 epit. Alfeni dig.*); 8.2.7 (Pomponius, *26 ad Quintum Mucium*) (?); Cicero, *de orat.*, 1.39.179.
[9] Cf. D.8.2.16; 8.2.7(?). [10] Cf. D.43.23.2 (Venuleius, *1 interd.*).
[11] Cf. D.39.3.2.10 (Paul, *49 ad ed.*).
[12] Cf. D.8.5.17pr (Alfenus, *2 dig.*). See for the Empire, D.8.2.2 (Gaius, *7 ad ed. prov.*).
[13] Cf. D.39.3.1.17 (Ulpian, *53 ad ed.*); Varro, *de ling. lat.*, 5.27; Cicero, *de leg.*, 1.4.14; *orator*, 21.72.
[14] Cf. D.39.3.1.17; Varro, *de ling. lat.*, 5.27.
[15] Cf. D.43.20.1.18 (Ulpian, *70 ad ed.*).

oneris ferendi[1] and possibly others. In later times servitudes were classified either as rustic, that is, attached to land, or urban, attached to buildings.[2] The classification itself will not have existed in our period but the basis of the classification – which was a natural development – did. Rustic servitudes were *res mancipi*, urban servitudes were *res nec mancipi*[3]; rustic servitudes were lost by non-use for two years, but non-use was not enough for the loss of urban servitudes and in this case the servient tenement had to be in positive breach of the servitude for the two years.[4]

Iter was the right to go across the neighbour's land on foot[5] and on horseback,[6] but did not give the right to drive animals or a cart across.[7] *Actus* was the right to drive animals or a cart across and was considered to include *iter*; hence a farmer with this right could cross his neighbour's land even without his animals.[8] *Via* is described in later texts as if it were the combination of *iter* and *actus*,[9] which causes a problem since *actus* is held to include *iter*.[10] It may be significant in this connection that when Cicero gives a list of servitudes he omits *via*.[11] But *via* had the peculiarity that the XII Tables provided the road was to be 8 feet wide on the straight, 16 feet on bends.[12] At some time – before, during or after our period cannot be determined – this provision was held to apply only if the parties had themselves made no agreement as to the width of the

[1] Cf. D.8.2.33 (Paul, *5 epit. Alfeni dig.*); 8.5.6.2 (Ulpian, *17 ad ed.*).
[2] Cf. e.g. G.2.14. Whether the land or building was in the town or country was irrelevant.
[3] Cf. G.2.14a, 17, 29; *Epit. Ulp.*, 19.1; *Vat. Fr.*, 45. It is sometimes argued that only the four original servitudes were *res mancipi* but this is contrary to the evidence of the texts.
[4] Cf. e.g. *P.S.*, 1.17.1, 2; D.8.2.6 (Gaius, *7 ad ed. prov.*); 8.2.7 (Pomponius, *26 ad Quintum Mucium*).
[5] Cf. D.8.3.1pr (Ulpian, *2 inst.*); 8.3.12 (Modestinus, *9 diff.*) J.2.3 pr.
[6] In classical law *iter* included the right to cross the land in a litter (*lectica*), or portable chair (*sella*) : D.8.3.7pr (Paul, *21 ad ed.*). But it is unlikely that the custom of being so carried was common enough in our time to be the subject of juristic discussion on the scope of *iter*.
[7] Cf. D.8.3.1pr; J.2.3pr.
[8] Cf. e.g. D.8.3.1.1; 8.3.12; J.2.3pr.
[9] Cf. D.8.3.1pr; J.2.3pr.
[10] Presumably *actus* was originally thought of only in respect of driving animals or carts across the land.
[11] *Pro Caecina*, 26.74 : cf. Watson, *Property*, p. 183 and n.3.
[12] D.8.3.8. (Gaius, *7 ad ed. prov.*); cf. 8.3.13.2 (Iavolenus, *10 ex Cassio*).

road.[1,2] *Aquae ductus* was the right to conduct water in a channel through a neighbour's land to one's own for drinking or irrigation purposes.[3] Servitudes did not impose on the owner of the servient tenement an obligation to do something so that it was the responsibility of the owner of the dominant tenement to keep the channel clean and in good repair.[4] It would seem, contrary to some modern opinion, that *aquae ductus* (and *aquae haustus*) did not reserve in any way the ownership of the water to the proprietor of the dominant tenement,[5] and this may explain why *aquae haustus* was not one of the original servitudes; it might appear technically to be nothing more than *iter*[6] since flowing water was common to all.[7] But *aquae haustus* was early recognized.[8] Of most of the remaining servitudes little need be said. *Lumen* was the right not to have one's light obstructed by a neighbour, and it differed from *prospectus* only in that for *lumen* the dominant land had to be higher than the servient.[9] *Stillicidium* was the right to let water drip from a height on to a neighbour's property whereas *flumen* was simply the right to let water flow on to that other's property.[10] It should be noted, too, that the extent of the servitude would often be determined by agreement; thus, in *pecoris ad aquam appellendi* the number of cattle which could be driven over the neighbour's land to water could be fixed.[11]

The servitude *oneris ferendi* was the right to have a wall on one's

---

[1] Cf. D.8.3.13.2, 3.

[2] In classical law most, but not all, jurists thought *via* included the right of transporting stones and building materials, and *rectam hastam referendi*: D.8.3.7pr (Paul, *21 ad ed.*).

[3] D.8.3.1pr; J.2.3pr.

[4] By the time of Servius at the latest the right of the owner of the dominant tenement to enter on the servient land to clean and repair the aqueduct was protected by the *interdictum de rivis* : D.43.21.3pr; cf. Watson, *Property*, pp. 191f.

[5] Cf. now Watson, *Property*, pp. 184ff.

[6] Cf. for a much later period, D.8.3.3 (Ulpian, *17 ad ed.*).

[7] It is almost universally held that originally servitudes were regarded as corporeal *res mancipi*. It seems to me that there is room for considerable doubt [cf. *Property*, pp. 92ff; 185f and 186 n. 3; supra, p. 60 n. 2] but in any event by our time the incorporeal nature of servitudes will have been fully recognized.

[8] Cf. e.g. Cicero, *pro Caecina*, 26.74; Watson, *Property*, p. 183.

[9] Cf. D.8.2.16.

[10] Cf. Varro, *de ling. lat.*, 5.27.

[11] Cf. D.3.20.1.18 for the first century BC.

land supported by a neighbour's, and in classical law it was exceptional in that it imposed a positive duty on the owner of the servient tenement to keep his wall in a satisfactory state of repair. In the first century B C there was, we know, a dispute between Gallus who wanted the obligation to repair to be on the owner of the dominant tenement and Servius who took the view which eventually prevailed.[1] Probably Gallus' view which treats *oneris ferendi* as being in this respect the same as other servitudes is the older, but the other is not likely to be much later. The problem is that the supporting wall would have been in existence before the creation of the servitude and would usually have performed other functions for the benefit of the owner of the servient land, hence the question of who should do repairs to the wall was not simple.[2]

A servitude had to be so used as to cause as little inconvenience as possible.[3] It had to be for the advantage of the dominant tenement, not just for the personal pleasure of the owner of that land, nor might it be to restrict the owner of the servient tenement.[4] One could not have a servitude over one's own land and so if two neighbouring estates came into the ownership of one man the mutual servitude rights and duties were extinguished and did not revive automatically if later the ownership was again split.[5]

Rustic servitudes could be created by *mancipatio* and *in iure cessio*, and *in iure cessio* could be used for urban servitudes.[6] Both kinds could also be brought into existence by *adiudicatio* in an *actio communi dividundo, familiae erciscundae* or *finium regundorum*, and by legacy,[7] and they were capable of being usucapted.[8] In addition, the owner of two estates might in transferring one by *mancipatio* or *in iure cessio* reserve a servitude right in favour of the estate which he was retaining[9] or grant one in favour of the

---

[1] D.8.5.6.2 (Ulpian, *17 ad ed.*); 8.2.33 (Paul, *5 epit. Alfeni dig.*) : cf. Watson, *Property*, pp. 198ff.

[2] For this and the apparent problem of the origins of *oneris ferendi* see now Watson, *Property*, pp. 198ff.

[3] Cf. e.g. D.8.1.9 (Celsus, *5 dig.*).

[4] Cf. e.g. D.8.1.15pr (Pomponius, *33 ad Sab.*).

[5] Cf. e.g. D.8.2.26 (Paul, *15 ad Sab.*); 8.6.1 (Gaius, *7 ad ed. prov.*).

[6] G.2.29, 31.

[7] Cf. D.8.2.31 (Paul, *48 ad ed.*).

[8] Until the *lex Scribonia* probably of 50 B C : cf. supra, p. 63 n. 8.

[9] Cf. e.g. D.8.3.30 (Paul, *4 epit. Alfeni dig.*).

estate he was transferring.[1] Servitudes were extinguished by *in iure cessio*, or by *remancipatio* for a rustic servitude, by *usucapio*,[2] by the same person becoming owner of both estates, and by a permanent change in the condition of the servient tenement which made the servitude impossible.

The action claiming a servitude was a variation of the *rei vindicatio*.[3]

[1] Cf. e.g. D.8.3.29 (Paul, *2 epit. Alfeni dig.*).

[2] Cf. supra, p. 63.

[3] Cf. e.g. Kaser, RPR, i, p. 374. Whether the formulary procedure was possible would depend in the first instance on whether the *formula* for *vindicatio* had come into being, but it is in any event most unlikely that the forms for the so called *actio confessoria* and *actio negatoria* were yet in the praetor's Edict : cf. e.g. Watson, *Property*, pp. 176ff; 'Praetor's Edict'. Later, servitudes were often protected by interdicts : for our knowledge of these in the Republic see Watson, *Property*, pp. 188ff.

CHAPTER 8

Other Property Rights

REAL SECURITY

Although the Romans depended upon personal security much more than we do,[1] this does not mean that the law of real security was neglected or slow to develop. Plautus, indeed makes a pun[2] on the two principal forms, *pignus* and *fiducia*.

> PERIPHANES. qua fiducia ausu's primum quae emptast nudiustertius
> filiam meam dicere esse? EPICUS. lubuit: ea fiducia.
> PE. ain tu? lubuit? EP. aio. vel da pignus, ni ea sit filia.

Old Periphanes asks the slave Epidicus on what account (or relying on what), *qua fiducia*, he dared to say that the girl bought the day before yesterday was Periphanes' daughter. Epidicus replies 'On that account, *ea fiducia*, I wanted to.' When Periphanes becomes cross, Epidicus says : 'Make a bet, *da pignus*, that she is not your daughter.' The lines using *fiducia* and *pignus* with meanings remote from their sense in real security have no comic point unless there is a hidden pun, hence these forms of pledge must have been in use. *Fiducia* is scarcely imaginable without a legal remedy, but the present text is in itself no real evidence that there was legal protection for *pignus*.

Fiducia was the form of security in which ownership of the thing to be pledged was transferred to the creditor by means of *mancipatio* and possibly also by *in iure cessio*. The wording of the

---

[1] Cf. infra, pp. 119ff.

[2] *Epid.*, 697-9. The date of the *Epidicus* is uncertain though it is earlier than the *Bacchides* which is one of Plautus' late plays : cf. e.g. Duckworth, *The Nature of Roman Comedy* (Princeton, 1952), p. 55.

mancipatio was not the same as that for a normal transfer of property but the creditor claimed in the *mancipatio* itself that the object had been bought for his faith and trust, *fide et fiduciae*, or some similar expression such as *fidi fiduciae causa*.[1] The significance of this is precisely that the transaction is within the scope of the provision of the XII Tables which declared that the law would enforce *nexum* or *mancipatio* in accordance with the words spoken.[2] This would mean that in the rather rigid proceedings by *legis actio*[3] which emphasized the words used rather than any intention which could be ascribed to the parties, the words *fide et fiduciae* would have to be interpreted, and so the creditor's good faith would be legally relevant in an action which technically was one of strict law. Hence from an early date, before the introduction of the *bonae fidei iudicia*, a debtor who had repaid the loan would be able to sue for the recovery of the thing pledged[4] and the judge could take into account in his judgement any injury caused to the thing or any misuse or abuse by the creditor.[5]

---

[1] Plautus, *Tri.*, 116-18; 140-44; *Aul.*, 584-6; *formula Baetica*, 1ff (Bruns, no. 135) : cf. for the argument, Watson, *Obligations*, pp. 172ff. Another Plautine joke on *fiducia* is in *Mos.*, 37 : cf. Watson, *Obligations*, p. 172.

[2] Tab. 6.1. *Cum nexum faciet mancipiumque, uti lingua nuncupassit, ita ius esto* : The original purpose of this clause was undoubtedly very different.

[3] See infra, pp. 161ff.

[4] For the duty of the creditor to remancipate the thing when the debt was paid see Erbe, *Die Fiduzia im römischen Recht* (Weimar, 1940), pp. 46ff.

[5] For this view of the origins of *fiducia* see Watson, *Obligations*, pp. 172ff. Kaser does not believe that there was a *legis actio* for *fiducia* : *T.v.R.*, xxxiv (1966), pp. 416f. He argues (1) though the *formula Baetica* shows that words like *fidi fiduciae causa* could be in the *mancipatio*, the tablets from Pompeii (Bruns no. 134) show this was not necessarily the case for *fiducia*. But the *tabulae* (and the *formula Baetica*) date from a time – first/second century AD – when the *legis actio* was obsolete, and the requirements for *fiducia* were no longer the same : Watson, *Obligations*, pp. 177f. (2) The sources talk of *pactum fiduciae* and where *pactum* refers to a subsidiary agreement, it means a formless agreement. But (*a*) *pactum fiduciae* does not appear in any of the surviving sources; cf. *Vocabularium Iurisprudentiae Romanae*, ii (Berlin, 1933), 851f : (*b*) even if the phrase *pactum fiduciae* was used in classical law this would be no indication of its existence in the time of the *legis actio* : (*c*) where an expression like *pactum conventum* is found in connection with *fiducia*, this may never refer to the *fidi fiduciae causa* clause in the *mancipatio* but to the side agreement between the parties which helped to determine the scope of that clause : cf. *formula Baetica*. (3) According to G.4.33 the *actio fiduciae* belongs to those actions which are not framed on the fiction of a *legis actio*, and Gaius gives as further examples the *actiones*

G

Whether or not *in iure cessio* could be, or was, used for *fiducia* at this time is doubtful though it certainly was so used in classical law.[1] There is no particular reason to think that in this respect the scope of *mancipatio* and *in iure cessio* must have been the same at this time, and it is difficult to know how the *addictio* could have been framed.[2] The point is of some importance since if *mancipatio* alone was used there could be no *fiducia* of *res nec mancipi*.

Fiducia was a reasonably satisfactory form of real security. For the creditor it had the advantage that he was owner of the thing and so in a strong position to protect his interest against both the debtor and third parties. Moreover he was able to give ownership to any purchaser and so would find it relatively easy to sell the thing at its full value. When the creditor did sell the thing he would naturally be liable to the debtor for whatever he obtained above the amount of the debt.[3] A disadvantage for the creditor was that when the thing was in his control he was not allowed to use it or take any profits from it,[4] but had the responsibility of looking after it.[5] This very fact, though, worked for the advantage of the debtor. The creditor might not wish to have the thing under his control and so might often hand the thing back informally to the debtor, or even hire it out to him, the *merces* for the hire presumably taking the place of interest on the loan.[6,7] Since the creditor remained owner he had adequate legal protection for his loan, and the debtor was able to make use of the thing, a matter of fundamental importance to him since *res mancipi* played the major rôle in agricultural production. Hence also the creditor was more likely to be paid. When the creditor retained the thing pledged in his

---

commodati and *negotiorum gestorum* which, it is admitted, were not actionable under the *legis actio* procedure. Kaser concludes that the *actio fiduciae*, no different from the other *bonae fidei iudicia*, would always have been actionable by *formula*. But it is difficult to read this into the Gaius' text since he has in it also discussed other actions – the *condictiones* – which are not formulated on a fiction of a *legis actio*, and the *condictio* certainly had a *legis actio* stage.

[1] G.2.59; 3.201; Isidorus, *orig.*, 5.25.23.
[2] This problem remains even for classical law.
[3] Cf. e.g. D.13.7.24.2 (Ulpian? Paul? *30 ad ed.*); *P.S.*, 2.13.1 : Erbe, *Fiduzia*, pp. 89f. [4] Cf. e.g. *P.S.*, 2.13.2.
[5] Whether he was liable only for *culpa* or also for *dolus* is uncertain : cf. Erbe, *Fiduzia*, pp. 51ff.
[6] Cf. G.2.59, 60.
[7] But not in every case was the thing at once restored to the physical control of the debtor : cf. e.g. G.2.59, 60; *P.S.*, 2.13.2.

physical control seizure of it by the debtor was not considered to be theft.[1] It is likely that this points to a belief that it was immoral for the creditor not to let the debtor have control of it.[2]

Disadvantages of *fiducia* for the debtor were first that if the creditor sold the thing – whether the debt had been repaid or not – no action for its recovery lay against the purchaser, and secondly that since he had transferred ownership he was unable to effect a second mortgage so long as the first remained uncancelled.

The debtor's action against the creditor was a personal, not a real, action. The appropriate *legis actio*, being tied to the *mancipatio* and the actual words used, was inevitably rather limited and the praetor at some stage issued a *formula in factum*. When this happened cannot be determined but I suspect it was early[3] – following the example of the *bonae fidei iudicia* – and before the end of our period, during which it will have existed side by side with the *legis actio*. Lenel's reconstruction of this *formula* is convincing : *Si paret Aulum Agerium Numerio Negidio fundum quo de agitur ob pecuniam debitam fiduciae causa mancipio dedisse eamque pecuniam solutam eove nomine satisfactum esse aut per Numerium Negidium stetisse quo minus solveretur eumque fundum redditum non esse negotiumve ita actum non esse, ut inter bonos bene agier oportet et sine fraudatione, quanti ea res erit, tantam pecuniam Aulum Agerium Numerio Negidio iudex condemna. Si non paret absolve.*[4, 5] Whether there was also a *formula* of the standard type for *bonae fidei iudicia* is very doubtful.[6]

---

[1] Cf. G.3.201 and 2.59-61.

[2] For the argument see Watson, *Property*, pp. 41ff.

[3] As was the case with *iniuria*. Of course, if the common view that there was no *legis actio* for *fiducia* is correct, then the Plautine texts would point to the existence of the *formula*.

[4] *Edictum*, pp. 291ff. Cf. Cicero, *top.*, 17.66; *de off.*, 3.15.61; *ad fam.*, 7.12.2. The use of *agier* in the most striking part of the *formula* is evidence that this clause at least is old. The rôle in *fiducia* of the formulation, *uti ne propter te fidemve tuam captus fraudatusve sim* (Cicero, *de off.*, 3.17.70) is uncertain : cf. Wubbe, *T.v.R.*, xxviii (1960), p. 37 and n. 67; Kaser, *T.v.R.*, xxxiv (1966), p. 416 n. 10; and the works they cite.

[5] The *actio contraria* (cf. Lenel, *Edictum*, p. 291) may well be a later development.

[6] Cf. now Watson, *Obligations*, pp. 176ff and the references given. But Kaser correctly points out that Watson's argument in favour of such a *formula* is based on a misunderstanding of G.4.33 and has no validity *T.v.R.*, xxxiv (1966), pp. 416f.

Fiducia could be used for purposes other than security; for instance a slave might be mancipated with the intention that he be manumitted by the recipient; an owner who thought he was in personal danger of having his property taken by the State might transfer things to a friend for safe keeping; in the absence of a law of agency *mancipatio fiduciae causa* could be useful in many ways where something was best done by a representative; and gifts *mortis causa* might be made. How far these uses had developed in our period cannot be determined.[1]

Plautus has many references to *pignus*,[2] the form of security in which physical custody of the thing pledged might but need not be given to the creditor but in which ownership was not transferred to him. In none of these Plautine texts, however, is there anything which serves as evidence that the creditor's right to the *pignus* was protected by an action, and the custom of giving a *pignus* could usefully exist even when it was devoid of legal protection. Many a creditor who was unwilling to make a loan without security might be happy to take a *pignus* though he knew that if it fell into a third party's hands he would have no action for its recovery, and that the debtor at any time had the legal right to sue by *vindicatio* for its return. In practice the debtor who had not repaid the debt was unlikely to bring a *vindicatio* and the creditor would keep the thing safe from third parties. The *pignus* will also have made it more likely that the debt would be repaid and, if it were not, the creditor in most cases could recoup himself by selling the pledge even if technically he had no right to do so.

But a real action on a *pignus* was available to a creditor at the latest when Cato's *de agri cultura* was written around 160 BC.[3] In this work[4] he recommends that particular provisions relating to *pignus* be added to certain contracts of sale, and in one text proposes that the parties agree that in the event of a dispute the *iudicium* be held at Rome.[5] Hence an action was certainly available and what

---

[1] On these see, e.g., Erbe, *Fiduzia*, pp. 121ff.

[2] *Amph.*, 68; *Cap.*, 655, 939; *Epid.*, 697ff; *Poe.*, 1285; *Ps.*, 87; *Ru.*, 581 : cf. *Truc.*, 239ff.

[3] This is to accept the traditional dating of the *de agri cultura*. But Daube suggests a much earlier date : *Forms of Roman Legislation* (Oxford, 1956), pp. 96f ; contra, Watson, 'The Imperatives of the Aedilician Edict', *T.v.R.* xxxviii (1970).

[4] 146.2; 149.2; 150.2.   [5] 149.2.

was involved was a real right since there could be little point in bolstering up a personal right (on the contract of sale) with a subsidiary, and equally shaky, personal right. Since the principal contracts are of sale not hire the remedy cannot be the *interdictum Salvianum*, but must be either the *actio Serviana* (or *actio hypothecaria*)[1] or a forerunner of this. There is no evidence of a civil law forerunner[2] so it seems we are concerned with a praetorian innovation which gave a real right. This makes the action in question the earliest known praetorian action which introduced a change in the substantive law.[3] In view of the slow development of the Edict before 100 BC[4] the balance of probability is that this *actio* was a recent innovation in 160 BC. It is worth stressing, though, for the general history of *pignus* that in Cato's texts the things which are to be pledged are not delivered to the creditor but are simply things belonging to the buyer which are brought onto the creditor's land.[5]

In Hadrian's Edict the *formula* of the *actio Serviana* very strangely appears in the section on interdicts where it is appended to the *interdictum Salvianum*.[6] This must mean that the action is later than the *interdictum Salvianum* which attracted it to that position[7]; and is confirmation that both the *interdictum* and *actio* go back to a time when the Edict was in its infancy and its arrangement was lax.[8] But the *interdictum Salvianum* is perhaps not much

---

[1] Cf. Watson, '*Actio Serviana* and *actio hypothecaria* (a hypothesis)', SDHI, xxvii (1961), pp. 356ff.

[2] The *actio Serviana* is formulated so completely *in factum* that it is most unlikely there was a civil law forerunner. Kaser, however, thinks that originally the pledge creditor had the *vindicatio* : e.g. *Eigentum und Besitz im älteren römischen Recht*, 2nd edit. (Cologne, Graz, 1956), pp. 21ff; 'The Concept of Roman Ownership', *Tydskrif vir Hedendaagse Romeins-Hollandse Reg* (1964), pp. 5f at p. 8. But see Watson, 'Praetor's Edict', n. 164.

[3] And it is probably significant that it was introduced without an edict : cf. Watson, 'Praetor's Edict'.   [4] Cf. Watson, 'Praetor's Edict'.

[5] Cf. Watson, *Obligations*, p. 181. It need not be thought that at some earlier stage actual delivery was needed to give a legal right for *pignus*.

[6] Cf. Lenel, *Edictum*, p. 493.

[7] The possibility that they date from the same year can be excluded first because one would then have expected that both would have a similar scope (though different functions) and secondly the names show that they are the work of different people.

[8] But the *interdictum* is usually thought to date from the first half of the first century BC : cf. e.g. Kaser, RPR, i, p. 395; Kelly, 'The Growth Pattern of the Praetor's Edict', *Irish Jurist*, i (1966), pp. 341ff at p. 347.

earlier than the *actio Serviana*. The interdict was given to an owner who had leased his land, to prevent the removal from the land of things belonging to the tenant which had been pledged for the rent when the rent had not been paid and security for its payment had not been given.[1]

USUFRUCT AND SIMILAR RIGHTS

Usufruct was the right to use and enjoy the fruits of another's property but not to alter its character fundamentally or destroy it. There is strong evidence for its existence in Plautus's *Casina* where one contender for the favours of a slave girl claims that she is his and the other retorts that first the *fructus* is his.[2]

Ususfructus was most frequently used, both originally and much later, to provide for the widow[3] so that she could live in the style she had been accustomed to during her husband's lifetime, and could continue to occupy what had been the matrimonial home.[4, 5] Accordingly, the commonest mode of creation was by legacy and it appears that the most usual form of this was *legatum per vindicationem*.[6] But there is no indication that legacy was the only way in which usufruct could originally be created and undoubtedly *in iure cessio* could be used to set up usufruct *inter vivos*.[7] Usufruct might also arise from the *adiudicatio* of an *actio communi dividundo*,

[1] Cf. Lenel, *Edictum*, pp. 490ff. But it is more likely that the interdict lay against anyone, not just the debtor : cf. Kaser, *loc. cit.* and the references given, n. 17.

[2] 836f. For the argument see Watson, *Property*, pp. 203f. The *Casina* is to be dated to 185 or 184 BC : cf. Duckworth, *Roman Comedy*, p. 55.

[3] Cf. e.g. Cicero, *top.*, 3.17; 4.21; *pro Caecina*, 4.11.

[4] It is generally believed that the origins of *ususfructus* are connected with the growth of marriage *sine manu*. But the arguments produced have no validity : cf. Watson, *T.v.R.*, xxxi (1963), p. 614.

[5] The owners of the property during the usufruct were therefore usually the usufructuary's children who had been instituted heirs by their father. This relationship between the usufructuary and the owner must have had its effect on the development of *ususfructus* and might help to explain why the usufructuary did not have *possessio* – the weaker position of women in litigation might also be relevant – and why the *cautio usufructuaria* apparently took so long to develop.

[6] See the texts referring to the Empire in *V.F.*, 41–93. For *legatum per vindicationem* see infra, pp. 108f.

[7] Cf. D.40.12.23pr (Paul, *50 ad ed.*) for the end of the second century BC : on the text see Watson, *Persons*, pp. 166ff.

familiae erciscundae or *finium regundorum*, or by a *mancipatio, in iure cessio* or *legatum* of a thing, *deducto usu fructu.*

The usufruct might be over immoveables or moveables, individual things or a complete *hereditas*,[1] but there could be no usufruct over things which are consumed or reduced by use, such as money or flasks of wine.[2] The usufructuary of a house could live in it or let it, and *fructus* was, in general, the ordinary produce of a thing such as crops and the young of animals.[3] In the middle of the second century BC there was a dispute over whether the offspring of a slave girl was to be counted as *fructus*,[4] and the origins of the dispute may go back to our time. The usufructuary had the duty of keeping the property in good condition where this was reasonable, and of paying the expenses.[5] If a building fell or became defective the owner was not bound to rebuild or repair.[6] Where the usufruct was of a flock the usufructuary had to replace those which died with young born to the flock.[7]

No usufruct could continue beyond the lifetime of the usufructuary and it ended on his death or on any prior occasion which had been arranged.[8] The usufruct also terminated if the subject matter was fundamentally changed, whether naturally or by human

[1] Cf. now Watson, *Property*, pp. 207ff.

[2] This was still the case in 44 BC when Cicero's *topica* was written : 3.17. But the law was sometime thereafter changed by a *senatus consultum* : cf. e.g. Watson, *loc. cit.*, pp. 207ff.

[3] For details of what might count as *fructus* see e.g. Grosso, *Usufrutto e figure affini nel diritto romano*, 2nd edit. (Turin, 1958), pp. 173ff. For the later Republic, D.7.1.9.7 (Ulpian, *17 ad Sab.*); 7.1.11 (Paul, *2 epit. Alfeni dig.*) : Watson, *Property*, pp. 213f.

[4] Cicero, *de fin.*, 1.4.12; D.7.1.68pr (Ulpian, *17 ad Sab.*); on the point see most recently Watson, 'Morality, Slavery and the Jurists in the Later Roman Republic', *Tulane Law Review*, xlii (1968), pp. 289ff at pp. 291ff.

[5] There is no evidence for the Republic but it is reasonable to assume that the law was the same as in the Empire : e.g. D.7.1.7.2 (Ulpian, *17 ad Sab.*).

[6] Cf. Cicero, *top.*, 3.15.

[7] No direct evidence for the Republic, but Cato, *de agri cultura*, 150 shows an express clause to this effect (with a qualification) in a contract of sale of the *fructus* of sheep : cf. Watson, *Property*, pp. 205f. So the idea was in existence. For the Empire see D.7.1.68.1; 7.1.69 (Pomponius, *5 ad Sab.*); 7.1.70 (Ulpian, *17 ad Sab.*); PS 3.6.20; J.2.1.38.

[8] Cf. D.7.4.3pr, 3 (Ulpian, *17 ad Sab.*) which provide evidence for a much later period.

activity,[1] or if it ceased to exist. Likewise the usufruct could be lost by non-use for the period of usucaption. *Ususfructus* was inalienable but whether an attempt to transfer it to another actually ended the usufruct or was simply regarded as a nullity cannot be determined.[2]

The usufructuary could claim his right by the *vindicatio usufructuaria* which was a variation of the *vindicatio rei*.[3] There may be a reference in Plautus' *Casina*[4] to the *legis actio* for usufruct and this probably ran : *Hunc ego usum fructum meum esse aio ex iure Quiritium*.[5]

Usus[6] was a more limited right and did not give the grantee any claim to the *fructus*. It would thus be of little value unless it were of a dwelling place which, in fact, was probably the common case. When the *usus* of a dwelling was granted to a man he could live in it with his wife,[7] but *usus* to a woman entitled her to live in it but did not entitle her husband to live there with her.[8]

Habitatio[9] in classical law was really *usus* of a dwelling, but to judge from a dispute in the later second century BC it was conceived of originally as being a very temporary right, for one year only, and probably gave no right *in rem*.[10, 11]

---

[1] Cf. D.7.1.71 (Marcellus, *17 dig.*) for the later Republic : cf. Watson, *Property*, pp. 212f, 218f.

[2] In classical law the effect was disputed : cf. D.23.3.66 (Pomponius, 8 *ad Quintum Mucium*); G.2.30.

[3] Cf. for the reconstruction of the classical *actio confessoria* and *actio negatoria* (which are probably later), Lenel, *Edictum*, pp. 191f.

[4] 836f : cf. supra, p. 90 and n.2.

[5] The reconstruction of Kaser, 'Geteiltes Eigentum im älteren römischen Recht', *Festschrift Koschaker*, i (Weimar, 1939), pp. 445ff at pp. 465f, who, however, brackets *usum* : contra, Grosso, *Usufrutto*, p. 395.

[6] There is no evidence that it existed in 200 BC. It probably did, but would be unimportant. For *usus* see in general, Grosso, *Usufrutto*, pp. 430.

[7] In the first century BC Tubero was of the opinion that the husband's freedmen could also live there.

[8] D.7.8.4.1 (Ulpian, *17 ad Sab.*). Quintus Mucius was the first to concede that *usus* to a woman entitled her to live with her husband in the dwelling.

[9] For *habitatio* see in general Grosso, *Usufrutto*, pp. 494ff.

[10] D.7.8.10.3 (Ulpian, *17 ad Sab.*). Rutilius (who almost certainly is the P. Rutilius Rufus who was praetor around 118 BC) declared it was for life : cf. now Watson, *Property*, pp. 220.

[11] Another particular form of *usus* was *operae servorum vel animalium* but this is not evidenced for the Republic and it probably developed later than the period covered in this book.

CHAPTER 9

Inheritances: Intestate Succession

Long before 200 BC succession at Rome could be under a will or on intestacy. The primary object of the law of succession is the discovery of the heir or heirs and, indeed, this is the only matter relevant for intestate succession. So important in succession is the position of the heir that we find in Cicero's *topica* the word *hereditas* defined in terms of the property which comes to the heir, not that belonging to the deceased at the time of his death.[1]

Closely linked in early Rome with taking the inheritance was the obligation to perform the private *sacra* of the deceased. The observance of the private *sacra* was under the supervision of the *pontifices*[2] who also developed rules – apparently from decisions on individual cases[3] – for determining who had to perform them. These rules varied from time to time but around 200 BC the main ones were that the heirs were primarily liable, then anyone who by the death or will took as much as all the heirs,[4] and thirdly, if there was no heir, that person who usucapted most of the deceased's property.[5, 6]

[1] Cicero, *top.*, 6.29. *Hereditas est pecunia quae morte alicuius ad quempiam pervenit iure nec ea aut legata testamento aut possessione retenta.* Cf. Watson, *Succession*, p. 1.

[2] Cf. e.g. Wissowa, *Religion und Kultus der Römer*, 2nd edit. (Munich, 1912), p. 400.

[3] The point is very much disputed but see above all, Franciosi, *Usucapio pro herede* (Naples, 1965), pp. 133ff, and the authors he cites: cf. Watson, *Property*, p. 33.

[4] This was the case as early as Tiberius Coruncanius who was active around 250 BC: Cicero, *de leg.*, 2.21.52. Previously the position had been different.

[5] Cicero, *de leg.*, 2.19.48–2.20.49. Whether by this time (as was later the case), in the absence of anyone usucapting the deceased's property, the creditor who recovered most from the deceased's property became liable in

The performance of the *sacra* was treated as a serious duty and hence was often regarded as troublesome. Plautus in two separate plays portrays characters regarding great delights as if they were a *hereditas sine sacris*[1] and the phrase seems to have been proverbial.[2] Either in our period or shortly afterwards ways were being sought to receive a *hereditas* or a *legatum* without becoming involved with the *sacra*.[3]

Heirs were classified as either *necessarii* or *sui et necessarii* or *extranei*.[4] The verbalization of the distinction is almost certainly later[5] but the basis and importance of the classification is very old. *Heredes necessarii* were slaves belonging to the testator who were both appointed heir and given their freedom under the will.[6] They automatically became heir and free on the testator's death, whether they wanted to or not.[7] *Heredes sui et necessarii* were those persons – sons, daughters, grandsons and so on – who were in the deceased's *potestas* or *manus* and who became *sui iuris* on his death.[8] They, whether succession was under a will or on intestacy, also automatically became heir and had no right to refuse.[9] All other heirs, whether on intestacy or under a will, were termed *extranei* and had the power of deciding whether to accept the inheritance or not.[10] Indeed, until they accepted they were not heir and the *hereditas* was without an owner. The main importance of the distinction is in fact that the Roman heir was fully liable for all the

---

the fourth place to perform the *sacra*, and the deceased's debtor who paid to no-one in the fifth place, cannot be determined. See now, Watson, *Property*, pp. 32ff; *Succession*, pp. 4ff.

[6] For the *usucapio* of property belonging to a person who has died see supra, pp. 63f.

[1] *Cap.*, 775; *Tri.*, 484.

[2] Cf. Festus, *s.v. Sine sacris hereditas*.

[3] For these see Cicero, *de leg.*, 2.20.50; 21. 53 : cf. now Watson, *Succession*, pp. 5ff; and also infra, pp. 111f.

[4] G.2.152.

[5] There is no sign of it in any text which refers to the Republic.

[6] The gift of liberty was essential if the slave was to be heir : cf. infra, p. 104.

[7] G.2.153.

[8] Thus, not also those persons in the *potestas* of, for instance, their grandfather, who fell into the *potestas* of their father on the grandfather's death : G.2.154.

[9] G.2.157. Later the praetor gave them the right to abstain from the *hereditas* : G.2.158.

[10] G.2.161, 162.

debts of the deceased even when they exceeded the assets. Frequently, a testator who was afraid he might not die solvent would, after instituting an *extraneus* heir, appoint one of his slaves as a substitute heir,[1] thus ensuring that if he did die insolvent he nonetheless would have an heir who – and not the testator – would suffer the disgrace if the assets were compulsorily sold.[2] Another importance of the distinction is that where the heir was *necessarius* or *suus et necessarius* the *hereditas* could never be *iacens* and so could not be usucapted.

The *heres extraneus* accepted the inheritance (made *aditio*) by a formal act called *cretio*. This was an oral declaration[3] which had to contain the words *hereditatem adeo cernoque*,[4] and Gaius gives as the form: *Quod me P. Mevius testamento suo heredem instituit, eam hereditatem adeo cernoque.*[5] It had to be unconditional[6] and it could not be made by any *extranea persona* on behalf of the heir.[7] But it could be made anywhere,[8] witnesses were legally unnecessary, and there was no time limit for its performance.[9] In practice, though, a will would almost invariably set a time limit,[10] and often specify that there had to be witnesses.[11, 12]

When the *heres scriptus* was a slave belonging to someone other

---

[1] For *institutio* and *substitutio* see infra, pp. 106ff.

[2] Cf. G.2.154.

[3] Cf. G.2.166; *Gai Inst. fragm. Augustod.*, 37, 38, 39, 42; Epit. Ulp., 22.28.

[4] Cf. G.2.166; *Gai Inst. fragm. Augustod.*, 38, 39, 42; *Epit. Ulp.*, 22.28: see also Pliny the Younger, *Epist.*, 10.75.2: the two wooden diptychs of AD 70 from Fayum, in Girard, *Textes de droit romain*, 6th edit. by Senn (Paris, 1937), pp. 809ff [Bruns, nos. 124A, 124B]; *PSI.*, 1027.

[5] G.2.166.

[6] Cf. D.50.17.77 (Papinian *28 quaest.*).

[7] Cf. Buckland, '*Cretio* and connected topics', *T.v.R.*, iii (1922), pp. 239ff at pp. 246ff; Lévy-Bruhl, 'Etude sur la *cretio*', NRDH, xxxviii (1914), pp. 153ff at pp. 161ff.

[8] Cf. *Gai Inst. fragm. Augustod.*, 42; Cicero, *ad Att.*, 11.2.1; 11.12.4: see now Watson, *Succession*, pp. 190ff.

[9] Cf. G.2.167. In Gaius' time, the praetor, at the request of the deceased's creditors, could fix a time limit for *cretio*.

[10] Cf. Cicero, *ad Att.*, 13.46.3; 15.2.4; G.2.164, 170.

[11] Cf. Cicero, *ad Att.*, 13.46.3; Varro, *de ling. lat.*, 6.81.

[12] In the Empire and also, it would appear, as early as the first century BC [cf. Watson, 'D.28.5.45 (44): an unprincipled Decision on a Will', *Irish Jurist*, iii (1968), pp. 377ff at pp. 378f] informal acting as heir, *pro herede gestio*, was enough to constitute *aditio* unless the will actually demanded a *cretio*. But it is unlikely that this is very old.

than the testator,[1] he – and not his owner – made the *cretio* but he
required the master's *iussum*. The slave was technically the heir
but the rights and duties of the inheritance descended upon his
dominus[2] who was liable *in solidum*, that is for the whole amount of
the debts. It is likely that the need for the *iussum*, which is presumably early,[3] was primarily intended for the protection of the
deceased's creditors and secondarily for the protection of the
heir's owner. In contractual situations, the activities of a slave did
not make the owner liable at all,[4] in delict the owner could escape
further liability by making noxal surrender of the slave to the injured party.[5] In the present context the danger was that a testator
who wished to benefit a third party might institute one of that
person's slaves as his heir, in the hope that the third party might be
able to take any advantage without incurring a liability. Hence
a special requirement was evolved, probably by the jurists,
which demanded the involvement (and responsibility) of the
master.[6]

An heir had the *hereditatis petitio* to protect his right, but it
could be brought only against a person who was holding the
property *pro herede*. That is, it was an action between parties both
of whom claimed to be heir.[7] In other circumstances the heir presumably was sufficiently protected by the *vindicatio*. The *hereditatis
petitio* lay to the centumviral court,[8] but probably only where the
value of the inheritance was above a certain amount.[9] The action
was a *legis actio sacramento in rem* though it is likely that already
the device of proceeding *per sponsionem* could also be used.[10] But

[1] Cf. infra, pp. 104f.
[2] Cf. D.28.5.60(59)pr (Celsus, *16 dig.*); 41.1.19 (Pomponius, *3 ad Sab.*) :
both of which relate to the later Republic and concern the special case of
the *liber homo bona fide serviens* : cf. Watson, *Persons*, pp. 222ff.
[3] Though there is no direct evidence.
[4] Cf. supra, p. 45.   [5] Cf. infra, p. 159.
[6] For a fuller discussion of the problem see Watson, *Succession*, pp. 193f.
[7] Cf. now Watson, *Succession*, pp. 195ff.
[8] Cf. Cicero, *de orat.*, 1.38.173, 175; 1.39.176, 177, 180; 1.56.238(?);
Brutus, 53.197; *de leg. agrar.*, 2.17.44; Valerius Maximus, 7.7.1, 2.
[9] Apparently 100,000 sesterces in classical law : *P.S.*, 5.9.1; cf. Kaser,
ZPR, pp. 38f and n. 24.
[10] Both the *legis actio in rem* and the action *per sponsionem* are mentioned
in Cicero, *in Verrem*, II, 1.45.115. For the action *per sponsionem* in general
see supra, pp. 71f.

Gaius tells us that in the procedure *per sponsionem* the challenge was actually by *sacramentum.*[1]

A very similar action was given to a person who claimed only to be heir to a share.[2]

When there was more than one heir and division of the estate could not be arranged among the *coheredes*, recourse could be had to the *actio familiae erciscundae.*[3] This had been established for the purpose by the XII Tables[4] which authorized proceedings *per iudicis postulationem.*[5] As with the *actio finium regundorum*[6] and the *actio communi dividundo*[7] all the parties were equally both plaintiff and defendant,[8] and the judge had considerable discretion in arranging the division.

INTESTATE SUCCESSION

Intestate succession, even among the wealthy, was common and important. The belief, dear to modern scholars, that the Romans regarded intestacy as disgraceful has been shown by Daube to be ill-founded,[9] and many monied Romans who had the capacity to make a will failed to do so.[10] Moreover, women who had not under-

[1] G.4.95. By a *lex Crepereia* of totally unknown date [cf. Rotondi, *Leges*, p. 479] the amount of the *sacramentum* was fixed at 125 sesterces. The idea that the sum is connected with the 500 *asses* for the highest *sacramentum* in a *legis actio* and that therefore the *lex* is later than 217 BC when the *as* was devalued to one fourth of a sesterce [cf. Girard, ZSS, xxix (1908), p. 167 n. 3] may or may not be correct. The argument against it is that the *lex Crepereia* would have been pointless if previously the *sacramentum* in the centumviral court was for 500 *asses*. Incidentally, it is not certain that the devaluation was in 217 BC.

[2] This action, the *petitio hereditatis partiaria*, would be as necessary as the *petitio hereditatis* and is unlikely to be much later. But it is not evidenced for the Republic except perhaps in D.5.4.9 (Paul, *3 epit. Alfeni dig.*) : cf. Watson, *Succession*, pp. 196ff.

[3] For the later Republic see D.10.1.16.6 (Ulpian, *19 ad ed.*) : Cicero, *pro Caecina*, 7.19; *lex Rubria*, cap. xxiii : cf. Watson, *Property*, pp. 121ff.

[4] D.10.2.1pr (Gaius, *7 ad ed. prov.*).

[5] G.4.17a : for this procedure, cf. infra, p. 163.   [6] Cf. supra, pp. 75f.

[7] Cf. supra, pp. 72f.   [8] Cf. D.10.2.2.3 (Ulpian, *19 ad ed.*).

[9] 'The Preponderance of Intestacy at Rome', *Tulane Law Review*, xxxix (1965), pp. 187ff; *Roman Law*, pp. 71ff.

[10] The evidence from Cicero is conclusive by itself since his writings give six apparent instances : *pro Flacco*, 36.89; *pro Cluentio*, 60.165; *in Verrem*, II, 1.45.115; *de orat.*, 1.39.176, 180; 2.70.283. Other significant cases occur in Cicero, *pro Cluentio*, 15.45 and *Rhet. ad Herenn.*, 1.13.23 : cf. Watson, *Succession*, pp. 175f.

gone *capitis deminutio* could not make a will,[1] nor could persons under puberty, and a will might be or might become void, or it might fail if the *heres scriptus extraneus* refused to take the inheritance or died before the testator.[2]

The law of intestate succession, both to *ingenui* and *libertini* was governed by the XII Tables.[3] For succession to *ingenui* there were two clauses. 5.4, *Si intestato moritur, cui suus heres nec escit, adgnatus proximus familiam habeto* : and 5.5, *Si adgnatus non escit, gentiles familiam [habento]*. Thus, the persons entitled to the inheritance in the first place were the deceased's *sui heredes*, that is, those persons in his *potestas* or *manus* who became *sui iuris* on his death. Among the *sui heredes* would be included any such person who was born after the testator's death.[4] All *sui heredes* who were children whether male or female of the deceased, and his wife *in manu*, took equal shares. *Sui* who were remoter descendants, i.e. whose father (or even father and grandfather) had predeceased the *paterfamilias* or been emancipated, took equally the share which would have come to their immediate ancestor if he had survived. These remoter *sui heredes* were not excluded from the inheritance by the survival of *sui* who were nearer in blood to the *paterfamilias*.[5] A woman did not have *patriapotestas*, hence she could have no *sui heredes*; and a man's illegitimate children were not in his *potestas* and not his *sui heredes*.[6] When there was no *suus heres* the inheritance went to the nearest agnate, and no distinction was made between male and female agnates.[7]

The term *adgnatus proximus* in the XII Tables' provision was interpreted narrowly to mean that only the nearest agnate was entitled to the inheritance and that if he died or failed to make *cretio*,

[1] Cf. infra, p. 103. Cicero, *pro Flacco*, 34.84, where Valeria had made no will, may be an instance of this; see also *ad fam.*, 7.21.

[2] On all this see infra, pp. 100ff.

[3] Though modifications were later made by the Edict : for the later Republic see Watson, *Succession*, pp. 176ff.

[4] No direct textual evidence for the Republic, but the point can be deduced from D.30.127 (Paul, *sing. de iure codic.*).

[5] For all this cf. G.3.1-8.

[6] Cf. Cicero, *de orat.*, 1.40.183.

[7] Rather later the law changed, either under a clause of the *lex Voconia* of 169 BC, or more likely, as a result of juristic interpretation from the *lex Voconia*, and among women only a *consanguinea*, a sister born of the same father, could succeed as an agnate : G.3.14; *P.S.*, 4.8.20; J.3.2.3a; cf. now Watson, *Succession*, pp. 177f.

the succession did not open to other a*gnati*[1] but went to the *gentiles*. The decisive moment, however, for finding the nearest agnate was the time when it was established that there was an intestacy, not the time of death.[2]

In the absence of an *agnatus proximus* the estate went to the *gentiles*, and it was clear that this was a common occurrence[3] (probably as a result of the narrow interpretation of *agnatus proximus*).[4,5]

The XII Tables (5.8) also regulated intestate succession to a freedman. If a *libertus* died intestate without having a *suus heres* the *hereditas* went to his patron. Any *suus heres*, including a wife *in manu* or an adopted child, would exclude the rights of the patron.[6] If the patron was dead, his rights of succession would pass to his son, grandson by a son, great-grandson by a grandson by a son,[7] his daughter, granddaughter by a son, great-granddaughter by a grandson by a son.[8,9] A freedwoman, of course, could have no *suus heres*, hence the rights of succession to her on intestacy would always descend to her patron. It should also be mentioned that in the circumstances in which she could make a will[10] she would require her *tutor*'s consent and he would be her *patronus*.

---

[1] Cf. G.3.11, 12, 13, 22. This restrictive interpretation probably indicates that originally there was no succession on intestacy by the agnates, and that the XII Tables' provision reduced the rights of the *gentiles*. But the matter is disputed and some scholars hold that the restrictive interpretation is not early : cf. the references given by Kaser, RPR, I, p. 90 n. 2; de Zulueta, *Institutes of Gaius*, ii (Oxford, 1953), pp. 124; Watson, *Succession*, pp. 178ff.

[2] At least there is evidence that this was the case from the time of Aquilius Gallus : D.30.127 (Paul, *sing. de iure codic.*); on the text see Watson, *Succession*, pp. 178ff.

[3] There is ample evidence that the *ius gentilicium* flourished as late as the first half of the first century BC : Cicero, *de orat.*, 1.39.176; *in Verrem* II, 1.45.115; Suetonius, *Divus Iulius*, 1.2; Catullus, 68.119ff; *Laudatio Turiae*, 13-16; probably, Cicero, *pro Flacco*, 34.84; cf. Varro, *de re rust.*, 1.2.8 : see on all this Watson, *Succession*, pp. 180f.

[4] The importance of the *gens* in intestate succession probably disappeared with the introduction of the edict, *Unde cognati* : cf. Watson, *Succession*, p. 181.

[5] The organization of the *gens* (and how its members took the *hereditas*) is not clear.

[6] Cf. G.3.40.   [7] Cf. G.3.45.

[8] Cf. G.3.46.

[9] The law of succession to a freedman was later modified by the Edict : see now, Watson, *Succession*, pp. 185ff.

[10] Cf. infra, p. 103.

CHAPTER 10

Wills

FORMS OF WILLS

There were two forms of will at this time,[1] one of which, the *testamentum in procinctu*, was a military will and could only be made by a soldier when the army was drawn up in battle array and the commander had taken the auspices.[2] This will required no formalities.[3, 4]

The other form, which was both much more frequent and important historically, was the *testamentum per aes et libram* which was a particular adaptation of *mancipatio*.[5] As a *mancipatio* it required five witnesses, a *libripens* and the person to whom the transfer was made, who was called the *familiae emptor*. Gaius gives us the wording of the act.[6] The *familiae emptor* said : '*Familiam pecuniamque tuam endo mandatela tua custodelaque mea esse aio,*

---

[1] The old *testamentum calatis comitiis* (cf. G.2.101, 102, 103; *Epit. Ulp.*, 20.2; Aulus Gellius, *N.A.*, 15.27.1, 2, 3; J.2.10.1; Theophilus, *Paraph.*, 2.10.1) presumably was already obsolete since it was so limited by its form that it could not long survive the emergence of the *testamentum per aes et libram* as a proper will : cf. Watson, *Succession*, p. 8.

[2] Appears from Cicero, *de nat. deor.*, 2.3.9 : cf. Watson, *Succession*, pp. 8ff.

[3] Appears from Cicero, *de orat.*, 1.53.228; cf. G.2.101, 102, 103; Aulus Gellius, *N.A.*, 15.27.3; J.2.10.1; Theophilus, *Paraph.*, 2.10.1.

[4] It was still in existence in the middle of the second century BC : Velleius Paterculus, *Hist. Rom.*, 2.5.2; Cicero, *de orat.*, 1.53.228; cf. Watson, *Succession*, pp. 8ff. The *testamentum in procinctu* became obsolete when, as a result of reforms, generals began to wage war only after they had laid down their *auspicia*.

[5] It seems that originally an heir could not be appointed under this form of will, but this would have changed by our time : for the early history see Kaser RPR, i, pp. 93f and the references he gives.

[6] G.2.104.

eaque, quo tu iure testamentum facere possis secundum legem publicam, hoc aere aeneaque libra esto mihi empta.' [1] He struck the scales with the bronze piece and gave it to the testator as the symbolic price. The testator, holding the tablets on which the will was written, then said '*Haec ita ut in his tabulis cerisque scripta sunt, ita do, ita lego, ita testor, itaque vos Quirites testimonium mihi perhibitote.'* This declaration was, Gaius says, called *nuncupatio* and by these general words the testator was thought to confirm the specific provisions written on the tablets. The antiquity of the proceedings is shown by the archaic phrase *endo mandatela tua custodelaque* of the *familiae emptor*'s declaration, and the *ita do, ita lego, ita testor* of the *nuncupatio* which must go back to a time when the *testamentum per aes et libram* did not institute an heir but only granted legacies.

The *nuncupatio* and the production of the tablets were fundamental to the ceremony just as were the *mancipatio* and the scales. [2] But the form of the *nuncupatio* was not invariable. A number of texts show that it was quite usual for the testator to name the heirs [3] and substitutes [4] or recite legacies [5] in the *nuncupatio*. In fact, the whole will might be given orally and there might be no writing or *tabulae* at all [6] – in which case the *nuncupatio* could not refer to *tabulae* – though in practice it seems that even where the whole contents of the will were recited orally the provisions were usually also put in writing. [7] The persons taking part in the ceremony had

---

[1] For questions of the wording see the references given by Kaser, RPR, i, p. 93, n. 4. On the form see also Stein, *Regulae iuris* (Edinburgh, 1966), p. 12 : Watson, *Succession*, pp. 11ff.

[2] Cf. Cicero, *de orat.*, 1.53.228 : *...tamquam in procinctu testamentum faceret sine libra atque tabulis.*

[3] Cf. D.28.1.21pr (Ulpian, *2 ad Sab.*); 28.1.25 (Javolenus, *5 post. Labeonis*); 28.5.1.1, 5 (Ulpian, *1 ad Sab.*); 28.5.9.2, 5 (Ulpian *5 ad Sab.*); 28.5.59(58)pr (Paul, *4 ad Vitellium*); 29.7.20 (Paul, *5 ad legem Iuliam et Papiam*). But the texts all refer to a later time.

[4] Cf. D.28.1.25 (Javolenus, *5 post. Labeonis*); 37.11.8.4 (Julian, *24 dig.*). Both concern a later period.

[5] Cf. D.28.1.21.1 (Ulpian, *2 ad Sab.*); 33.8.14 (Alfenus Varus, *5 dig.*). Both concern a later time.

[6] Cf. D.28.1.25; 28.6.20.1 (Ulpian, *16 ad Sab.*); C.6.13.1 (Gordian, AD 239); 6.11.2.1 (Gordian, AD 242). All concern a later time.

[7] D.28.5.1.5 (Ulpian, *1 ad Sab.*); 28.5.9.2, 5 (Ulpian, *5 ad Sab.*); 29.7.20 (Paul, *5 ad legem Iuliam et Papiam*); 37.11.8.4 (Julian, *24 dig.*). All concern a later period.

H

to be present for the whole time, for the *nuncupatio* as well as for the *mancipatio*.[1]

Though the written *tabulae* were subordinate to the oral *nuncupatio* they were much more than simply evidence of the terms of the *nuncupatio*; as we have just seen, the *nuncupatio* in its traditional form did not give the terms of the provisions recorded in the *tabulae*. Accordingly it is not surprising that the *tabulae* had their own formalities. Thus, like the *mancipatio familiae* and the *nuncupatio* themselves[2] the *tabulae* had to be in Latin[3]; and provisions appearing before the institution of the heir were ignored.[4]

As the form of the proceedings shows, originally the *familiae emptor* became owner of the testator's property as soon as the *mancipatio* was made.[5] The difficulties inherent in this[6] were overcome, probably by the jurists and courts treating the act as creating a valid will and having no other effect, but also I submit by the help of a statute.[7] This statute is, I think, referred to in the wording of the *mancipatio familiae* : *quo tu iure testamentum facere possis secundum legem publicam*[8]; and it also, I believe, contained a clause that if the witnesses to the *mancipatio*, the *libripens* and the *familiae emptor* all put their seals on an appropriate written document this document would be accepted as being the *tabulae* referred to in the *mancipatio*.[9] The purpose of this last provision would be to en-

[1] Argued from D.28.1.20.8 (Ulpian, *1 ad Sab.*) which refers to the *veteres* : cf. Watson, *Succession*, p. 12.

[2] No direct evidence but the fact can be deduced since there is no indication anywhere that Greek was ever allowed for the formal act of *mancipatio*.

[3] Greek was allowed only after AD 439 : C.6.32.21.6 (Theodosius and Valentinian).

[4] Cf. G.2.229, 230, 231.

[5] G.2.103 says that originally the *familiae emptor* acted as heir and that to him the testator gave instructions for the distribution of the estate after his death.

[6] E.g., subsequent alienation of things which had belonged to the testator. There is also no sign that any action was available against a *familiae emptor* who acted fraudulently.

[7] Some traces of the original conception may have remained, for instance in the rule that an object left as a *legatum per vindicationem* had to be owned by the testator when he made the will as well as when he died : cf. infra, p. 109; and in the rules about revocation : cf. infra, p. 116.

[8] Cf. Watson, *Succession*, pp. 13ff.

[9] The statute which is being postulated was in existence some considerable time before 73 BC because it had previously been referred to in an edict on

courage the witnesses etc. to put their seals on the *tabulae*, thus providing a valuable safeguard for wills, though the *lex* would not deny validity to *tabulae* which were not so sealed.

The institution of an heir (or heirs) was essential to the validity of a will,[1] but a will could also properly include clauses of substitution[2], legacies,[3] the appointment of tutors,[4] and gifts of liberty to slaves.[5, 6] All these clauses, to be valid, required the use of particular formal words.[7]

TESTAMENTARY CAPACITY

Only a Roman citizen[8] above puberty and *sui iuris* could make a will which was valid according to Roman law. Women who were *sui iuris* could not make a will unless they had undergone *capitis deminutio*.[9] The reason for this seems to be that originally a woman could not make a will at all[10] but some time after the emergence of the *testamentum per aes et libram* it was felt that she should be able to do so in the common case where her heirs on intestacy would not be her natural relatives, that is when she had undergone *capitis deminutio*, usually by entering a marriage *cum manu*.[11] When a woman did have capacity to make a will, the will nonetheless required the consent of her *tutor*.[12]

A person who went into exile ceased to be a citizen and he could

---

bonorum possessio secundum tabulas which had become *tralaticium* : Cicero, *in Verrem*, 11, 1.45.117 : cf. Watson, *Succession*, pp. 13ff. This would not constitute evidence that the statute goes back to our period, unless the further identification of it with that referred to in the wording of the *mancipatio familiae* is correct, and unless that statute did, as was suggested above, do something to turn the *mancipatio* and *nuncupatio* into a proper will.

[1] Cf. infra, pp. 106ff.
[2] Cf. infra, pp. 107f.
[3] Cf. infra, pp. 108f.
[4] Cf. supra, p. 35. [5] Cf. supra, pp. 48f.
[6] Perhaps there could also be clauses of adoption but it is unlikely that these clauses were true adoptions, or that the clauses were in use as early as 200 BC: see Kaser, RPR, i, p. 293, n. 26. *Fideicommissa* did not become legally enforceable until Augustus : cf. now Watson, 'The Early History of *fideicommissa*', *Index*, i (1970), pp. 179ff.
[7] Nowhere actually stated for gifts of liberty.
[8] Cf. Cicero, *pro Archia*, 5.11.
[9] Cf. Cicero, *top.*, 4.18; G. 1.115a.
[10] A woman could not appear before the *comitia calata*.
[11] But the reason for the development is a matter of dispute : cf. Watson, *Persons*, pp. 132ff. [12] Cf. G.2.112.

not make a will and any previously made will became void.[1] The
same was true of persons captured by the enemy since they were
regarded as foreign slaves.[2, 3] Also, if a testator subsequently became *alieni iuris*, say by adoption, the will became inoperative.[4] A
different kind of incapacity was that resulting from physical or
mental disability : thus, a lunatic could not make a will,[5] nor a
person who was deaf[6] or dumb,[7] nor a *prodigus* who was interdicted
from dealing with his property.[8] In cases where the incapacity was
not due to the testator's status, but to his mental or physical condition, loss of capacity after the will was made did not affect the will's
validity.[9]

A will was an act of the *ius civile* and hence peregrines could not
take anything under a Roman will.[10] But members of communities
which had Latin city rights – whether the city had the old Latin
rights or was in the newer and less favoured category[11] – could.
A slave belonging to the testator could be appointed heir provided
he was also given his freedom by the will[12]; and a slave belonging to
another could be appointed heir[13] provided his master had the
capacity to take under the will.[14] Similarly legacies could validly be

[1] Cf. Cicero, *top.*, 4.18; Mommsen, *Römisches Strafrecht* (Berlin, 1899),
pp. 68ff, 964ff.
[2] The *lex Cornelia de captivis* (82–80 B C) ordered the execution of the
will of a person who had been a Roman citizen and who had died in
captivity : cf. now, Watson, *Succession*, p. 26.
[3] At the beginning of the first century B C it was an open question whether
a person condemned on a criminal charge could make a will : *Rhet. ad
Herenn.*, 1.13.23; cf. Watson, *Succession*, pp. 23f.
[4] Cf. G.2.146.
[5] Cf. e.g. Valerius Maximus, 7.8.1; *Epit. Ulp.*, 20.13; Watson, *Succession*,
pp. 24f.
[6] Because he could not hear the words of the *familiae emptor* : cf. *Epit.
Ulp.*, 20.13.
[7] Because he could not speak the words of the *nuncupatio* : cf. *Epit. Ulp.*,
20.13; D.28.1.25 (Javolenus, *5(?) post. Labeonis*).
[8] Cf. e.g. *Epit. Ulp.*, 20.13.
[9] Cf. e.g. D.28.1.25 : Watson, *Succession*, pp. 25f.
[10] Hence Cicero's argument that Archias was a Roman citizen because he
had accepted Roman inheritances : *pro Archia*, 5.11.
[11] Cf. e.g. Cicero, *pro Caecina*, 35.102. See above all for Latin city rights,
Mommsen, *Römisches Staatsrecht*, iii, 3rd edit. (Leipzig, 1887), pp. 623ff.
[12] Plautus, *Poe.*, 839; cf. G.2.186.
[13] Cf. D.28.5.60 (59)pr. (Celsus, *16 dig.*); 41.1.19 (Pomponius, *3 ad Sab.*).
[14] Cf. e.g. D.28.5.31pr (Gaius, *17 ad ed. prov.*) : cf. Watson, *Succession*,
Chapter 3. For *cretio* by a *servus alienus*, see supra, pp. 95f.

left to slaves. The *servus alienus*, of course, could not be made free under the will, and it was his master who became owner of the property bequeathed to him.[1]

There was no incapacity to take on the part of pupils,[2] persons *alieni iuris*[3] – though ownership would go to the *paterfamilias* – or women.[4] Bequests could also be made to an unborn person who would be a *suus heres* of the testator,[5] but not to other unborn persons.[6] Deities could not take under a will,[7] but the *populus Romanus* could be appointed heir, even by a foreign king.[8]

The witnesses to a *testamentum per aes et libram*, the *familiae emptor* and the *libripens* had to have the qualifications normally required of witnesses to a *mancipatio*, that is, they had to be Roman citizens above puberty.[9] Further, a person in the *potestas* of the *familiae emptor* or of the testator could not be a witness, nor could the *paterfamilias* of the *familiae emptor* nor anyone in the same *potestas* as the *familiae emptor*.[10] The heir and legatees were competent witnesses though the practice was probably discouraged.[11] Socially it was regarded as a friendly act to invite someone to witness one's will.[12]

---

[1] See on this topic, Watson, *Succession*, pp. 27ff.
[2] Cf. Cicero, *de inven.*, 2.21.62; *in Verrem*, II, 1.50.131f.
[3] Cf. G.2.244; D.28.5.47(46) (Africanus, *2 quaest.*).
[4] Restrictions were introduced by the anti-feminist *lex Voconia* of 169 BC : see now Watson, *Succession*, pp. 29ff.
[5] Cf. D.28.2.29pr (Scaevola, *6 quaest.*).
[6] Cf. G.2.241, 242. There is no direct evidence for the Republic at all. D.30.127 (Paul, *sing. de iure codic.*) relates only to intestate succession.
[7] Cf. Mommsen, *Staatsrecht*, ii, pp. 61f.
[8] The earliest recorded instance is from 133 BC. There is in fact no real evidence for the Republic that the *populus Romanus* could be instituted heir by a Roman private citizen : cf. Voci, *Diritto ereditario romano*, i, 2nd edit. (Milan, 1967), pp. 416ff.
[9] Cf. G.2.104.
[10] All this appears from G.2.105-8.
[11] Cf. Cicero, *pro Milone*, 18.48; *ad Att.*, 7.2.3; G.2.108; D.34.5.14(15) (Marcian *6 inst.*) : see now Watson, *Succession*, pp. 33f. By the time of Justinian, the heir or a person in his *potestas* could not be a witness; J.2.10.10; D.28.1.20pr (Ulpian, *1 ad Sab.*) (interpolated : cf. works cited by Watson, *Succession*, pp. 33 n.6).
[12] Cf. Cicero, *ad Att.*, 12.18a.2; 14.3.2. Nonetheless a stranger might be asked to act as a witness; Cicero, *pro Cluentio*, 13.37.

INSTITUTION OF THE HEIR AND DISINHERISON

A clause instituting the heir or heirs was essential to the validity of a will, and any provision written in the will before the *institutio heredis* was ineffective.[1] Formal words were required : '*Titius heres esto*'; and possibly as an alternative : '*Titium heredem esse iubeo*.'[2]

Sui heredes who were not instituted heir had to be expressly disinherited.[3] Again formal words were necessary : '*Titius filius meus exheres esto*'[4]; but a general clause disinheriting all *sui* who were not instituted was sufficient : '*Ceteri omnes exheredes sunto*.'[5,6] If a *suus* was neither instituted heir nor disinherited the will was void.[7] A *suus* born after the will was made who was neither instituted heir nor disinherited caused the will to be *ruptum*.[8,9]

Any number of persons might be instituted heir,[10] and the inheritance could be divided in whatever proportions the testator

---

[1] Cf. for the Empire the statement of Gaius : *testamenta vim ex institutione heredis accipiunt, et ob id velut caput et fundamentum totius testamenti heredis institutio*: G.2.229. See now Watson, *Succession*, p. 40. The Proculians allowed the appointment of a *tutor* to precede the *institutio heredis*.

[2] Cf. G.2.117; Watson, *Succession*, pp. 40f.

[3] For the rules in classical law which are very different but permit inferences as to the development, see G.2.123-137.

[4] Cf. G.2.127.

[5] Cf. G.2.128.

[6] Only later was it established that a *filius in potestate* had to be expressly disinherited by name, though other *sui* could be disinherited by a general clause : appears from Cicero, *de orat.*, 1.38.175; cf. C.6.28.4.2 [Justinian, AD 531]; Watson, *Succession*, pp. 42f.

[7] The rule that, if a daughter or remoter descendant was passed over in silence, the will was not void but the person concerned came in for a share of the inheritance (G.2.124) is, I think, later, and was one aspect of the distinction made by the *centumviri* (cf. supra p. 106, n. 6) between *filii* and other *sui heredes*. An argument that the will was originally void when any *suus* was passed over in silence can be drawn from the rules on *postumi*.

[8] Cf. Cicero, *de orat.*, 1.38.175; 1.39.180; 1.57.241; *pro Caecina*, 25.72; *de inven.*, 2.42.122; D.28.2.29pr (Scaevola, *6 quaest.*) : cf. Watson, *Succession*, pp. 43ff. The rule that a female *postuma* would be sufficiently disinherited by the general clause provided a legacy was left to show she had not been overlooked (G.2.132) is also, I suggest, a later modification.

[9] The *querella inofficiosi testamenti*, which could be brought when a testator who was under a moral obligation to provide for a person failed to do so, is almost certainly a later invention though it existed by the middle of the first century BC : Valerius Maximus, 7.7.2; 7.8.4; Quintilian, *Inst. Orat.*, 9.2.9; 9.2.34, 35 : cf. Watson, *Succession*, pp. 62ff.

[10] Cf. D.5.4.9 (Paul, *3 epit. Alfeni dig.*); Suetonius, *Divus Iulius*, 83.

wished, but it was traditional to divide the estate into twelfths (*unciae*), and this was called *solemnis assis distributio*.[1] A person could not die partly testate and partly intestate and problems might arise if the estate was not wholly divided or the proportion of a share was not specified, but these could usually be solved by juristic interpretation in a way which made the will cover the whole estate and so be valid.[2] Likewise since an heir was a universal successor he could not be instituted heir to a specific thing (*ex certa re*), but the institution was treated as valid, the reference to the specific thing being ignored.[3] The institution had to be of a *certa persona* and the will was void if the institution was too vague.[4] The institution of the heir could be subject to a condition.[5]

SUBSTITUTIO

Substituto was a precaution against intestacy and it took one of two forms. In *substitutio vulgaris* the testator, after instituting the heir, appointed another person to be heir if the institution failed to take effect. It was, therefore, in a way a conditional institution, and could operate only if the institution failed. Hence if the *institutus* made *cretio* and then died, the inheritance would descend to his heirs and not open to the *substitutus*.[6] The practice of naming a *substitutus* was probably very common,[7] and it was legally possible to provide for a succession of *substituti*.

In *substitutio pupillaris*, the testator appointed a *substitutus* to take

---

[1] On this see Voci, *Diritto ereditario romano*, ii, 2nd edit. (Milan, 1963), pp. 134ff.

[2] Cf. e.g. D.28.5.13.7 (Ulpian, *7 ad Sab.*); 28.5.17.1 (*idem*).

[3] No textual evidence for the Republic, but cf. e.g. D.28.5.1.4 (Ulpian, *1 ad Sab.*); 28.5.9.13 (Ulpian, *5 ad Sab.*).

[4] Cf. D.28.5.32pr (Gaius, *1 de test. ad. praet. urb.*) : Watson, *Succession*, pp. 48f.

[5] This is denied for the period before about the end of the Republic by Buckland, 'Cretio and connected topics', *T.v.R.*, iii (1922), pp. 239ff, especially from p. 256; contra, Watson, 'D.28.5.45(44) : an unprincipled Decision on a Will', *Irish Jurist*, iii (1968), pp. 377ff at pp. 384ff. Cf. the instances of *substitutio* – which is itself conditional *institutio* – and D.28.7.28 (Papinian, *13 quaest.*), which concerns Servius.

[6] Cf. for *substitutio vulgaris* in the later Republic, D.28.6.39.2 (Javolenus, *1 ex post. Labeonis*); 28.1.25 (Javolenus, *5 post. Labeonis*); Cicero, *ad Att.*, 15.2.4. See in general, Buckland, *Textbook*, pp. 300ff.

[7] At least, it appears to have been standard in the time of Cicero : *ad Att.*, 15.2.4.

the inheritance if the *institutus*, who had to be a *suus impubes* of the testator, died before reaching puberty.[1] An open answer must be returned to the question whether this *substitutus* was legally regarded as the heir of the testator or of the *impubes*, but it is likely that the jurists decided each problem as it arose on practical grounds and that theory was of limited significance.[2]

LEGACIES

There were at least four (or just possibly, only three[3]) types of legacy, and each had its own characteristics.

A *legatum per vindicationem* was left in one of these forms : '*Titio hominem Stichum do lego*',[4] '*sumito*',[5] '*sibi habeto*',[6] '*capito*'.[7] From the wording of G.2.193 it is often held that '*do lego*' was the proper, regular or typical form of the legacy but this is not borne out by the texts.[8]

In this type of legacy the ownership of the property legated passed straight from the testator to the legatee and never came to the heir. But whether the legatee became owner automatically as soon as the heir made *cretio* or only when the legatee himself accepted the legacy is not clear.[9] The action available to the legatee for the thing was the *vindicatio rei* and this could be brought

---

[1] Cf. for the later Republic, D.28.6.39pr (Javolenus, *1 ex post. Labeonis*); Cicero, *in Verrem*, II, 1.41.104f; *de inven.*, 2.21.62ff; *top.* 4.21; between 93 and 91 BC was fought the famous *causa Curiana* on the question whether a *substitutio pupillaris* would operate as a *substitutus vulgaris* if the *suus institutus* was in fact never born : Cicero, *de orat.*, 1.39.180; *de inven.*, 2.42.122; *Brutus*, 52-53, 194-8. See now Watson, *Succession*, pp. 53ff.

[2] See now, Watson, *Succession*, pp. 59f. For examples of the kinds of problems which could arise see Cicero, *de inven.*, 2.21.62; *top.*, 4.21.

[3] It has been argued that the *legatum per praeceptionem* did not emerge before the Empire, but see infra, p. 111.

[4] Cf. for the first century BC, D.40.7.39pr (Javolenus, *4 ex post. Labeonis*) : refers, *inter alios*, to Quintus Mucius; 32.100.2 (Javolenus, *2 ex post. Labeonis*); 33.7.15pr (Pomponius, *6 ad Sab.*). D.33.2.40 (Alfenus Varus, *8 dig. a Paulo epit.*) has only '*lego*'. Cf. G.2.193; *Epit. Ulp.*, 24.3.

[5] Cf. D.33.5.20 (Labeo, *2 post. a Iavoleno epit.*) : refers to Aufidius and has '*sumito sibique habeto*'. Cf. G.2.193.

[6] Cf. D.33.5.20; 33.8.14 (Alfenus Varus, *5 dig.*); 32.29.4 (Labeo, *2 post. a Iavoleno epit.*). Cf. G.2.193.

[7] Not evidenced at all for the Republic, but see G.2.193.

[8] On this whole question see now Watson, *Succession*, pp. 122f.

[9] The matter was disputed in classical law, the Sabinians taking the former view, the Proculians the latter : cf. e.g. G.2.195.

against any person, including the heir, who held the thing.[1] Things so legated had to be in the Quiritary ownership of the testator at the time of his death, and non-fungibles also had to be owned by him when he made the will.[2] But *ususfructus* and similar rights and servitudes could be the object of a *legatum per vindicationem*.[3]

In *legatum per damnationem* the form of words used was either '*heres meus Stichum servum meum dare damnas esto*' or '*dato*' of which the latter – contrary to modern scholarly opinion[4] – was overwhelmingly the more common.[5]

This time the legatee did not become owner automatically but only when the heir transferred the thing to him as, of course, the heir was under an obligation to do.[6] Again in distinction to *legatum per vindicationem*, a *legatum per damnationem* could be left of property which did not belong to the testator.[7] When this happened the heir had to buy the thing and give it to the legatee. If the owner refused to sell, the legatee could bring the relevant action, the *actio ex testamento*, the *iudex* would condemn the heir to give the value of the thing,[8] and the heir was released from his obligation by

[1] Cf. G.2.194; no textual evidence for the Republic.
[2] Cf. G.2.196; no textual evidence for the Republic but the rule is probably a survival from the time when the *mancipatio familiae* transferred ownership at once to the *familiae emptor*.
[3] Sole textual evidence for Republic is D.33.2.40 which concerns the first century B C, and refers to *habitatio*.
[4] Based on G.2.201.
[5] Cf. Watson, *Succession*, pp. 123ff. Of texts concerned with the Republic which give the actual wording, 22 have *dato*, 2 have *damnas esto dare*. For the former : Cicero, *de inven.*, 2.40.116; *Rhet. ad Herenn.*, 1.12.20; D.35.1.28pr (Paul, *2 epit. Alfeni dig.*); 33.1.22 (Alfenus Varus, *2 dig. a Paulo epit.*); 31.74 (Papinian, *27 quaest.*); 32.29.2 (Labeo, *2 post. a Iavoleno epit.*); 35.1.40.1, 2, 3, 4, 5 (Javolenus, *2 ex post. Labeonis*); 33.6.7.1 (*idem*); 30.30pr (Ulpian, *19 ad Sab.*); 30.5.1 (Paul, *1 ad Sab.*); 32.30.2, 5 (Labeo, *2 post. a Iavoleno epit.*); 34.5.14(15) (Marcian, *6 inst.*); 35.1.8 (Pomponius, *5 ad Sab.*); 35.1.38 (Paul, *sing. de iure codic.*); 33.4.6pr, 1 (Labeo, *2 post. a Iavoleno epit.*); 32.62 (Julian, *sing. de ambig.*). None refers to a time before the early first century B C. For the latter : D.33.1.7 (Pomponius, *8 ad Quintum Mucium*) refers to Quintus Mucius; 33.1.17pr (Labeo, *2 post. a Iavoleno epit.*). The validity of '*reddito*' and '*damnas esto reddere*' was apparently not suggested until the first century B C : argued from D.30.106 (Alfenus Varus, *2 dig. a Paulo epit.*).
[6] Cf. G.2.204.
[7] Cf. D.32.30.6 (Labeo, *2 post. a Iavoleno epit.*).
[8] Cf. for the Empire, D.30.71.3 (Ulpian, *51 ad ed.*).

paying the amount of the judgement. It is likely that if the owner was prepared to sell, but only at an inflated price, the heir was under an obligation to buy at that price and give the thing to the legatee.[1] Incorporeal rights and future things could also be the object of this legacy.[2]

The legatee's action here against the heir for non-performance was the *actio ex testamento*.[3] This was a civil law *actio in personam* and it could be framed either for a *certum* or an *incertum*.[4] When the action was brought under a *legatum per vindicationem* for a *certum*, the heir suffered condemnation *in duplum* if he wrongly denied liability.[5]

If the legatee in a *legatum per damnationem* was prepared to release the heir from the obligation without performance, this could not be done informally by the simple agreement of the parties. In the law of contracts, too, an obligation which could be created only with the aid of certain formalities could be ended only by reverse formalities.[6] Since the *testamentum* was made *per aes et libram* release of the *legatum per damnationem* likewise could only be made *per aes et libram*.[7] The form of words was : '*Quod ego tibi tot milibus sestertiorum testamento damnatus sum, me eo nomine a te solvo liberoque hoc aere aeneaque libra. Hanc tibi libram primam postremamque expendo secundum legem publicam.*'[8]

Legatum sinendi modo[9] took the form: '*Heres meus damnas esto sinere L. Titium hominem Stichum sumere sibique habere.*'[10] It was midway in character between the *legatum per vindicationem* and

---

[1] This is argued from D.32.30.6 and 30.45pr (Pomponius, *6 ad Sab.*) (which concern the first century BC) and the more relaxed attitude in the Empire; cf. Watson, *Succession*, pp. 126f.

[2] Cf. G.2.203; *Epit. Ulp.*, 24.9; *P.S.*, 3.6.10.

[3] Cf. G.2.204, 213; D.33.1.7 (Pomponius, *8 ad Quintum Mucium*).

[4] Cf. Lenel, *Edictum*, pp. 367f. Presumably some action was competent from the date of introduction of such legacies, hence there was probably a relevant *legis actio*. Whether this had yet given way to *formulae* cannot be determined.

[5] Cf. G.4.9, 171.

[6] Cf. infra, pp. 122f.

[7] Cf. Cicero, *de leg.*, 2.20.51; 2.21.53; G.3.175.

[8] G.3.174.

[9] For which there is no evidence in the Republic but its antiquity is not seriously doubted : cf. e.g., Bammate, *Origine et nature du legs sinendi modo* (Lausanne, 1947), pp. 147ff; Kaser, 'Das *legatum sinendi modo* in der Geschichte des römischen Vermächtnisrechts', zss, lxvii (1950), pp. 320ff.

[10] Cf. G.2.209.

legatum per damnationem since by it the testator could legate anything which belonged to himself or his heir, but not something which belonged to a third party.[1] Unlike the *legatum per damnationem* it seems never to have occasioned condemnation *in duplum* though both legacies were enforced by the same remedy, the *actio ex testamento*. In view of the language of the legacy – *sinere* – it was probably enough if the heir allowed the legatee to take the thing, and so the heir was not obliged to make a formal conveyance even when the thing was a *res mancipi*.[2] The *legatum sinendi modo* is unlikely ever to have been much used.

Legatum per praeceptionem was in all probability also in existence at this time.[3] The form was '*L. Titius hominem praecipito*'[4] and since it was a direction to 'take in advance' the legacy could be left only to an heir.[5] The purpose was that one *coheres* should have a particular thing among his share of the estate, and hence the appropriate action was the *actio familiae erciscundae*,[6] and the thing had to belong to the testator at the time of his death.[7]

It is impossible to decide whether *legatum partitionis* was in existence, though in a more subtle form it was known to Publius Mucius Scaevola[8] who was consul in 133 BC. *Legatum partitionis* was a direction to the heir to share the inheritance with the legatee and hence was a legacy of an uncertain amount. The form was

---

[1] Cf. G.2.210.

[2] The point was disputed in classical law but was decided in favour of the above position: G.2.214; *Epit. Gai.*, 2.5.6.

[3] But its antiquity is very much disputed, some scholars even holding that it did not exist before the beginning of the Empire: cf. the references given by Leuba, *Origine et nature du legs per praeceptionem* (Lausanne, 1962), p. 145nn. 2, 3, 4. The more acceptable view, as Leuba, *Origine*, pp. 145ff (and the scholars he cites) shows, is that it is ancient. The difficulty, as one can see from the two texts which concern the Republic and which may well be relevant, is to distinguish this legacy from other possible forms of *praelegata* to the heir: Pliny the Elder, *Hist. Nat.*, 33.11.38 (refers to 133 BC); Valerius Maximus, 7.8.4; for *praelegata* see e.g. Kaser, RPR, i, p. 624; Leuba, *Origine, passim*.

[4] Cf. G.2.216.

[5] This was the Sabinian view in the Empire (G.2.217) though the Proculians thought such a legacy could be left to anyone. The Sabinian view is the older: cf. Kaser, RPR, i, pp. 622f.

[6] Cf. G.2.219; for the *actio familiae erciscundae* see supra, p. 97.

[7] Cf. G.2.220. Though it was probably enough for the thing to be *in bonis testatoris*. [8] Cicero, *de leg.*, 2.20.50.

something like '*Heres meus cum Titio hereditatem partito, dividito*'.[1] Its original function may have been to enable someone to take as much as the heir without becoming liable for the performance of the *sacra*, in which case it might appear to be earlier than 250 BC by which time the more subtle form of *partitio* under a small deduction would be needed since then a legatee who took as much as the heir was also liable to perform the *sacra*. But it is equally plausible to hold that it was introduced in response to the *lex Voconia* of 169 BC which would have made it useful in at least two cases.[2] If *legatum partitionis* did exist in our period it was probably treated as a *legatum per damnationem*.[3]

Another legacy which may or may not have existed was *legatum optionis*[4] : '*Attia uxor mea optato Phylargyrum puerum, Agatham ancillam*.' This gave the legatee a right of choice and he became owner as soon as the choice was made. The object of the legacy could only be slaves and there could be no conditional *legatum optionis*.[5, 6]

A legacy might be of a single thing or of a number of things or of an agglomeration under a generic name or of incorporeals such as usufruct (and similar rights)[7] and servitudes.[8] There was inevitably very considerable scope for interpreting the extent of bequests and for establishing principles of interpretation, not only because of the natural imprecision of language, but also because wills were often rather badly drafted by amateurs and at the crucial moment the testator was no longer there to explain his intention. Regrettably we have no precise information about which prin-

---

[1] *Epit. Ulp.*, 24.25.   [2] See now Watson, *Succession*, p. 128ff.

[3] As it apparently was in the first century BC [D.32.29.1 (Labeo, *2 post. a Iavoleno epit.*); for the argument see Watson, *Succession*, pp. 130ff.] and later.

[4] It was known to Alfenus in the first centry BC : D.35.1.28.1 (Paul, *2 epit. Alfeni dig.*).

[5] For details see e.g. Bolomey, *Le legs d'option* (Lausanne, 1945); for the Republican evidence, cf. Watson, *Succession*, pp. 132f.

[6] In the Empire, *legatum optionis* was construed as a *legatum per vindicationem* : cf. Kaser, RPR, i, p. 620 and the references he gives, n. 7.

[7] Cf. e.g. D.33.2.12 (Alfenus Varus, *2 dig. a Paulo epit.*); 33.2.31 (Labeo, *2 post. a Iavoleno epit.*); 7.8.4.1 (Ulpian, *17 ad Sab.*); Cicero, *top.* 3.17; 4.21. All concern the first century BC.

[8] Cf. D.8.2.16 (Paul, *2 epit. Alfeni dig.*); 8.3.29 (*idem*) : Lenel, *Palingenesia Iuris Civilis*, i, (reprinted, Graz, 1960), 46; Watson, *Property*, pp. 194f. Both texts concern the first century BC.

ciples of interpretation could be regarded as established[1] – though presumably in the normal case male would be construed to include female, singular plural, and so on[2] – nor on whether as a general rule more weight would be given to the literal meaning of a bequest or to the apparent intention of the testator if the two seemed to conflict.[3]

An obvious place for juristic discussion on the extent of a bequest is legacies of agglomerations under a generic name, such as *penus*, stores, *suppellex*, furniture, *fundus cum instrumento*, a farm with its equipment. But equally obviously, any such discussion will reveal less about principles of interpretation or even of attitudes to interpretation than about the social, moral or religious outlook of the time and of the particular jurist. This is true of the two instances which have come down to us.

In the first century BC and later a legacy of *penus* was, in the main, confined to what could be eaten and drunk,[4] but we know that Sextus Aelius Catus[5] who was consul in 198 BC[6] was of the opinion that the legacy also included frankincense and candles provided for family use.[7] Now it seems that originally there was a connection between *penus* and *penates*[8] – *penates* are the gods who

[1] For the principles of interpretation of wills which can be seen to have existed in the first century BC, see Watson, *Succession*, pp. 85ff.

[2] But even this cannot be taken absolutely for granted. Thus, it was certainly accepted for early statutory interpretation that male included female but doubts were raised (and problems consequently could arise) by 287 BC: cf. e.g. Watson, *Obligations*, pp. 246f; Yaron, '*Si pater filium ter venum duit*', *T.v.R.*, xxxvi (1968), pp. 57ff at pp. 61f.

[3] On wide and narrow interpretation (not only for wills) in the Republic see Watson, *Limits of Juristic Decision in the Later Roman Republic* (University of Edinburgh Inaugural Lecture no. 36); 'Narrow, Rigid and Literal Interpretation in the Later Roman Republic', *T.v.R.*, xxxvii (1969) pp. 351ff.

[4] Cf. D.33.9.3 (Ulpian, *22 ad Sab.*); Aulus Gellius, *N.A.*, 4.1.16-23; Ormanni, '*Penus legata*', *Studi Betti*, iv (Milan, 1962), pp. 579ff; Watson, *Succession*, pp. 134ff.

[5] *Sextus Caecilius* in D.33.9.3.9 must be a scribal error for *Sextus Aelius*; cf. Aulus Gellius, *N.A.*, 4.1.20.

[6] Cf. e.g. Kunkel, *Herkunft und soziale Stellung der römischen Juristen*, 2nd edit. (Graz, Vienna, Cologne, 1967), p.8.

[7] D.33.9.3.9; Aulus Gellius *N.A.*, 4.1.20. Ormanni, '*Penus*', p. 676, takes *cerei* to mean wax images of the god or sacrificial victim, but the common meaning of *cereus* is wax candle : *Thesaurus Linguae Latinae*, iii, 862.

[8] Cf. Ormanni, '*Penus*'.

live in and rule over the store room[1] – and it has been suggested[2] that the early function of *legatum penus* was to enable the legatee to carry out the family religious rites without too much expense, when the heir was an *extraneus*. This conception of the legacy was apparently still important in the time of Sextus Aelius and influenced his opinion because the use of frankincense and candles in domestic worship is well-known.[3] Incidentally, the early connection of *legatum penus* with worship probably explains why even[4] in the Empire this legacy could be, and often was, validly cast in the form of a *legatum poenae nomine*[5] though *legata poenae nomine* were void.[6, 7]

The attribution of the other instance to our period is itself the result of a consideration of the social outlook of the time. The jurist Paul wrote that at one time neither a silver mixing bowl nor any silver vessel was counted as *suppellex*, furniture, 'because of the severity of the time'.[8] Something has dropped out of the text and Mommsen conjectured,[9] plausibly enough, that the decision was Sextus Aelius'. Certainly we know that the period in question was before Quintus Mucius, who excluded from a legacy of *argentum factum* those pieces of silver which counted as *suppellex*,[10] and that in our time the owning of much silver was frowned upon as being over-luxurious. Sextus Aelius himself refused the silver dishes presented to him by envoys of Aetolia, and the only silver he ever owned were the two drinking vessels given him by his father-in-law on account of his courage when Perseus was defeated.[11]

There was no restriction on the number of legacies in a will but

---

[1] Cf. Wissowa, *Religion und Kultus der Römer*, 2nd edit. (Munich, 1912), p. 162.

[2] By Ormanni, '*Penus*', at e.g. pp. 696f, 689f.

[3] Cf. e.g. Cato, *de agri cult.*, 84; Cicero, *de off.*, 3.20.80; Watson, *Succession*, p. 136. The candles might well have been kept in the store-cupboard, in which case material and religious reasons would complement each other.

[4] It must be a survival: see for the Republic: D.45.1.115.2 (Papinian, *2 quaest.*).

[5] That is, '*Heres meus penum dato; si non dederit, centum dato*', or '*Heres meus, si penum non dederit, centum dato.*'

[6] G.2.235; *Epit. Ulp.*, 24.17.

[7] Cf. Ormanni, '*Penus*', at e.g. p. 617; Watson, *Succession*, p. 141.

[8] D.33.10.3.5 (*4 ad Sab.*).

[9] *Digesta Iustiniani Augusti*, ii (reprinted, Berlin, 1963), p. 140 n. 1.

[10] D.34.2.19.9 (Ulpian, *20 ad Sab.*).

[11] Pliny the Elder, *Hist. Nat.*, 33.50.142.

whether there was a restriction in our period on the value of the property which could be left in any one legacy depends on the date of the *lex Furia testamentaria*, which was a plebiscite proposed by C. Furius[1], a tribune who is otherwise unknown. This *lex* is earlier than the *lex Voconia* of 169 BC[2] and is likely to be close in time to the *lex Cincia de donis et muneribus* of 204 BC[3] with which it has some similarities, and whose general social purpose it might share. The plebiscite enacted that no one, apart from certain excepted classes, could take by legacy (or *mortis causa*) more than 1,000 *asses*, and it gave a *legis actio per manus iniectionem* (in the form of *manus iniectio pura*)[4] to the heir against anyone who did so take for four times the amount taken above 1,000 *asses*.[5] The excepted classes, who could take larger legacies, were all those persons within the sixth degree of relationship,[6] and one from the seventh, the child of a *sobrinus*, a cousin on the mother's side[7]; and probably also relatives by marriage, husband and wife, fiancé and fiancée, parents-in-law, children-in-law, step-parents and step-children.[8] The *lex Furia* was a *lex minus quam perfecta*,[9] that is, a statute which forbade some act and provided a penalty for contravention, but did not declare the act, if done, void.

The purpose of the statute, according to Gaius, was to protect the heir who might find his status financially worthless if the

---

[1] Cicero, *pro Balbo*, 8.21.

[2] Emerges from G.2.225, 226.

[3] For the *lex Cincia* see supra, pp. 73f. The *lex Furia* is generally thought to be later than the *lex Cincia* [cf. e.g. Steinwenter, *s.v. Lex Furia*, RE, xii, 2356f; Kaser, RPR, i, p. 629] but this is rightly declared an unproven hypothesis by Wesel; 'Über den Zusammenhang der *lex Furia, Voconia* und *Falcidia*', ZSS, lxxxi (1964), pp. 308ff at p. 310 n. 2.

[4] Cf. Watson, *Succession*, pp. 163ff. For this procedure see infra, pp. 163f.

[5] G.2.225; 4.23; *Epit. Ulp., praef.* 2; J.2.22pr; Theophilus, *par.*, 2.22pr. It is not expressly stated that the person to whom the action lay was the heir: see now Watson, *Succession*, pp. 163ff. Steinwenter, *Lex Furia*, 2357, appears to hold that the *lex* did not apply to legacies *per damnationem* and *sinendi modo*, but this is implausible: cf. Watson, *Succession*, p. 166 n. 1.

[6] Degrees of relationship were calculated by counting up to the common ancestor and down again.

[7] *Vat. Fr.*, 301 (Paul, *71 ad ed., ad Cinciam*).

[8] No textual evidence, but there is for the *lex Cincia* – *Vat. Fr.*, 302 (Paul *71 ad ed.*) – and it is likely that the *lex Furia* was no less generous: cf. Steinwenter, *Lex Furia*, 2356. The *lex Cincia* also allowed *tutores* to make gifts to their wards: *Vat. Fr.*, 304 (*idem*).

[9] Cf. *Epit. Ulp., praef.* 2.

testator had left too large legacies.[1] It is likely that the *lex* also had another aim, akin to that of the *lex Cincia*, and was one of the laws passed after the second Punic War with the social and political motive of restricting greed and liberality.[2]

Legacies could be left subject to a condition.[3, 4]

REVOCATION OF WILLS

We have already seen the factors which might cause a will to be void from the beginning, or make a valid will subsequently void. But a will could also be revoked by the testator. For this, it was not enough simply to destroy the *tabulae* on which the will was written with the intention of revoking it, but a new will had to be made.[5] The reason for this, it is thought,[6] is that the validity of the will derived from the ceremony *per aes et libram* and the *nuncupatio*, and did not depend on the continuing existence of the *tabulae*. Logically one might have expected that the first will remain valid until the *familiae emptor* remancipated the estate to the testator, but so much was not demanded.[7]

[1] G.2.225. This is often disputed, but it seems plausible enough : cf. Watson, *Succession*, pp. 163ff.

[2] See above all Steinwenter, *Lex Furia*, 2358f; Wesel, 'Zusammenhang', pp. 310ff : cf. Watson, *Succession*, p. 165.

[3] For the texts concerning conditional legacies in the later Republic see now, Watson, *Succession*, pp. 101ff.

[4] In some legacy context Cato – who may be Cato the Censor or his son – gave the opinion that, if the legacy would have been unenforceable had the testator died at the moment of making the will, then the legacy was void. The context of the opinion cannot be determined but we know that only much later was the opinion generalised into a *regula*. G.2.244 is especially instructive though we do not know that Servius' opinion would have prevailed earlier. See also D.34.7.1pr (Celsus, *35 dig.*) : cf. now Hausmaninger, 'Celsus und die *regula Catoniana*', *T.v.R.*, xxxvi (1968), pp. 469ff.

[5] This was the position at civil law even in Gaius' time : G.2.151.

[6] Cf. e.g. Kaser, RPR, i, p. 578; Voci, *Diritto ereditario*, ii, pp. 492f.

[7] At least, not in classical law. It may have been originally, but if so the requirement was almost certainly obsolete even by our time.

CHAPTER II

The Sphere of the *Condictio*

The *condictio* was a general action which did not state the basis of the plaintiff's case, but declared the plaintiff's claim that the defendant was under an obligation to give him something. This was the appropriate action for three separate Roman contracts and was also available in a number of non-contractual situations. My intention is first to deal with the contracts, then with the non-contractual cases, and lastly with the nature of the *condictio*.

STIPULATIO

The Romans had no general theory of contract and for an agreement to be valid and legally enforceable it had to fall within the framework of some particular recognized contract. The *stipulatio*, which is probably the oldest Roman contract,[1] was a formal unilateral contract of strict law. As is usual in Roman law, the formalities were of a simple kind, this time being that the contract was oral, in question and answer form (with no delay between the question and answer), the substance of the answer had to correspond to the question and the verb used in the reply had to be the same as that of the question. Neither writing nor witnesses were required for the contract's validity, but no one possessing ordinary caution would fail to avail himself of one of these modes of proof.[2] The reply did not have to repeat everything said in the question: thus, '*Ducentos nummos aureos Philippos probos dabin?*' '*dabo*'[3] and even '*Viginti minas dabin?*', '*dabuntur*'[4] created valid

---

[1] It was known at the time of the XII Tables: cf. G.4.17a.
[2] Aulus Gellius, *N.A.*, 14.2.21, 26, which concerns Cato the Censor. Cf. *Rhet. ad Herenn.*, 2.9.13.
[3] Plautus, *Ba.*, 881ff; cf. Plautus, *Ps.*, 117f; Cicero, *pro Caecina*, 3.7.
[4] Plautus, *Ps.*, 1077f; cf. Plautus, *Ba.*, 882f.

I

stipulations. Any verb could be used for this question and answer,[1] though the form '*spondesne*'?, '*spondeo*' was apparently by far the most common[2] and had the peculiarity that it created a stipulation only when the words were spoken by Roman citizens.[3] Undoubtedly this form had a very different origin from the others,[4] but by this time it was treated no differently apart from its restriction to citizens.[5]

Since the *stipulatio* was *stricti iuris* the contract was valid if the formalities were observed and it was irrelevant that the promisor had entered the contract as a result of fraud or fear. Indeed, it was not until the first century BC that any remedy was available[6] when the contract was improperly induced. Likewise, great stress was laid on the words actually used and, partly as a consequence,[7] implied terms scarcely developed. But we can be reasonably certain that when a promissee made it impossible for the promisor to fulfil a condition under which the promisee was to be paid, the promisor was not bound to pay.[8]

A stipulation might be void if it was for an immoral[9] or illegal purpose, or if it was impossible or subject to an impossible condition.[10] Also, it could not be made on behalf of a third person who was not the promissee's *paterfamilias* or *dominus*: not only did the

---

[1] Denied by Nicholas even for the whole of the classical period: 'The Stipulation in Roman Law', LQR, lxix (1953), pp. 63ff; contra, e.g., Winkler 'Gaius III. 92', RIDA, v (1958), pp. 603ff; Watson, 'The Form and Nature of *acceptilatio* in classical Roman Law', RIDA, viii (1961), pp. 391ff; Feenstra, 'L'*epistula* comme preuve d'une stipulation', *Studi Betti*, ii (Milan, 1961), pp. 407ff at p. 407 n. 4.

[2] Thus, of the some 100 instances in the Digest where the verb used is given, 85 have '*spondes?*' '*spondeo*' : Nicholas, 'Stipulation', p. 73.

[3] Cf. G.3.93.

[4] Cf. above all, Kaser, *Das altrömische Ius* (Göttingen, 1949), pp. 267ff.

[5] Cf. Watson, *Obligations*, p. 1.

[6] By the *edictum quod metus causa* of around 78 BC and the *edictum de dolo* of about 66 BC.

[7] But also because the stipulation could be used to cover any kind of situation.

[8] Cf. for the first century BC, D.4.8.40 (Pomponius, *11 ex var. lect.*); 22.2.8 (Ulpian, *77 ad ed.*); Watson, *Obligations*, p. 2. The rule that a *statuliber* was to become free if the heir stopped the condition being fulfilled goes back to the XII Tables. See also in general, Daube, 'Condition Prevented from Materializing', *T.v.R.* xxviii (1960), pp. 271ff.

[9] This appears indirectly from the disappearance of an action on betrothal : supra, pp. 14f. [10] Cf. G.3.97, 97a, 98.

third person acquire no rights under the contract, but it could not be enforced by the promissee.[1] It is probable, too, that there could be no valid stipulation which was to be performed after the death of the promisor or the promissee.[2] But when the stipulation could be performed or come into operation during the lifetime of the parties it was valid and the rights and duties under it descended on death to the parties' heirs. Thus, Cato[3] held that if a promisor died leaving a number of heirs and one of them committed a breach of the stipulation for which a fixed monetary penalty had been arranged, and the stipulation admitted of division (for instance *'amplius non agi'*) then only the person in breach was liable, and that only for his share; but if the stipulation did not admit of division (for instance, *'iter fieri'*) all would be liable for their respective shares in the *hereditas*.[4]

Since *stipulatio* was a verbal contract neither the promisor nor the promisee could be deaf or dumb[5]; and in other respects it was subject to the general rules of contractual capacity which have been dealt with in earlier chapters.[6]

The stipulation could be used to achieve a variety of ends : thus, a whole contract of sale might be incorporated in mutual stipulations, or certain terms in a sale – especially warranties against eviction and against latent defects[7] – might be the subject of one stipulation, and so might a personal guarantee.

Personal security, in fact, was more important at Rome than it is today, mainly because the Romans attached much more weight to the duties of friendship,[8] and it was accepted that one friend should readily act as guarantor for another. Two verbs could be used, either *spondere* or *fidepromittere*,[9] and both required that the principal obligation was also created *verbis*.[10] The creditor who was not

---

[1] Cf. D.50.17.73.4 (Quintus Mucius, *sing.* ὅρων) (concerns early first century BC); G.3.103.

[2] No Republican evidence, but see G.3.100 which suggests a history of development.

[3] Who might be Cato the Censor or his son.

[4] D.45.1.4.1 (Paul, *12 ad Sab.*); cf. Watson, *Obligations*, pp. 5f.

[5] Cf. G.3.105. [6] Cf. G.3.104-9. [7] Cf. infra, pp. 135f.

[8] For the importance of friendship, e.g. in politics, see Taylor, *Party Politics in the Age of Caesar* (Berkeley, 1949), pp. 7ff; in *mandatum*, Watson, *Contract of Mandate in Roman Law* (Oxford, 1961), pp. 20f.

[9] The use of *fideiubere* is later : cf. Watson, *Obligations*, pp. 6ff.

[10] Cf. G.3.119. The rule is ancient and is one reason for the later creation of the more flexible *fideiussio*.

paid had the choice of exacting the debt either from the principal debtor or the guarantor. He was not legally bound to sue the debtor first though it is likely that it was thought improper to proceed first against the guarantor[1] unless it was probable that the debtor was insolvent. An action brought against the principal debtor automatically released the *sponsores* and *fidepromissores* even if the debtor turned out to be insolvent.[2] By the *lex Publilia*[3] a *sponsor* who had paid the debt and was not reimbursed within six months had an *actio depensi* against the principal debtor.[4] He had the right of *manus iniectio pro iudicato*[5] and this was one of the cases in which the defendant's denial of liability doubled the sum due from him.[6] The *actio depensi* was not available to the *fidepromissor* who, if he paid, had no remedy against the debtor,[7] and this probably means that when the *actio depensi* was established the *sponsor* was the only personal guarantor. Since the guarantor presumably decided the form in which his guarantee was couched he would normally choose '*spondesne?*' '*spondeo*' if this were available to him. Hence we can conclude that in practice '*fidepromittis?*' '*fidepromitto*' was largely confined to peregrines.[8]

The burden of a *sponsio* or *fidepromissio*,[9] unlike that of other stipulations, did not descend to the heir[10] (unless the *fidepromissor* was a peregrine whose city had a different rule), and during the Republic statutes were passed which made the lot of a *sponsor* or *fidepromissor* easier. The *lex Furia* which is probably slightly older

[1] As it certainly was in Cicero's day : *ad Att.*, 16.15.2

[2] Cf. Cicero, *ad Att.*, 16.15.2 (which mentions only *sponsores*).

[3] Of unknown date, but certainly before our time. The *actio depensi* is perhaps a development after the *lex Publilia* : cf. Kaser, RPR, i, p. 155.

[4] For double the amount according to G.3.127 but this may be in error because *lis crescit infitiando*.

[5] Cf. infra, p. 163.

[6] G.3.127; 4.9, 22, 171.

[7] Until the introduction of the *actio mandati* : cf. Watson, *Obligations*, pp. 7ff. The suggestion in that book that there may have been an edictal remedy can probably – certainly for our period – be excluded if the development outlined in Watson, 'Praetor's Edict', is accurate.

[8] Cf. Watson, *Obligations*, pp. 7ff.

[9] The use of the terms is convenient but it must be emphasised that the word *sponsio* with the meaning of a contract of surety does not exist in the sources, legal or lay, and that *fidepromissio* does not occur at all : Daube, *Roman Law*, pp. 24ff.

[10] Cf. G.3.120.

than 200 BC[1] and applied only to Italy[2] relieved a *sponsor* and *fidepromissor* of liability after 2 years, and further laid down that the debt, when it fell due, was to be divided into as many parts as there were guarantors, and each was to be liable only for an aliquot share.[3] If the creditor exacted more from a guarantor than his rateable share, the latter could proceed against him by *manus iniectio pro iudicato*.[4] Earlier than the *lex Furia*,[5] the *lex Appuleia* had introduced a kind of partnership between *sponsores* and *fidepromissores* : any one of them who paid more than his share of the debt had an action against the others for the excess. After the *lex Furia*, the sole importance of the *lex Appuleia* was outside Italy. The *lex Cicereia* was consequential upon the *lex Furia* and so, presumably, only slightly later. This enacted that a person taking *sponsores* or *fidepromissores* had to give advance public notice and declare both the matter for which he wanted guarantees and the number of *sponsores* and *fidepromissores*. If the creditor failed to do this, the guarantors were allowed 30 days in which to ask for a *praeiudicium* to determine whether proper notice had been given, and if the finding was against the creditor, the *sponsores* and *fidepromissores* were released.[6, 7]

It would appear from this volume of legislation – unparalleled in any other branch of private law in the Republic – that there was a strong feeling that the moral obligations to help a friend were leading too many persons into financial difficulties. The *lex Furia* and *lex Cicereia* took away so much of the creditor's advantage that borrowing (with personal, rather than real, security) would be more difficult and eventually, perhaps more than two centuries later, a new form of personal security using the verb *fideiubere* was introduced to which these statutes did not apply.

A further use of *stipulatio* was to provide another person, termed *adstipulator*, whom the debtor might pay as an alternative to

---

[1] But not certainly. Cf. e.g. Rotondi, *Leges*, pp. 475ff; Kunkel, *Festschrift Koschaker*, ii (Weimar, 1939) p. 12 n. 25; de Zulueta, *The Institutes of Gaius*, ii (Oxford, 1953), p. 161; Frezza, *Le garanzie delle obbligazioni, i, Le garanzie personali* (Padua, 1962), p. 16.

[2] G.3.121a.

[3] G.3.121.

[4] G.4.22.

[5] G.3.122 : cf. e.g. Rotondi, *Leges*, p. 246; Kunkel, *loc. cit.*

[6] G.3.123.

[7] The subsequent *lex Cornelia* dates from about 81 BC.

paying the creditor. After the principal *stipulatio* was made, the second *stipulatio* was taken and in this the promisor promised to give the same thing to the *adstipulator*. Release by either the first promissee or the *adstipulator* ended the obligation under both *stipulationes*. The same main verb did not have to be used in the *stipulatio* and the *adstipulatio*, and the *adstipulatio* could be for a lesser, but not greater, obligation. The right of action on the *adstipulatio* did not descend to the heir of the *adstipulator* and an *adstipulatio* to a slave was of no effect.[1] There was no recognized contract[2] between the *stipulator* and the *adstipulator* but if the latter released the debtor and did not hand over what was due, the stipulator had a delictal action under Chapter 2 of the *lex Aquilia*.[3]

Roman obligations in early times were discharged by a *contrarius actus*, a reverse act in similar form to that which created the obligation. Performance of the obligation was legally irrelevant. The *contrarius actus* of *stipulatio* was *acceptilatio* and in all probability it was still necessary in our period for the extinction of the obligation.[4] The usual form was '*Habesne acceptum?*', '*habeo*' but any form of words would do which declared that there had been performance.[5] In view of its nature there could be no conditional *acceptilatio*,[6] and no partial *acceptilatio*,[7] nor could *acceptilatio* be made on behalf of someone other than the *dominus* or *paterfamilias*.[8] Also, of course, only verbal obligations were extinguished by *acceptilatio*.[9] And just as a slave could not bind his *dominus* by

[1] For all this see G.3.110-14.
[2] Until the introduction of *mandatum*, probably in the second half of the second century B C.
[3] Infra, p. 152.
[4] It is clear that it was necessary in 287 B C though it was not by the time of Servius in the first century B C : cf. Watson, *Obligations*, pp. 212f. The disappearance of the requirement was not the result of statute or edict; presumably people gradually ceased to take the trouble to make *acceptilatio* – a practice which eventually found acceptance in the courts. So the development was presumably slow.
[5] Cf. Watson, '*Acceptilatio*', pp. 391ff. The point would become more significant once *acceptilatio* become recognized as the mode of extinguishing a stipulation when there was no performance.
[6] Cf. D.46.4.4 (Pomponius, *9 ad Sab.*); 46.4.5 (Ulpian, *34 ad Sab.*); Watson, *Acceptilatio*, p. 400.
[7] Argued from G.3.172; Watson, *loc. cit.*
[8] Cf. D.46.4.3 (Paul, *4 ad Sab.*) (interpolated); 46.4.13.10 (Ulpian, *50 ad Sab.*); 46.4.8.4 (Ulpian, *48 ad Sab.*); Watson, '*Acceptilatio*', p. 401f.
[9] Cf. G.3.170.

entering a contract so he could not release a debtor of the *dominus* by *acceptilatio* even at his owner's command.[1] Where a guardian's consent was needed for a *stipulatio* promised by the ward, so the consent would be required for an *acceptilatio* by the ward.[2, 3, 4]

THE CONTRACT LITTERIS

This rather strange Roman contract is of obscure origins,[5] but, in view of its *stricti iuris* nature and its other peculiarities, an early date is indicated. There is textual evidence for its existence around the beginning of the first century B C.[6] Like *stipulatio*, the literal contract was unilateral but its formalities required writing, not an oral question and answer. Moreover, it was rather a way of reconstituting an existing obligation than of creating an entirely new one.[7]

It was created in one of two forms. First, when a creditor made an entry in his account books to the debit of a person who had contracted with him of the amount owed him under the existing contract of, say, purchase or partnership.[8] No payment was in fact made to the apparent recipient. This form was known as *a re in personam*. The entry cancelled the existing obligation which would – usually at least – be *bonae fidei*, and substituted a new one which was *stricti iuris*. The consent of the other contracting party was necessary to this arrangement, and in practice evidence would be required, usually perhaps writing which would be retained by the creditor.[9] The literal contract had sound advantages for the creditor : it might give an opportunity for providing better evidence

---

[1] Cf. D.46.4.22 (Gaius, *3 de verb. obl.*); Watson, '*Acceptilatio*', p. 403.
[2] Cf. G.3.171; Watson, '*Acceptilatio*', pp. 403f.
[3] *Novatio* was, I think, a late development, arising only after *acceptilatio* ceased to be needed to release a *stipulatio* : cf. Watson, *Obligations*, pp. 214ff.
[4] For *condictio* – otherwise named *actio certae creditae pecuniae* – as the action on a *stipulatio* for a *certum* see Cicero, *pro Roscio com.*, 4-5.13-14; Watson, *Obligations*, pp. 14ff. For a possible alternative and for the action for an *incertum* see infra, p. 128.
[5] See now on the literal contract in general, Watson, *Obligations*, pp. 18ff, which stresses the extent to which our knowledge is limited.
[6] Cicero, *de off.*, 3.14.58-60 : cf. now Watson, *Obligations*, pp. 29ff.
[7] Cf. Watson, *Obligations*, p. 21.   [8] Cf. G.3.129.
[9] Argued from the tablets of Herculaneum which, admittedly, concern a much later period : cf. Watson, *Obligations*, pp. 22f. And see Cicero, *pro Roscio comoedo*, 1.1, 2; Watson, *Obligations*, pp. 25f : Valerius Maximus, 8.2.2; Watson, *Obligations*, p. 34.

than existed for the earlier obligation, the action would be for the fixed sum stated in the account books – not as in the *bonae fidei* obligations for what ought to be given in accordance with good faith – and the debtor could no longer oust the creditor's claim on the ground that it was fraudulent. No such benefits obtained for the debtor, but presumably he would agree to the literal contract only if he was given some incidental advantage, such as more time to pay.

The second form of literal contract was called *a persona in personam* when the creditor debited to a third party what was already owed him by another. In this case both the third party and the existing debtor must have agreed to this assignment of debt.[1]

How formalised the writing had to be is not certain but the balance of the evidence strongly supports the view that the entry actually had to be in the creditor's (monthly) account books, and that writing in, say, his daily ledger was not sufficient.[2] No entry in the debtor's books was needed.[3] A peregrine could not be the creditor in the literal contract[4] and also apparently not the debtor.[5]

The literal contract could not be made subject to a condition.[6, 7]

Though there is no real evidence (for any period) it is likely that a *contrarius actus*, a written record of repayment in the creditor's account books, was needed for the extinction of the literal contract.[8, 9]

[1] This is expressed for the third party by G.3.130.

[2] Cf. Cicero, *pro Roscio comoedo*, 1-5.1-14; for the argument, Watson, *Obligations*, pp. 24ff, pp. 38f.

[3] This appears from Cicero, *de off.*, 3.14.58-60; cf. Watson, *Obligations*, p. 37.

[4] This appears from G.3.132, 133; cf. Watson, *Obligations*, p. 24; but see also p. 32 and n.1.

[5] In classical law it was accepted that a peregrine could not be the debtor in *a persona in personam*, but Sabinus and Cassius held, against Nerva, that he could in *a re in personam* : G.3.133.

[6] Cf. *Vat. Fr.*, 329. Buckland, *Textbook*, p. 459, suggests on the basis of Cicero, *ad fam.*, 7.23.1, that it might be subject to *dies*, but the text, as he says, is not conclusive.

[7] Livy, 35.7.2, 3; Plautus, *Truc.*, 70ff; 749f; *Most.*, 304f; are not directly helpful for the literal contract : cf. now, Watson, *Obligations*, pp. 18ff.

[8] Cf. Buckland, *Textbook*, p. 572. The use of *acceptum referre* to mean 'to place one's credit' is not in itself significant for the release of the literal contract.

[9] For *condictio* (*actio certae creditae pecuniae*) as the action on the literal contract see Cicero, *pro Roscio comoedo*, 4-5.13-14; Watson, *Obligations*, pp. 14ff.

MUTUUM

This was a contract of loan of money and other fungibles, the debtor being bound to restore not the same things, but goods of the same quality and quantity.[1] The contract was *stricti iuris* and unilateral, only the recipient coming under an obligation. The contract came into being not on agreement but on delivery of the goods and then only if ownership was actually transferred to the borrower. It follows from this that the risk of damage or destruction was always on the borrower and he was not excused repayment because of any subsequent injury to the things.

Loan for consumption was, of course, common,[2] but it does not follow that the contract of *mutuum* was itself common – at least in its pure form – and we have only one text of Cicero which actually shows that it was actionable in the Republic.[3] The explanation lies in the nature of the *condictio*[4] as an action against the unjustified retention of something which should be given to the plaintiff; hence it lay only for the equivalent of the goods delivered and did not cover interest payments. But businessmen would normally want interest so the practice was to accompany the loan with a *stipulatio* providing for this, and the *stipulatio* would normally be framed to cover the principal as well, and also all other relevant clauses such as the date of repayment. Hence the basic contract involved would be *stipulatio*, not *mutuum*. It is very probable, in fact, that no terms could be attached to the *mutuum* and that technically repayment was due as soon as the loan was made.[5, 6]

It will have been observed that the contractual element in *mutuum* was not of great significance; and little separates this contract from the non-contractual cases where the *condictio* was given.[7]

[1] Cf. G.3.90.
[2] Cf. Plautus, *Ps.*, 294f; *St.*, 256; *Tri.*, 727; 761f; Terence, *Heaut.*, 601. See also, Plautus, *Per.*, 37f; *Ps.*, 85f.
[3] *pro Roscio comoedo*, 4-5.13-14; cf. Watson, *Obligations*, pp. 14ff.
[4] Cf. infra, pp. 126f.
[5] Cf. Kaser, '*Mutuum* and *stipulatio*', *Eranion Maridakis*, i (Athens, 1963), pp. 155ff.
[6] For *mutuum* see in general, Buckland, *Textbook*, pp. 462ff; Kaser, RPR, i, pp. 442ff.
[7] This also emerges from Gaius' treatment of obligations *re* at G.3.90f.

THE CONDICTIO IN NON-CONTRACTUAL SITUATIONS

In other cases, with one exception to be looked at shortly, the *condictio* was given when there had been a handing over, a *datio*, to the defendant, and ownership had actually been transferred to him, and when however it was yet proper according to the civil law that the thing or the sum of money be returned to the plaintiff.[1]

Thus, the *condictio* would be available to a person who had by mistake paid a debt that was not owed[2]; or who had given money or a thing in return for some promised performance and the recipient failed to carry out his side of the agreement[3]; or who had given money or a thing for a performance which involved dishonourable conduct by the recipient but not by the giver.[4]

The exceptional case was the *condictio* against a thief for the recovery of stolen property. This time there had been no *datio*, the thief had not become the owner and, in fact, the action was available only to the true owner.[5] The *condictio* here was alternative to, and not cumulated with, the *vindicatio*.[6] The reason for this exceptional case is much disputed but it is most reasonable to see it as a survival from a time when the *condictio* had a wider scope, and which remained because of disapproval of thieves.[7]

THE NATURE OF CONDICTIO

The *legis actio* for *condictio* was introduced by the *lex Silia* for *certa pecunia* and by the later *lex Calpurnia* for other *certae res*.[8] Both statutes are to be dated before our period.[9] The procedure *in iure*

---

[1] For our very limited knowledge of *condictio* in the Republic, see Watson, *Obligations*, pp. 10ff.

[2] Cf. G.3.91. See also Digest, title 12.6.

[3] Cf. Digest, title 12.4.

[4] Cf. Digest, title 12.5.

[5] Cf. G.4.4; D.13.1.1 (Ulpian, *18 ad Sab.*); and in general, Digest, title 13.1.

[6] Cf. d'Ors, 'The *odium furum* of Gaius 4.4', RIDA, xii (1965), pp. 453ff, especially at pp. 457ff.

[7] This opinion is taken over from Daube's (unpublished) lectures on *condictiones*.

[8] G.4.19.

[9] Not universally accepted : cf. the authors cited by Kaser, ZPR, p. 81 nn. 4, 5. The conclusive argument is, I submit, that the formulary *condictio* was in existence by the time of Plautus, *Rudens*, [cf. infra p. 127 n. 3] and that a *legis actio per condictionem* would not be introduced later.

was as follows. The plaintiff declared : '*Aio te mihi sestertiorum x milia dare oportere : id postulo aies aut neges.*' The defendant denied the obligation. The plaintiff : '*Quando tu negas, in diem tricensimum tibi iudicis capiendi causa condico.*' The parties then had to appear on the 30th day to choose a *iudex*.[1] Thus, even in the old *legis actio* procedure, the action did not state the ground of the plaintiff's claim.[2]

But as early as this it was already possible to proceed by a *formula* for the *condictio*,[3] though the *legis actio* would also continue to be used.[4] When the action was for *certa pecunia* the *formula* ran : *Si paret Numerium Negidium Aulo Agerio sestertium decem milia dare oportere, iudex Numerium Negidium Aulo Agerio sestertium decem milia condemna, si non paret absolve.*[5] For *certa res* : *Si paret Numerium Negidium Aulo Agerio tritici Africi optimi modios centum dare oportere, quanti ea res est, tantam pecuniam Numerium Negidium Aulo Agerio condemna, si non paret absolve.*[6]

To restrain rash litigation by plaintiffs and pointless defence by defendants, a *sponsio* for one third of the sum sued for was made available to parties in the action for *pecunia credita*.[7] It seems certain that the *sponsio* also existed in the *legis actio*.[8]

---

[1] For all this see G.4.17b.

[2] Cf. e.g. Kaser, z p R, p. 81 and the references he gives.

[3] Cf. Watson, 'Some Cases of Distortion by the Past in Classical Roman Law', *T.v.R.*, xxxi (1963), pp. 69ff. The basic argument is that the *legis actiones* did not have *exceptiones*, '*ut nunc*' as Gaius says [G.4.108], and yet Plautus, *Rudens*, 1376ff, which involves a *stipulatio*, shows the existence of the *exceptio legis Laetoriae*. Hence the action must have been under a *formula*. Kaser [z p R, p. 54 and n. 1], who thinks the formulary *condictio* is later, holds that the Plautine passage shows that factual situations which later could give rise to specific *exceptiones* could at that time be opposed to the success of civil law actions. But he does not explain by what means, nor does he attempt to show in what way the defence to be put up in the *Rudens* differed from a classical *exceptio*. As a matter of fact the argument of Labrax, if put into the third person appropriate for a *formula*, has exactly the form of a classical *exceptio* : '*ni dolo malo instipulatus sis nive etiamdum siem quinque et viginti annos natus.*

[4] Probably until the *lex Aebutia* of around 140 B C ; cf. now above all, Kaser, z p R, pp. 54f.; but add to the references, Watson, 'Distortion', p. 73.

[5] Cf. Lenel, *Edictum*, p. 237.

[6] Cf. Lenel, *Edictum*, p. 240.

[7] G.4.171.

[8] Cf. for all, Kaser, z p R, p. 213.

Since the *condictio* lay only in respect of *certa pecunia* or *certa res* it could not be used when a *stipulatio* had been given for an incertain prestation. In this case there was an *actio ex stipulatu* with an *intentio* running: *quidquid ob eam rem Numerium Negidium Aulo Agerio dare facere oportet*.[1] It is often maintained, moreover, that when the stipulation was for a *certum* there was an *actio certa ex stipulatu* to which the *condictio* was an alternative, but the argument is very insecure.[2]

[1] G.4.136; cf. Lenel, *Edictum*, pp. 151ff.
[2] For literature on the question see Kaser, ZPR, p. 256 n. 56; and add Watson, *Obligations*, pp. 14ff.

CHAPTER 12

The *Bonae Fidei* Contracts

Apart from the *actio tutelae*,[1] actions in which the defendant was to be condemned to pay a sum equivalent to what he ought to give or do in accordance with good faith were restricted to a few contracts of which sale, hire and partnership alone existed around 200 BC.[2,3] The significance of the formulation, *quidquid ob eam rem Numerium Negidium Aulo Agerio dare facere oportet ex fide bona, eius iudex Numerium Negidium Aulo Agerio condemna &c.*, is two-fold. First, it makes the measure of damages very flexible. The judge, in condemning the defendant, has to take into account factors which ought morally to mitigate or increase the damages. Thus, a plaintiff's fraud will automatically have an adverse effect on his claim, though it would be irrelevant in an action on a stipulation.[4] Secondly, the words *ex fide bona*[5] by virtue of con-trolling the measure of damages (and in the absence of any other relevant clause) will govern the standard of liability. When in the

---

[1] Cf. supra, p. 39.

[2] For a summary of the arguments in favour of the existence of the contracts of sale, hire and partnership see now Watson, *Obligations*, respectively at pp. 40f, 100f and 126. *Mandatum* can scarcely be much older than 126 BC: cf. now Watson, *Obligations*, p. 147. And the *bonae fidei* actions for *commo-datum* and *depositum* probably date from the Empire: cf. e.g. Watson, *Obligations*, p. 160. Even the edictal *actiones in factum* for these last two contracts are likely to be little earlier than 100 BC; cf. Watson, 'Praetor's Edict'. For the XII Tables' provision concerning deposit see infra, p. 157.

[3] The not altogether dissimilar *actio rei uxoriae* had an *intentio* in *quod eius melius aequius erit*; and the *actio fiduciae* had *ut inter bonos bene agier oportet et sine fraudatione*.

[4] And even later, after the advent of the *edictum de dolo*, the *exceptio doli* would have to be specifically pleaded in the *formula* of a *stricti iuris* action.

[5] For the *bonae fidei* nature of the consensual contracts, cf. e.g. Cicero, *de off.*, 3.17.70; *de nat. deor.*, 3.30.74; *top.*, 17.66.

circumstances of a particular case it appears right that the defendant should be liable only for fraud, the award of damages 'in accordance with good faith' will be nil when he has been merely negligent. And similarly when negligence ought morally to ground liability, he will be liable to pay damages *ex fide bona*.[1] Of course, for the stock situations of each contract the standard of liability will appear fixed, as being either for *dolus* only or for *culpa* as well.

The contracts of sale, hire and partnership shared a further characteristic in that they required no binding element of form, but their validity derived solely from the agreement of the parties, however it might be expressed, plus the essential matters of substance.

EMPTIO VENDITIO (SALE)

Sale needed a price, a thing to be sold, and agreement.

The price had to be in money since otherwise it would not be possible to tell who was buyer and who was seller – an essential point, since, as we shall see, their duties were different.[2] But it is likely that the price might consist primarily of money and partly of some other thing.[3] The price had to be fixed[4] and, we can assume, had to be seriously meant,[5] but the sale was not affected if the price was too low or highly inflated [6]

The thing to be sold had to be *in commercio* and hence could not be a free man, a *res sacra*, *res religiosa* or *res publica*. The point is important since at this time the contractual actions, the *actio empti* and the *actio venditi*, were available only if there was an actual valid contract of *emptio venditio* and otherwise, for instance, a de-

---

[1] Cf. Watson, *Contract of Mandate in Roman Law* (Oxford, 1961), pp. 195ff, especially at p. 215.

[2] The Sabinian view that the price need not be in money (G.3.141) is a later attempt to extend the advantages of *emptio venditio* to *permutatio*.

[3] Cf. Cato, *de agri cult.*, 146; 150 : for the argument see Watson, *Obligations*, pp. 42f.

[4] Though in the first century B C Ofilius thought that there was a valid sale if the price was agreed as the value to be put on the thing by a named third party : G.3.140.

[5] That is, if the seller did not intend to exact the price because he was really making a disguised gift of the thing, the sale would be void. Despite the *lex Cincia* this point would become of real significance only when gifts were prohibited between husband and wife.

[6] Cf. Cicero, *ad Att.*, 14.13.5.

frauded buyer who had paid the price had to fall back on some other remedy such as the *condictio*.[1]

Likewise there could be no sale of a thing which did not exist, for example an unknown monster or a slave who had died before the contract was concluded, but there could be sale of incorporeals such as debts[2] and inheritances[3] and also of future things, for instance the *fructus* of a flock of sheep,[4] olives on the tree,[5] grapes on the vine[6] and winter fodder which was still growing.[7] Modern analysis classifies the sale of *res futurae* either as *emptio spei* or *emptio rei speratae*. In the former case the sale is to be valid even if the hoped-for thing does not come into being – what is bought is the hope – but in the latter the sale fails unless the thing comes to exist. Both forms of sale existed in classical law but the surviving texts do not show that *emptio spei* existed in our period,[8] though at least *emptio rei speratae*, which presents fewer difficulties for legal theory, must have done.

Since *emptio venditio* was a consensual contract it was formed as soon as the parties reached agreement, and no formalities were required. In practice, though, important sales would usually be recorded in writing for evidentiary purposes,[9] or the terms and agreement made known to witnesses. The common giving of *arra*, earnest money, served a different evidentiary purpose in demonstrating to the parties themselves that final agreement had been reached – like shaking hands on concluding a bargain –

---

[1] There is no direct authority for these statements but the propositions appear clearly from the pattern of development which can be seen in classical law : on this see now above all, Stein, *Fault in the Formation of Contract in Roman Law and Scots Law* (Edinburgh, 1958), pp. 61ff. Plautus' *Persa*, 135ff; 329ff; 577ff; and 714f should not be taken as good evidence that there could be a valid sale of a free person misrepresented as a slave : see Watson, *Obligations*, p. 44.

[2] Cf. Cicero, *ad Att.*, 12.3.2; 12.31.2; D.44.4.4.6 (Ulpian, *76 ad ed.*) (refers to first century BC).

[3] Cf. Cicero, *ad fam.*, 14.5.2. In classical law (and probably earlier) the sale of the *hereditas* of a person who was still alive was void : D.18.4.1 (Pomponius, *9 ad Sab.*).

[4] Cato, *de agri cult.*, 150.

[5] Cato, *de agri cult.*, 146.

[6] Cato, *de agri cult.*, 147.

[7] Cato, *de agri cult.*, 149.

[8] Cf. Watson, *Obligations*, 45.

[9] For the importance of writing as evidence of a contract see Aulus Gellius, *N.A.*, 14.2.21, 26.

though it had no specific legal function. But *arra* acted as part-payment of the price and had the additional social purpose of making it more likely that the bargain would be kept on both sides.[1,2]

Ownership of the thing sold did not pass to the buyer when the contract was concluded but only when the appropriate delivery was made, *mancipatio* (or *in iure cessio*) for *res mancipi*, *in iure cessio* for incorporeal *res nec mancipi*, *traditio* (or *in iure cessio*) for corporeal *res nec mancipi*.[3] For transfer of ownership by *traditio* following upon a sale, physical delivery was not sufficient by itself, and payment of the price or the giving of security by the buyer to the seller was also needed. This particular rule goes back to the XII Tables.[4]

Risk of destruction, however, passed to the buyer, not with ownership[5] but at the moment the contract became perfect. Normally this would be the time of agreement but when the contract was under a suspensive condition it did not become perfect until the condition was realized; when the sale was of goods from a larger stock the contract became perfect only when specific goods were appropriated to the contract; and when a stock was sold, the quantity being then unascertained and the price fixed at so much per unit, the sale became perfect only when the quantity sold became known. Destruction of the subject matter of the contract before the *emptio venditio* became perfect would stop the sale coming into being because *emptio venditio* needed a thing to be sold. But risk of deterioration passed to the buyer at the moment of agreement even when the sale was *imperfecta* since the thing continued to exist and there was a *res quae veneat*.[6]

[1] For the dispute on the function of *arra* in the time of Plautus see now Watson, *Obligations*, pp. 47ff. The texts are Plautus, *Rud.*, 554ff.; 859ff; 1281ff; *Mos.*, 637f; 643ff; 659; 662ff; 669ff; 795ff; 813; 915ff; 977ff; 1010ff; 1021; 1026d; 1085; *Cur.*, 612; *Ps.*, 1183; Varro, *de ling. lat.*, 5.175.

[2] We have no information whatever on the effect of error on the contract.

[3] For these modes of acquisition of ownership see supra, pp. 61ff.

[4] On this much disputed topic see Watson, *Obligations*, pp. 61ff. The main texts are J.2.1.41; D.18.1.19 (Pomponius, *31 ad Quintum Mucium*); Varro, *de re rust.*, 2.1.15. The restriction became obsolete in practice due to juristic activity in the very late Republic or early Empire.

[5] Cf. D.18.6.12(11) (Alfenus Varus, *2 dig.*) which concerns the first century BC.

[6] There is very little evidence for the rules about risk in the Republic – though see D.18.6.15(14).1 (Paul, *3 epit. Alfeni*); cf. Watson, *Obligations*,

The obligations of the buyer were to pay the price, pay interest if he was late in paying[1] and pay the seller's expenses if it was the buyer's fault that delivery of the thing sold was delayed. Thus, Sextus Aelius Paetus, the consul of 198 BC, declared that if it was due to the buyer that a slave was not delivered, the seller could recover from him the cost of the slave's keep.[2]

The duties of the seller[3] were to look after the thing until delivery and to deliver it. He was certainly liable if the thing was damaged or destroyed through his own negligence – though the negligence of his slaves was not imputed to him – but we cannot determine whether he was liable for all injury to the thing apart from that caused by what is termed *vis maior*.[4]

As for the duty of delivery it was enough that the seller allow the thing to be taken away.[5] He was, moreover, not under any legal obligation to make the buyer owner nor even to ensure that the buyer was legally entitled to physical control of the thing. Thus, if a third party successfully asserted a legal claim to the thing and the buyer was deprived of it, he had no claim on the contract of sale against the seller.[6] The situation was not quite the same when the seller had acted fraudulently, at least from the time of Cato the Censor's decision against Tiberius Claudius Centumalus. Claudius had been ordered by the augurs to demolish that part of his house on the Caelian hill which obstructed their view. He sold the building to Publius Calpurnius Lanarius without warning him, and the buyer was also served with the augurs'

---

p. 68 – and the foregoing is a statement of what seems to be the classical law which is unlikely to be different. There is a lack of information in the sources on deterioration. But see D18.6.8pr (Paul, *33 ad ed.*); cf. e.g. de Zulueta, *The Roman Law of Sale* (Oxford, 1945), p 32; Arangio-Ruiz, *La compravendita in diritto romano* (Naples, 1956), pp. 250ff. It can be argued that when the sale was *imperfecta* but not conditional the risk of deterioration remained with the seller.

[1] No evidence until much later: cf. D.19.1.13.26 (Ulpian, *32 ad ed.*); *Vat. Fr.*, 11 (Papinian, *3 resp.*).
[2] D.19.1.38.1 (Celsus, *8 dig.*).
[3] The parties' duties were probably reciprocal: cf. now Watson, *Obligations*, p. 69.
[4] For all this see D.18.6.12(11) (Alfenus Varus, *2 dig.*) (refers to first century BC); Watson, *Obligations*, pp. 71f.
[5] Cf. D.18.6.1.4 (Ulpian, *28 ad. Sab.*), which refers to the *veteres*: Watson, *Obligations*, p. 70.
[6] Cf. e.g. Watson, *Obligations*, pp. 73ff.

K

order. Calpurnius demolished the parts of the building as required and then discovered that Claudius had sold the house after he received the augurs' order, and he brought the *actio ex empto* against him. Cato as *iudex* held that 'since he was aware of that matter when he made the sale and did not declare it, he was bound to make good the buyer's loss'.[1] But the action in respect of silence was given only for legal defects affecting land,[2] for instance when the seller did not disclose a servitude over the land, which he knew about.[3] But it is very likely that the *actio ex empto* was given against the buyer for positive mis-statements even when the thing sold was not land and when he was not acting fraudulently.[4]

Whether in a sale of *res mancipi* the seller was bound to mancipate cannot be determined.[5] But when a *res mancipi* was transferred by *mancipatio* and the buyer was evicted he had an action resulting from that ceremony[6] though not from the contract.

In general the seller was not liable for any latent defect in the thing sold, even when he was aware of it. But he was liable for *promissa* (guarantees given by *stipulatio*) and *dicta* (express statements) made during the negotiations even, it seems, if they were without fraud.[7] Mere puffery, however, was not actionable.[8] But a special liability was introduced by the Edict of the curule aediles for sale of slaves in the market place.[9] The earliest form of this probably goes back to our period (or it might be only slightly later)[10] and it seems to have run : '*Titulus servorum singulorum scriptus sit curato ita, ut intellegi recte possit quid morbi vitiive cuique*

---

[1] Cicero, *de off.*, 3.16.67.

[2] Cicero, *de off.*, 3.16.65, 66, 67; cf. now Watson, *Obligations*, pp. 87f.

[3] Cicero, *de orat.*, 1.39.178; *de off.*, 3.16.67 (refer to 91 BC); cf. Watson, *Obligations*, pp. 79f.

[4] This appears from D.21.2.69.3 (Scaevola, *2 quaest.*) (refers to Servius) taken together with the rules about *dicta promissave* : cf. Watson, *Obligations*, pp. 76ff, 88f, 89 n. 7.

[5] Cf. e.g. Watson, *Obligations*, pp. 74f.
   Cf. supra, pp. 61f.

[7] Cf. D.21.2.69.3; Cicero, *de off.*, 3.14.58, 59, 60; Watson, *Obligations*, pp. 88f.

[8] Cf. Cicero, *de off.*, 3.13.55.

[9] That is, within the jurisdiction of the aediles.

[10] Against the conjecture of Daube [*Forms of Roman Legislation* (Oxford, 1956), pp. 91ff] favouring 199 BC see Watson, 'The Imperatives of the Aedilician Edict' *T.v.R.* xxxviii (1970). But some form of this edictal clause was known to Cato the Censor or his son : cf. infra, p. 135.

sit, quis fugitivus errove sit noxave solutus non sit.[1] It thus apparently imposed a duty on the seller to make the buyer aware of those defects included in the terms *morbus* and *vitium* and to let him know if the slave was a runaway, given to wandering off, or liable to be noxally surrendered. There would inevitably be considerable discussion as to what constituted a *morbus* or *vitium,* and we have an opinion of Cato that a slave who had lost a finger or a toe was *morbosus.*[2] At some point (unknown, but certainly in the Republic) this aedilician edict was replaced by another,[3] and a further clause relating to the sale of *iumenta* was added.[4]

The law was so unsatisfactory as to warranties against eviction and against latent defects that it was very common in important sales for the buyer to take a stipulation from the seller in respect of both of these. That part concerning eviction would usually be for double the price if what was sold was a *res mancipi* and for the buyer's interest in other cases. The *stipulatio* was given even when the thing sold was transferred by *mancipatio* (and hence the *actio auctoritatis* would lie) partly at least because it was customary for the seller to give guarantors, and *sponsio* and *fidepromissio* were effective only when they guaranteed a verbal obligation. The part

---

[1] Aulus Gellius, *N.A.*, 4.2.1.

[2] D.21.1.10.1 (Ulpian, *1 ad ed. aed. cur.*). Whether this is Cato the Censor or his son cannot be determined.

[3] According to D.21.1.1.1 (Ulpian, *1 ad ed. aed. cur.*); this read : '*Qui mancipia vendunt certiores faciant emptores, quid morbi vitiive cuique sit, quis fugitivus errove sit noxave solutus non sit : eademque omnia, cum ea mancipia venibunt, palam recte pronuntianto, quodsi mancipium adversus ea venisset, sive adversus quod dictum promissumve fuerit cum veniret, fuisset, quod eius praestari oportere dicetur : emptori omnibusque ad quos ea res pertinet iudicium dabimus, ut id mancipium redhibeatur. si quid autem post venditionem traditionemque deterius emptoris opera familiae procuratorisve eius factum erit, sive quid ex eo post venditionem natum adquisitum fuerit, et si quid aliud in venditione ei accesserit, sive quid ex ea re fructus pervenerit ad emptorem, ut ea omnia restituat. item si quas accessiones ipse praestiterit, ut recipiat. item si quod mancipium capitalem fraudem admiserit, mortis consciscendae sibi causa quid fecerit, inve harenam depugnandi causa ad bestias intromissus fuerit, ea omnia in venditione pronuntianto : ex his enim causis iudicium dabimus. hoc amplius si quis adversus ea sciens dolo malo vendidisse dicetur, iudicium dabimus.*' But the text is not in perfect form. For possible reconstructions see, above all, Nicholas, '*Dicta promissave*', *Studies in the Roman Law of Sale dedicated to the Memory of de Zulueta* (Oxford, 1959), pp. 91ff at pp. 94f. His third suggestion seems the most persuasive.

[4] Cf. D.21.1.38pr (Ulpian, *2 ad ed. aed. cur.*).

of the *stipulatio* concerning defects varied according to the object sold and in the case of slaves would specify that they were not given to running away or liable to be noxally surrendered. Some idea of the forms may be drawn from the later writer, Varro. Thus in the sale of sheep, '*illasce oves, qua de re agitur, sanas recte esse, uti pecus ovillum, quod recte sanum est extra luscam surdam minam, id est ventre glabro, neque de pecore morboso esse habereque, recte licere, haec sic recte fieri spondesne?*'[1]; in the sale of she goats, '*illasce capras hodie recte esse et bibere posse habereque recte licere, haec spondesne?*'[2] It is noteworthy that even in these *stipulationes* the seller guaranteed the buyer only quiet enjoyment and not ownership.

That such *stipulationes* were so necessary in practice was a grave defect in the contract of sale since it meant that *emptio venditio*, too, had to be made by the parties face-to-face and could not be effected satisfactorily by their slaves[3] or by letter. Other terms including the price[4] were also frequently cast in the form of a *stipulatio*.

From the earliest days of *emptio venditio* there were certain standard clauses, some in favour of the buyer, some in favour of the seller. In favour of the buyer was the *pactum displicentiae*, that the goods could be returned if the buyer was dissatisfied,[5] and *emptio ad gustum*, a clause in sale of wine that the buyer was to taste within a specified time and could reject if the wine was sour or musty.[6] In favour of the seller was *in diem addictio*, that he could withdraw from the contract if he received a better offer,[7] and the *lex commissoria*, that he could avoid the contract if the price was not paid within a fixed time.[8] A clause particularly favouring neither the one nor the other was *arbitrium boni viri*, the referring either of a

---

[1] *de re rust.*, 2.2.6.

[2] *de re rust.*, 2.3.5. Cf. *de re rust.*, 2.4.5; 2.5.10, 11; 2.9.7. See also now, Watson, *Obligations*, pp. 83ff. The particular forms in Varro are taken from Manilius (*de re rust.*, 2.3.5) but it is likely that he only collected or improved existing forms.

[3] Since the *actiones adiecticiae qualitatis* were not yet in existence.

[4] Cf. Varro, *de re rust.*, 2.2.5.

[5] Plautus, *Merc.*, 418f: cf. D.9.2.52.3 (Alfenus, *2 dig.*) (refers to first century BC); Watson, *Obligations*, pp. 96f

[6] Cato, *de agri cult.*, 148; cf. now Watson, *Obligations*, p. 97.

[7] Plautus, *Cap.*, 179ff: cf. Watson, *Obligations*, p. 98.

[8] Though this clause is not evidenced for the Republic.

dispute to,[1] or the fixing of a specific provision by,[2] the judgement of a *bonus vir*.

LOCATIO CONDUCTIO (HIRE)

Locatio conductio was a wide-ranging contract and included hire of a thing, of services and of work to be done. In general it will be simplest to look at these three manifestations separately – though this is not to be taken to mean that there was more than one kind of *locatio conductio* – but first we can deal with the reward for the hire.

The reward, conveniently termed *merces*,[3] probably had to consist of money[4] except in the case of *negotia partiaria*, where the *merces* could be a proportion of the product of the work of one partly expended on the property of the other.[5] But the *merces* did not have to be wholly in money.[6] The *merces* had to be fixed, not in the sense that it was known to the parties, but that at least it would be calculable according to some determined scheme.[7]

In *locatio conductio rei* the duty of the *conductor*, that is, the hirer, was not only to pay the rent but also to take proper care of the thing hired. What standard of liability was normally demanded

[1] Cato, *de agri cult.*, 148, 149.

[2] Cf. D.18.1.7pr (Ulpian, *28 ad Sab.*) (refers to the *veteres*); Watson, *Obligations*, pp. 98f, and the references given, p. 99 nn. 2, 3.

[3] As it often, but not invariably, was: cf. Kaufmann, *Die altrömische Miete* (Cologne, Graz, 1964), pp. 136ff.

[4] The strongest argument is probably the parallelism between *emptio venditio* and *locatio conductio*, and the way this is brought out by G.3.139–47. In the case of hire, too, the idea that the reward might consist of something other than money is probably a development. Nonetheless, it should be emphasized (1) that the argument drawn by Watson, *Obligations*, pp. 102f, from D.19.2.35.1 (Africanus, *8 quaest.*) for the proposition that the *merces* had to be in money in the Republic is rather tenuous: (2) that Varro, *de re rust.*, 3.16.10 (ignored by Watson) does show a lease of apiaries for a fixed rent of 5,000 pounds of honey [though Varro is concerned only with the fact, not the form of the contract which might be based on *stipulationes*]; and (3) that the situation in G.3.144, where the question whether there is a *locatio conductio* is raised, concerns the exchange of user and the entire problem may relate to that – scince who is *locator* and who *conductor* cannot be determined – and not to the absence of a money *merces*.

[5] Cato, *de agri cult.*, 16, 136, 137. These *negotia partiaria* relate to *locatio operis faciendi* and *locatio operarum*, so the scope is wider than the *colonia partiaria* in classical law, which was always *locatio rei* (*immobilis*): cf. Watson, *Obligations*, pp. 104f.

[6] This appears from Cato, *de agri cult.*, 144.5; 145.3.

[7] Cf. Cato, *de agri cult.*, 14: Watson, *Obligations*, pp. 103f.

cannot be directly discovered,[1] but the parties were free to fix their own standard in the contract.[2] And when the *conductor* acted in breach of an express term of the contract, for instance loaded mules above a fixed weight, and injury resulted, he would be *ipso facto* liable to the *actio ex locato*.[3] As in sale, the negligence of his slaves was not imputed to the fault of the *conductor*.[4]

The *locator* did not have to be owner and it was enough that he could give the *conductor* physical control of the thing and keep him in control. Hence, sub-leases were possible[5] and no special term developed to denote these.[6] The lease could continue even if the *locator* sold the *res locata* provided he arranged that the *conductor* remain in control[7]; but it should be noticed that the *conductor* never had a right to the thing enforceable *in rem* and was limited to the contractual remedy against the *locator*.[8] The *res locata* had to be fit at the outset for the purpose of the lease or no rent was payable,[9] and if the *locator* could not enable the *conductor* to enjoy the object for the whole period of the lease he lost his right to rent *pro rata*.[10] But the *conductor* could not deduct from his *merces* for minor inconveniences.[11] All this assumes that the *locator* was free from fault.

---

[1] There is, in fact, no evidence at all for the Republic, and little more for classical law. *P.S.*, 2.18.2 shows that the *conductor* was liable for *culpa* but the nature of the text is such that it cannot be taken to mean there was no liability for *custodia*. This is also true of D.19.2.25.4 (Gaius, *10 ad ed. prov.*) but for a different reason, namely that the *conductor* would be liable if *culpa* could be imputed to him but not otherwise, even if the standard of liability was for *custodia*. But the text is usually held interpolated: cf. Mayer-Maly, *Locatio conductio* (Vienna, Munich, 1956), pp. 178f. C.4.65.28 [AD 294] and J.3.24.5 make the *conductor* liable for *custodia*. Some authorities, e.g. Buckland, *Textbook*, p. 500, declare that in classical law the *conductor* was liable for *culpa levis*; others, e.g. Kaser, RPR, i, p. 473, that he was liable for *custodia*. The matter will be left open.

[2] Cf. D.19.2.30.4 (Alfenus, *3 dig a Paulo epit.*) (concerns first century BC): Watson, *Obligations*, pp. 118f.

[3] Cf. D.19.2.30.2. (concerns the first century BC); cf. Watson, *Obligations*, pp. 236f.   [4] Cf. D.19.2.30.4; Watson, *Obligations*, pp. 118ff.

[5] Cf. D.19.2.30pr (concerns the first century BC).

[6] Cf. Mayer-Maly, *Locatio conductio*, pp. 27ff.

[7] Cf. D.19.1.13.30 (Ulpian, *32 ad ed.*) (concerns the first century BC).

[8] Cf. Kaser, RPR, i, p. 473.

[9] Cf. D.19.2.19.1 (Ulpian, *32 ad ed.*) (concerns first century BC); Watson, *Obligations*, pp. 113f.

[10] Cf. D.19.2.30pr, 1 (Alfenus, *3 dig. a Paulo epit.*) (concerns the first century BC); D.19.2.27 (Alfenus, *2 dig.*).

[11] Cf. D.19.2.27pr; Watson, *Obligations*, pp. 115f.

But if he knew or ought to have known that the thing was unfit for the purpose of the lease or unnecessarily prevented the enjoyment of the *conductor* – for instance, demolished a building which did not have to be pulled down, in order to build better – then he was also liable in damages.[1,2]

Locatio operarum was hire of services, the *locator* being the person who hired out his services and took the *merces*. Contracts of employment (whether of this type or of *locatio operis faciendi*) were even at this time not so important at Rome as in the modern world partly because so much unskilled and even skilled work was performed by slaves, and partly because what were regarded as 'liberal professions' – for instance land-measuring, medicine, advocacy – could not be the subject of a contract of *locatio conductio* when performed by a free man.[3] And the hire of a slave doctor[4] would often be *locatio rei*. In *locatio operarum*, the *conductor* still had to pay the *merces* if the intended result was not achieved and this was due to factors external to the *locator*.[5]

Locatio operis faciendi which might be a contract with the same aim as a contract of *locatio operarum* was different and the *merces* was due only if the intended result was actually achieved.[6] This time the person who did the work and took the *merces* was the *conductor*. When gold or silver was delivered to a smith to be worked ownership was at once transferred to the smith,[7] perhaps because he was not expected necessarily to return exactly the same gold or silver but only *eiusdem generis*.[8] Contracts for the carriage

[1] Cf. D.19.2.19.1; 19.2.30pr; 19.2.35pr (Africanus, *8 quaest.*); Watson, *Obligations*, pp. 116f.
[2] *Remissio mercedis*, the release of the *conductor* in limited circumstances from the duty of paying rent when he was allowed to enjoy the thing but something went wrong and he received no profit from it, is, I believe, a juristic development and was known to Servius in the first century BC: D.19.2.15.2 (Ulpian, *32 ad ed.*); Watson, *Obligations*, pp. 110ff. But it is, I feel, unlikely to be very old, and hence its scope need not be discussed.
[3] Cf. now Watson, *Obligations*, pp. 109f.
[4] Cf. Varro, *de re rust.*, 1.16.4.
[5] No authority till much later, but see D.19.2.38pr (Paul, *1 reg.*).
[6] No early authority, but the proposition can be deduced for the early Empire from D.19.2.58.1 (Labeo, *4 post. a Iavoleno epit.*).
[7] At least this was the case in the time of Quintus Mucius and of Alfenus though not in classical law : D.34.2.34pr (Pomponius, *9 ad Quintum Mucium*); 19.2.31 (Alfenus, *5 dig. a Paulo epit.*); cf. now Watson, *Obligations*, pp. 106ff.
[8] Cf. D.19.2.31.

of goods by sea might, one would think, fall within any of the manifestations of *locatio conductio* but the only two Republican instances where we can be specific concern *locatio conductio rerum vehendarum, that is, locatio operis faciendi.*[1,2]

Before we leave hire it should be noticed that in practice the dividing line between *emptio venditio* and *locatio conductio*[3] was not always drawn exactly where we would expect. Thus, Cato describes a sale of winter pasturage[4] and of the increase of a flock of sheep[5] where one might have looked for contracts of *locatio conductio.*[6,7]

SOCIETAS (PARTNERSHIP)

Neither *emptio venditio* nor *locatio conductio* had a pre-*formula* stage. The *legis actiones* were not flexible enough, it is thought, to deal with the *bonae fidei* nature of the obligations.[8] But this is not true of partnership. Gaius tells us that at one time when a *paterfamilias* died his *sui heredes* were in a kind of partnership—which he describes as *legitima simul et naturalis*—called *ercto non cito*, that is, 'undivided ownership'.[9] Later, other persons who wished to set up a similar partnership could do so by means of a definite *legis actio* before the praetor.[10] These partnerships differed from the consensual contract in that when one partner manumitted a slave belonging to the partners he became free and the freedman of all the partners, and that *mancipatio* by one partner of a *res mancipi*

---

[1] D.19.2.31; 14.2.2pr (Paul, *34 ad ed.*) (both concern first century BC); cf. now, Watson, *Obligations*, pp. 121f.

[2] From at least the first century BC the shipowner's liability under the contract was obscured in sea-carriage cases by the acceptance of the principles of average of the *lex Rhodia de iactu*: cf. D.14.2.2pr, 3; 19.2.31. How much earlier this acceptance was cannot be determined.

[3] A matter of fundamental importance to the parties since it was essential to sue on the right *formula*.

[4] *De agri cult.*, 149.

[5] *De agri cult.*, 150.

[6] Kaufmann holds, indeed that originally sale and hire were not distinguished: *Miete*, at e.g. pp. 303ff.

[7] Contracts of letting with the State as one party were common – cf. e.g. Livy, 23.48.10–49.4 – but though these may have been influential for the origins of the consensual contract, they are of a different nature and cannot be discussed here.

[8] But see the origin suggested for *fiducia*, supra, pp. 84f.

[9] G.3.154a.

[10] G.3.154b.

belonging to the partners made the *res mancipi* the property of the transferee.[1] Since the non-existence of these rules in consensual *societas* cannot be attributed to anything essential in the nature of that contract, nor their presence in the older contracts to anything in the *legis actio*, it would seem that they were no longer thought desirable. Thus, the old forms, especially that created by *legis actio*, would have no reason for existence once the consensual contract was available and they would not long continue. If they were still in being around 200 B C it must have been only as archaic survivals.

Consensual *societas* differed from our modern partnership in several respects but above all in that it was almost entirely concerned with the relationship of the partners *inter se* and not with the dealings of a partner and a third party. Thus, if a contract within the scope of the partnership was made with a third party, the rights and duties under the contract were acquired only by that third party and the partner who contracted with him. The third party, for instance, could not bring an action against another partner or the partnership itself.[2] But the contracting partner would be responsible for the contract to his partners.

Ercto non cito among *sui heredes* would be, in the very nature of things, a partnership of all the partners' assets. Presumably the same was true of a partnership created by *legis actio*. The *praetor urbanus* issued only one *formula* for *societas* and that, we know, was also for a *societas omnium bonorum*.[3] This suggests that the consensual partnership was originally envisaged primarily for farming concerns among relatives and very close friends, and not for mercantile ventures among men whose main tie was the hope of mutual business profit.[4] The *formula*, to judge from its later appearance,[5] read : '*Quod Aulus Agerius cum Numerio Negidio societatem omnium bonorum coiit, qua de re agitur, quidquid ob eam*

[1] G.3.154b.
[2] For *societates argentariorum* see infra, pp. 142f.
[3] Cf. above all, Lenel, *Edictum*, pp. 297ff; and also, Arangio-Ruiz, *La società in diritto romano* (Naples, 1950), p. 29; Watson, 'Consensual *societas* between Romans and the Introduction of *formulae*', R I D A, ix (1962), pp. 431ff at pp. 432f.
[4] This is one of the main facts pointing to an early date for the introduction of consensual *societas* between Romans.
[5] But the strong possibility of its having undergone some changes must be emphasized: cf. Watson, 'Praetor's Edict', and infra, p. 142 n. 1.

*rem Numerium Negidium Aulo Agerio (alterum alteri) dare facere
(praestare?) oportet ex fide bona,*[1] *eius iudex Numerium Negidium
Aulo Agerio condemna, si non paret absolve.*'[2]

Whether from the start lesser partnerships were possible and
were actionable under this *formula* cannot be determined but it
seems that they existed in our period.[3] *Societates publicanorum*
indeed flourished,[4] though it is perhaps unwise to argue too much
from them since we know that in classical law they[5] differed from
other partnerships in having corporate personality.[6] Partnerships,
other than of all the partners' assets, might be of everything which
came from trade or employment (*universorum quae ex quaestu
veniunt*)[7] or of one kind of business (*unius negotiationis*)[8] or even
of a single transaction (*unius rei*).[9] This last kind (which is not
recognized in the law of Scotland or England) could have a
particular usefulness at Rome where the law of agency was always
underdeveloped. It appears likely that there was no conditional
partnership.[10] *Societas omnium bonorum* gave rise to special problems; for instance if one partner was married and had received a
substantial dowry and the partnership was terminated during the
continuance of the marriage.[11] By the beginning of the first century

---

[1] The classical formula here contained a clause giving *beneficium com-
petentiae*, namely, '*dumtaxat quod Numerius Negidius facere potest*', but this
is due to a clause of the Edict [cf. Lenel, *Edictum*, pp. 298f] and hence is
likely to be later [cf. Watson, 'Praetor's Edict'].

[2] Cf. above all, Lenel, *Edictum*, pp. 297ff.

[3] Emerges from Plutarch, *Cato maior*, 21.6.

[4] Cf. Livy, 23.48.10–49.4 (refers to 215 BC). They may antedate the
consensual contract.

[5] No text throws any light on their legal structure in the Republic.

[6] D.3.4.1.pr, 1 (Gaius, *3 ad ed. prov.*); cf. e.g. Mitteis, *Römisches Privatrecht
bis auf die Zeit Diokletians*, i (Leipzig 1908), pp. 403ff (who observes that
their general characteristics were those of private law *societas*); Duff,
Personality in Roman Private Law (Cambridge, 1938), pp. 141ff; Bonet,
'*Societas publicanorum*', *Anuario de Historia del Derecho Español*, xix (1948–
9), pp. 218ff.

[7] Cf. D.17.2.71.1 (Paul, *3 epit. Alfeni dig.*) (refers to first century BC);
17.2.11 (Ulpian, *30 ad Sab.*) : cf. Watson, *Obligations*, p. 135.

[8] Plutarch, *Cato maior*, 21.6.   [9] Cf. Cicero, *pro Roscio comoedo*.

[10] Whether there could be or not was disputed throughout classical law :
C.4.37.6 [Justinian, AD 531]. Paul apparently gave an affirmative answer :
D.17.2.1pr (*32 ad ed.*); cf. now Watson, *Obligations*, pp. 130f.

[11] Cf. e.g. for the first century BC, D.17.2.65.16 (Paul, *32 ad ed.*); *P.
Grenf.* 2.107 recto; D.17.2.52.18 (Ulpian, *31 ad ed.*); Watson, *Obligations*,
pp. 136f.

BC – but how much earlier cannot be decided – bankers' partnerships, *societates argentariorum* had the particular characteristic that a contract of one partner with a third party bound all the partners.[1, 2]

In many cases – perhaps in most, especially in *societas omnium bonorum* – the financial contributions of the partners would be equal, though we need not presume that this had to be the case.[3] The partnership profits or losses would be divided equally[4] unless the parties made a special arrangement,[5] but it is likely that it was not permitted for the partners to agree that one partner take a larger share of any profit and a smaller share of any loss.[6]

The partnership action was the *actio pro socio* which lay at this time only for fraud[7], but this was no particular hardship since the *actio communi dividundo* was always available to settle accounts and in it the judge would be able to take account of a partner's negligence.[8] A partner condemned in the *actio pro socio* probably suffered some kind of censorian disgrace.[9]

---

[1] *Rhet. ad Herenn.*, 2.13.19, which attributes the rule to custom; cf. D.2.14.25pr (Paul, *3 ad ed.*); 2.14.27pr (*idem*); Arangio-Ruiz, *Società*, pp. 82f.

[2] In classical law a partnership for taxfarming, *societas vectigalium*, did not end with the death of one partner (unless he were the manager or held the contract with the State), and it might be agreed at the outset that the heir of a deceased partner was to become one: D.17.2.59pr (Pomponius, *12 ad Sab.*); 17.2.63.8 (Ulpian, *31 ad ed.*). This is possibly a survival of a once general rule: cf. infra, p. 144.

[3] Though, Plautus, *Rud.*, 549ff, suggests that at least for *societas omnium bonorum* equality of assets had special significance, legal or social: cf. Watson, *Obligations*, p. 143.

[4] Cf. e.g. G.3.150; D.17.2.29pr (Ulpian, *30 ad Sab.*).

[5] Assuming this to be possible.

[6] At least, this was the view of Quintus Mucius, disapproved of by Servius: G.3.149; J.3.25.2; D.17.2.30 (Paul, *6 ad Sab.*) cf. 17.2.29.1 : see now Watson, *Obligations*, pp. 137ff.

[7] This emerges from the fact that later condemnation in the *actio pro socio* automatically brought with it praetorian *infamia* (which could not at first be avoided by the defendant's appointing a representative). Hence *culpa* was not appropriate for liability when the praetorian edict *Qui nisi pro certis personis ne postulent* was issued, probably after 200 BC; cf. Watson, 'Some Cases of Distortion by the Past in Classical Roman Law', *T.v.R.*, xxxi (1963), pp. 69ff, at pp. 76ff : *Obligations*, pp. 144ff.

[8] For the *actio communi dividundo* cf. supra, pp. 72f.

[9] It seems most likely that praetorian *infamia* was based on censorian *infamia* : cf. e.g. Greenidge, *Infamia in Roman Law*, (Oxford, 1894), pp. 114ff.

The very bringing of the *actio pro socio* terminated the partnership automatically at *litis contestatio*,[1] as did renunciation by one partner even where the partnership was for a period which had not yet come to an end.[2] Whether, as in classical law, death of a partner ended the partnership,[3] or whether it continued in the person of the heir, is open to question, but the probability is that it continued.[4] But *capitis deminutio* even *minima* ended the contract,[5] and so presumably did compulsory sale of a partner's property on bankruptcy.[6]

Since the consensual contracts had no requirements of form, there was no formal *contrarius actus*. Performance of the contract would itself extinguish the obligation. When the parties agreed that the obligation should be wiped out without performance (by one party), it was presumably *mala fide* to raise the action.[7]

[1] Cf. D.17.2.63.10 (Ulpian, *31 ad ed.*); 17.2.65pr (Paul, *32 ad ed.*) (refer to a much later period).

[2] Cf. D.17.2.65.8 (refers to first century BC); Watson, *Obligations*, pp. 133f.

[3] Cf. e.g. G.3.152. In classical law it could not even be agreed that the heir of a partner should become a partner: D.17.2.35 (Ulpian, *30 ad Sab.*); 17.2.59pr (Pomponius, *12 ad Sab.*).

[4] Argued from Cicero, *pro Quinctio*, especially at 16.52; 24.76: Watson, *Obligations*, pp. 131ff.

[5] Cf. e.g. for classical law, G.3.153.

[6] Cf. e.g. for classical law, G.3.154.

[7] Of course, if the contract had from the start been a disguised gift the whole contract was void.

CHAPTER 13

Delicts

FURTUM (THEFT)

Roman law tended to leave within the scope of private actions a great deal of what would in modern law be considered most proper for criminal law. The clearest example of this is theft, and we know that the private *actio furti* goes back at least as far as the XII Tables.[1]

The original material element of *furtum* was asportation[2] but before the end of the Republic this had been changed to handling,[3] a wider approach which would mitigate the absence of any action for attempts. This changeover cannot be precisely dated but the balance of probability is in favour of its being after our period.[4] Whichever requirement applied there is no reason to think it was not strictly adhered to.[5]

Land could not be stolen[6] since there had to be asportation; and the taking of *res publicae* and *res sacrae* was not *furtum* but gave

---

[1] Cf. e.g. G.3.190, 191, 192; Aulus Gellius, *N.A.*, 11.18.8.

[2] The most obvious derivation of *furtum* is from *ferre*, 'to carry'; comparative law suggests a need for asportation [cf. e.g. Daube, CLJ, vi (1963), p. 222 n. 10] and since Sabinus uses the verb *adtrectare* [Aulus Gellius, *N.A.*, 11.18.20, 22, 23] *contrectatio* cannot yet have been the technical term and thus handling is unlikely to have been the standard for long.

[3] Appears from D.47.2.21pr (Ulpian, *40 ad Sab.*); for the argument see Watson, *Obligations*, pp. 220 and the works cited.

[4] Since Sabinus uses the verb, *adtrectare*: cf. supra, p. 145 n. 2.

[5] For the later Republic see above all Watson, *Obligations*, pp. 221ff and the references cited. The most important text is D.47.2.67(66).2 (Paul, *7 ad Plautium*).

[6] With the changeover to *contrectatio* some jurists (unsuccessfully) held that land could be stolen: D.41.3.38 (Gaius, *2 rer. cott.*); Aulus Gellius, *N.A.*, 11.18.13.

rise to actions for *peculatus*[1] and *sacrilegium*[2] respectively.[3] Further, *res hereditariae* could not be the object of theft.[4] But as well as things, persons who were subject to another, such as children *in potestate*, wives *in manu*, *iudicati* and *auctorati*, might be stolen.[5]

Furtum was wider than our modern theft since there need be no intention to deprive the owner permanently; temporary deprivation of the owner, or even use for an unauthorised purpose was enough for the action. Thus, Brutus (praetor in 142 BC) used to observe that a man was condemned for theft who had led an animal to a place other than where he had been given it to use, and so was one who had driven the animal further than he had asked permission for.[6] And it was *furtum* to make use of something given for safekeeping.[7] A text which concerns the first century BC tells us that it was theft even to accept a pledge knowing it did not belong to the borrower who had no right to pawn it.[8] In all these cases what was stolen was the thing taken or improperly used, a fact of some consequence since when the owner brought the *actio furti* the sum awarded was a multiple of the value of the stolen thing, not a multiple of the owner's interest. At the beginning of the Empire, the jurist Labeo described the Republican jurists' decisions on theft in this connection as *acria et severa*.[9]

---

[1] Cf. *Rhet. ad Herenn.*, 1.12.22; for the argument, Watson, *Obligations*, pp. 226f.

[2] Cf. Cicero, *de inven.*, 1.8.11; 2.18.55; for the argument, Watson, *loc. cit.*

[3] For *peculatus* and *sacrilegium* see above all, Mommsen, *Römisches Strafrecht* (reprinted, Graz, 1955), pp. 760ff.

[4] Cf. D.47.2.69 (Marcellus, *8 dig.*); 47.2.70 (Scaevola, *4 quaest.*); 47.2.72 (Javolenus, *15 ex Cassio*). The texts providing direct evidence all concern a much later period, but the rule is obviously early : cf. supra, pp. 63f. But a pledge-creditor, usufructuary or other such person still had his *actio furti* when the thing stolen was a *res hereditaria*, though this is likely to have been an innovation after our period.

[5] Cf. G.3.199. Though there is no early evidence the rule is obviously old. One might doubt whether *auctorati* occurred as early as this, though there were numerous free gladiators in the very late Republic : cf. e.g. Friedländer, *Darstellungen aus der Sittengeschichte Roms*, ii, 8th edit. (Leipzig, 1910), pp. 371f; Treggiari, *Roman Freedmen during the Late Republic* (Oxford, 1969), pp. 141f.   [6] Aulus Gellius, *N.A.*, 7.15.1.

[7] Cf. Aulus Gellius, *N.A.*, 7.15.2 (refers to Quintus Mucius); see also Valerius Maximus, 8.2.4; Symmachus, *Epist.*, 7.69.1; G.3.196.

[8] D.12.6.36 (Paul, *5 epit. Alfeni dig.*). This is not *furtum ope consilio* since the borrower's theft had been committed earlier.

[9] Aulus Gellius, *N.A.*, 7.15.1.

For theft to be committed there had to be a wrongful intention, and hence the wrongdoer had to have the mental capacity to form the intention. Thus, the XII Tables enacted that when an *impubes* was caught in an act of stealing he was to be flogged at the discretion of the praetor and the damage made good.[1] So, though the child was not regarded as free from fault, his behaviour was not treated as a simple case of *furtum manifestum*.[2] At some later (unknown) time it was questioned whether an *impubes* could commit *furtum* and the general opinion was that he could only do so if he were close to puberty and so understood that he was acting wrongly.[3] Theft necessarily involved an act done without the consent of the owner (or other person who had right to an *actio furti*),[4] but we cannot tell whether a defendant would be liable if he wrongly thought – with or without justification – that the owner, if asked, would have given his consent. The thief's *dolus*, though, had to be of a fairly specific kind and he had to envisage an advantage accruing to himself or another; the mere intention to deprive another of his property was never enough.[5]

Not only the owner but also certain persons with lesser rights

---

[1] Aulus Gellius, *N.A.*, 11.18.8. For the historical accuracy of the text see Watson, *Obligations*, pp. 224f.

[2] For which see infra, pp. 148f.

[3] G.3.208. There is, pace Watson, *loc. cit.*, no inherent contradiction between Aulus Gellius, *N.A.*, 11.18.8 and G.3.208. A natural historical evolution can be seen.

[4] *Invito domino* say the (later) texts : G.3.197; D.47.2.46.7 (Ulpian, *42 ad Sab.*).

[5] Pace, Thomas, '*Contrectatio*, Complicity and *furtum*', *Iura*, xiii (1962), pp. 70ff at p.87; '*Contrectatio* – my last word', *Iura*, xiv (1963), pp. 180ff at pp. 183f; Stein, *Roman Law and English Jurisprudence Yesterday and Today* (Inaugural lecture, Cambridge, 1969), p. 17 : contra, Watson, '*Contrectatio* again', SDHI, xxviii (1963) pp. 331ff at pp. 335f and 340f : cf. also *Obligations*, pp. 225f. Most recently Thomas regards the notion of *lucrum* as implicit in the *animus furandi* but *lucrum* for him signifies 'unwarranted appropriation, not simply in an economic sense' : '*Animus furandi*', *Iura*, xix (1968), pp. 1ff. There is no specific evidence for our period, though D.4.3.7.7 (Ulpian, *11 ad ed.*) may possibly be relevant for the views of Quintus Mucius : Watson's argument against Albanese's opinion [cf. most recently, *Obligations*, p. 226 n. 1] goes too far : see the language of D.17.2.65.8 (Paul, *32 ad ed.*). But contrast D.15.1.7.1 (Ulpian, *29 ad ed.*); and it is still doubtful whether *Quintus* means *Quintus Mucius*. Thomas thinks *Quintus* is a later jurist : '*Animus furandi*', p. 5. For gaps in the law's protection see infra, p. 160.

could bring the *actio furti*,[1] and these would probably include at least[2] the pledge-creditor,[3] the usufructuary[4] and the usuary,[5] but it seems that an *actio furti* available to an owner who then died did not transmit to his heir.[6]

The XII Tables drew a distinction between *furtum manifestum* and *furtum nec manifestum*, but did not define these terms, thus giving scope for discussion in later generations. Gaius, indeed, tells us of four opinions as to what constituted *furtum manifestum*; when it was detected during commission, or in the place of commission, or when the thief had not yet carried the stolen thing to the place he intended for it, or if the thief was seen at any time with the thing in his hands.[7] This last opinion was not accepted, says Gaius, and the third was apparently also not approved. But the wide last view was current in our time, if any reliance can be placed on Plautus' *Poenulus*.[8] The deceived brothel-keeper, Lycus, takes into his house the money and purse which he is later alleged to have stolen. He comes out again still holding the purse and its owner

---

[1] This emerges from D.47.2.77(76).1 (Pomponius, *38 ad Quintum Mucium*) which shows a dispute between Quintus Mucius and Servius as to whether a thief who had the thing stolen from him could himself bring the *actio furti*. That such an extreme case could be discussed shows that the principle that persons with a right less than ownership could sue was firmly established: cf. Watson, *Obligations*, p. 228.

[2] There is no textual evidence until much later for any of these persons.

[3] Cf. e.g. D.47.2.52.18 (Ulpian, *37 ad ed.*) (refers to first century AD): 47.2.12 (Ulpian, *29 ad Sab.*).

[4] Cf. e.g. D.47.2.46.1 (Ulpian, *42 ad Sab.*).

[5] Cf. D.47.2.46.3.

[6] This situation is the one more likely to be under discussion in Cicero, *ad fam.*, 7.22, and this opinion is probably the one obsolete in Cicero's time but held by Sextus Aelius, M'. Manilius and M. Brutus: cf. now Watson, *Obligations*, pp. 228f.

[7] G.3.184. The original meaning of *manifestus* would easily be forgotten; and it is still a matter of great controversy: cf. Kaser, *Das altrömische Ius* (Göttingen, 1949), pp. 213f. and the authors he cites; a remarkably implausible view is in Pugsley, '*Furtum* in the XII Tables', *Irish Jurist*, iv (1969), pp. 139ff.

[8] 711–85. With reserve, I would accept the accuracy of the representation of the law. The fun in an elaborate legal scene like this lies in the audience's perception that someone will be enmeshed in a trap. Hence the legal points should be in the mind of the audience in advance, and this can be so only if the playwright's representation of the law is reasonably accurate, or corresponds to a folk-image of the law. But for Plautus' ability to get his law wrong see *infra*, p. 149 n. 5.

claims he is a *manufesto fur*, presumably because he is caught with the supposedly stolen property in his hands.[1] *Furtum nec manifestum* was any theft which was not *manifestum*. The distinction was fundamental since the penalties were vastly different.

For manifest theft the XII Tables laid down capital penalties.[2] A free man was scourged and the magistrate made *addictio* of him to the victim. A slave was similarly scourged and then put to death. These punishments were eventually replaced by the praetor, in both cases with a four-fold penalty.[3] This changeover seems to have occurred in two stages; for free men sometime in the Republic[4] and quite possibly before our period, for slaves not until the Empire.[5] The penalty in an *actio furti nec manifesti* brought by the owner was always double the value of the thing stolen,[6] even when the owner's interest was less.[7] When a non-owner was allowed the *actio furti* the condemnation was in a multiple of his interest, not in a multiple of the thing's value.[8]

The XII Tables also gave other actions in connection with theft, which continued to exist in our period and later. The *actio furti concepti* lay for a three-fold penalty when a stolen thing was searched for and found on a man's premises in the presence of witnesses. Whether he was the thief or not was irrelevant for the action.[9] But in his turn, the person on whose property the stolen thing was found had the *actio furti oblati*, also for a three-fold

---

[1] Not because witnesses earlier saw the slave give Lycus the purse.

[2] G.3.189; cf. Aulus Gellius, *N.A.*, 11.18.8; 20.1.7, 8; G.4.111: cf. Daube, 'Some Comparative Law – *Furtum conceptum*', *T.v.R.*, xv (1937), pp. 48ff at p. 64 n. 2; *Studies in Biblical Law* (Cambridge, 1947), p. 241 and n. 126.

[3] G.3.189.

[4] Cf. Watson, *Obligations*, p. 231; 'Praetor's Edict'.

[5] Plautus, *Aul.*, 465–9; D.12.4.15 (Pomponius, *22 ad Sab.*): cf. Watson, *Obligations*, pp. 231ff. The *Aulularia* passage demonstrates the dangers of relying heavily on Plautine law since the cock is killed on the spot as a *fur manifestus* yet it was never permitted to kill at the time a thief caught in the act just because he was a *fur manifestus*.

[6] G.3.190; Aulus Gellius, 11.18.15; Plautus, *Poe.*, 1351; Cato, *de agri cult. praef.*, 1.

[7] Though possibly this penalty was reduced when a person other than the owner also had the right to an *actio furti*: cf. for a much later period, e.g. D.47.2.36.1 (Ulpian, *42 ad Sab.*). Perhaps, too, the owner could sue only when he had some interest: cf. for a much later period, e.g. D.47.2.46.4.

[8] Cf. e.g. for a much later period D.47.2.46.4.

[9] G.3.186, 191; Aulus Gellius, *N.A.*, 11.18.12.

L

penalty, against the person who had passed the goods off on him.[1] In the absence of an effective police force this seems a most practical arrangement. Usually the *paterfamilias* on whose premises stolen property was found would be the thief, or one of his family would be; and where this was not the case he would nonetheless often be in a better position than the victim to trace the thief. The XII Tables also provided for a ritual search, conducted by an almost naked priest wearing a fillet round his temples and having with him a bowl for sacrificial wine. If stolen property was found the theft was treated as *manifestum*.[2] This ritual search – at least in theory – continued in our time.[3, 4] It was presumably resorted to only if an informal search – finding during which would give rise to the *actio furti concepti* – was refused.[5]

The XII Tables also allowed a thief by night to be killed on the spot, but a thief by day only if he defended himself with a weapon and even then only if first a shout had been given. This rule survived without alteration into classical law and was accepted by Gaius[6] though it was restricted by the time of Ulpian.[7]

Complicity in theft, *furtum ope consilio*, was established as an

---

[1] G.3.187, 191; Aulus Gellius, *N.A.*, 11.18.12. The qualification in G.3.187 that the action lies *utique si ea mente data tibi fuerit, ut apud te, potius quam apud eum qui dederit, conciperetur*, is obviously later than the XII Tables [cf. Daube, 'Some Comparative Law', p. 70; *Biblical Law*, p. 269] and, I would hazard the guess, after our period.

[2] G.3.192, 193, 194; Aulus Gellius, *N.A.*, 11.18.9. This is to accept completely the opinion of J.G. Wolf on the hitherto mysterious search *lance et licio*: '*Lanx* und *licium*. Das Ritual der Haussuchung im altrömischen 'Recht' *Sympotica Franẓ Wieacker* (Göttingen, 1970), pp. 59ff. No oath was required from the person whose house was to be searched: Macrobius, *Sat.*, 1.6.60 has no Roman legal significance; cf. Daube, 'Some Comparative Law', pp. 53ff.

[3] This appears from Aulus Gellius, *N.A.*, 16.10.8 who tells us that the *lex Aebutia* (of about 140 BC?) 'put to sleep' the *quaestio 'lance et licio'*. But e.g. Wolf thinks it already obsolete: '*Lanx*', p. 61.

[4] The edictal *actio furti prohibiti* (G.3.192) will be later: Watson, 'Praetor's Edict.'

[5] Cf. Daube, 'Some Comparative Law', pp. 68ff; *Biblical Law*, pp. 259ff.

[6] Cicero, *pro Tullio*, 20.47, 48; 21.49, 50; *pro Milone*, 3.9; Aulus Gellius, *N.A.*, 11.18.7, 8; 20.1.7, 8; Seneca, *Controv. lib.*, 10, *excerpta controv.* 6; Macrobius, *Sat.* 1.4.19; D.9.2.4.1 (Gaius, *7 ad ed. prov.*); 47.2.55(54).2 (Gaius, *13 ad ed. prov.*).

[7] D.9.2.5pr (Ulpian, *18 ad ed.*); *Coll.* 7.3.2, 3; D.48.8.9 (Ulpian, *37 ad ed.*); cf. Watson, 'Two Studies in Textual History', *T.v.R.*, xxx (1962), pp. 209ff at pp. 218ff.

offence and we know the wording of the *legis actio* from Cicero :
'*ope consilioque tuo furtum aio factum esse.*'[1,2]

In addition to the *actio furti* the owner of the stolen property
could bring either the *vindicatio* or a *condictio*.[3] Condemnation in
the *acti furti* would bring censorian *infamia* upon the defendant.[4,5]

THE LEX AQUILIA[6]

This statute in its final form is a *plebiscitum* of 287 BC[7] but it had
passed through at least one earlier stage of development.[8] It had
three chapters.

[1] *de nat. deor.*, 3.30.74; cf. above all, Lenel, *Edictum*, pp. 324ff. especially
at p. 327. For a very different view of the significance of the text see the
references given by Thomas, '*Contrectatio* – my last Word', p. 182 n. 9. See
also for *furtum ope consilio* in the Republic; G.3.202 [cf. Watson, *Obligations*,
p. 222]; 50.16.53.2 (Paul, *59 ad ed.*) [cf. Watson, *Obligations*, p. 229 and
n. 7].
[2] Plautus, *Ru.*, 1021-9, 1259f, implies that it was theft to know of theft and
not report it. But it might be dangerous to draw conclusions from this.
[3] Cf. e.g. G.4.8 (refers to a much later period).
[4] Cf. supra, p. 143 n. 9.
[5] Later at least, when the praetorian *actio rerum amotarum* existed the
actio furti was excluded between spouses.
[6] The original scope of the *lex Aquilia*, especially of the third Chapter, has
recently been the subject of a radical article by Kelly, 'The Meaning of Lex
Aquilia', LQR, lxxx (1964), pp. 73ff [contra, Watson, *Obligations*, p. 246
n. 7 at pp. 246f] which in turn has given rise to the rather more extreme
views of Pugsley, '*Damni injuria*', *T.v.R.*, xxxvi (1968), pp. 371ff; 'The
Origins of the *Lex Aquilia*', LQR, lxxxv (1969), pp. 50ff. Essential to their
case is the rejection as original of the wording of the statute as it has come
down to us, and especially the rejection of '*si quis alteri damnum faxit*'. Hence
the fundamental significance for them of their argument that 'in Plautus the
phrase "to inflict loss" is always *damnum dare*; while *damnum facere*, which
occurs seven times, *invariably means exactly the opposite*, *viz.* to suffer a
loss' : Kelly, '*Meaning*', p. 79; cf. Pugsley, '*Damni injuria*', p. 372. The argument thus demands close attention [cf. already Watson, *Obligations*, p. 247].
Damnum facere literally means to make a loss, and one could expect it to be
used both with the meaning 'to inflict a loss' or 'to suffer a loss'. In the *lex
Aquilia* itself the presence of the word *alteri* means there is no possibility of
confusion and the provision unambiguously means 'if anyone will have
inflicted a loss on another'. In Plautus, the use of *damnum facere* (or rather,
quid damni facere)is not helpful to their case in the way that Kelly and
Pugsley assert. In six of the seven texts where the phrase occurs, its use is
plainly causative, 'to inflict loss on oneself'. Thus, *Asin.*, 182, *neque ille scit
quid det, quid damni faciat*; *Merc.*, 784, *non miror si quid damni facis aut
flagiti*; *Pseud.*, 440f, *nam tu quod damni et quod fecisti flagiti populo viritim*

Chapter 1 enacted that one who killed another's male or female slave or four-footed animal of the kinds which go in herds had to pay to the owner the highest value which the slave or animal had had in the previous year. Gaius gives the wording as[1]: '*Ut qui servum servamve alienum alienamve pecudem iniuria occiderit, quanti id in eo anno plurimi fuit, tantum aes dare domino damnas esto.*' And further on the statute provided that the action would be given for double the amount against a defendant who denied liability.[2] At this stage of the discussion it is enough to notice that this is the earliest Roman statute known to us which expressly lists male and female and it does not do so systematically (or it should have begun '*ut qui quaeve*'); that the use of *aes*[3] to denote money is consistent with a date before the introduction of coined money; that the occurrence of the noun *dominus* (also in Chapter 3) restricted the scope of the action (in contrast to the *actio furti*) in that only an owner could be the plaintiff; and that *pecudes* meant sheep, goats, cattle, horses, mules and asses.[4]

Chapter 2 gave an action against an *adstipulator* who received the money from the debtor, released him by *acceptilatio*, and then fraudulently failed to hand the money over to the principal creditor.[5] The action was for the creditor's interest and the condemnation was again doubled if the defendant denied liability.[6]

---

potuit dispertirier; cf. *Bacch.*, 1032; *Capt.*, 327; *Merc.*, 237. In the remaining instance, *Merc.*, 422, the phrase's use might be consequential, 'to suffer loss' but it is at least as likely to be causative. Thus in Plautus, as in the *lex Aquilia* the meaning (or, at least, primary meaning) of *damnum facere* is 'to inflict a loss'. Incidentally, *damnum dare* occurs in Plautus twice only: *Cist.*, 106; *Truc.*, 228.

[7] Theophilus, *Paraph.*, 4.3.15. There is no evidence to suggest any other date.

[8] The strange position of Chapter 3 after Chapter 2 can be explained only on the hypothesis that Chapter 3 is an addition: cf. Daube, 'On the Third Chapter of the *Lex Aquilia*', LQR, lii (1936), pp. 253ff at pp. 266ff.

[1] D.9.2.2pr (Gaius, *7 ad ed. prov.*).

[2] D.9.2.2.1; cf. 9.2.23.10 (Ulpian, *18 ad ed.*).

[3] And not in a specialised phrase such as *aes alienum*.

[4] Cf. D.9.2.2.2: later extended to pigs, elephants and camels, but not to dogs or wild beasts such as bears, lions or panthers.

[5] Cf. G.3.125. For this understanding of the Chapter see Levy-Bruhl, 'Le deuxième chapitre de la loi Aquilia', RIDA, v (1958), pp. 507ff. For *adstipulatio* see supra, pp. 121f.

[6] G.3.216. Chapter 2 became obsolete in classical law: cf. D.9.2.27.4 (Ulpian, *18 ad ed.*).

The original and later scope of Chapter 3 has been the subject of considerable controversy but by far the most satisfactory explanation of the early history is that of Daube.[1] He argues that to begin with the Chapter was concerned with the wounding of a slave or animal and that the measure of damages was the financial loss which became apparent within 30 days of the infliction of the injury. In the second half of the first century B C the action was extended to cover damage and destruction of inanimate things.[2] According to Ulpian,[3] this Chapter ran: '*Ceterarum rerum, praeter hominem et pecudem occisos, si quis alteri damnum faxit, quod usserit fregerit ruperit iniuria, quanti ea res erit in diebus triginta proximis, tantum aes domino dare damnas esto.*' But the first seven words are not original.[4] As in the other chapters, a defendant who denied liability was condemned *in duplum*.[5] Only with regard to living creatures can the distinction between *frangere* and *rumpere* ever have had any point, though in the *lex Aquilia* the words are not so precisely defined as in the XII Tables with its *os frangere* and *membrum rumpere*.[6] Injuries by burning would be common in a society which relied largely upon flaming torches for artificial lighting.[7]

Under both Chapter 1 and Chapter 3 the defendant was liable only if he had acted *iniuria*, that is, without right. Even much later there were traces of this conception, though as early as the first century B C the basis of liability was negligence or deliberate wrong-doing.[8]

[1] 'Third Chapter'; followed by Watson, *Obligations*, pp. 234f [contra, e.g. Kaser, *T.v.R.*, xxxiv (1966), p. 418]; and now Daube, *Roman Law*, pp. 66ff.
[2] Ulpian tells us '*Lex Aquilia omnibus legibus quae ante se de damno iniuria locutae sunt derogavit, sive duodecim tabulis sive alia quae fuit: quas leges nunc referre non est necesse*': D.9.2.1pr (*18 ad ed.*). Probably in our period some statutory provision, now lost to us, covered damage and destruction of inanimate things. [3] D.9.2.27.5 (*18 ad ed.*).
[4] Cf. e.g. Lawson, *Negligence in the Civil Law* (Oxford, 1950), p. 8, and the authorities he cites: Kelly, 'Meaning', p. 78; Pugsley, '*Damni injuria*', p. 372. For the radical attitude of the two last-mentioned scholars to the remainder of the wording, see supra, p. 151 n. 6. [5] Cf. G. 4.9; *P.S.*, 1.19.1; J.3.27.7.
[6] Cf. Daube, 'Third Chapter', pp. 255, 260. For *membrum ruptum* and *os fractum* see infra, p. 155.
[7] Torches would frequently be used as weapons of assault simply because at the decisive moment that was what the wrongdoer had in his hand: cf. bottles at football matches today.
[8] For *non iure* in the first century B C; D.19.2.30.2 (Alfenus, *3 dig. a Paulo epit.*); 9.2.39pr (Pomponius, *17 ad Quintum Mucium*) (Quintus Mucius):

The *actio legis Aquiliae* required *damnum*, financial loss,[1] caused by killing (*occidere*) for Chapter 1, by burning, snapping or breaking (*urere, frangere, rumpere*) for Chapter 3. *Occidere, urere, frangere* and *rumpere* were given their natural meaning.[2,3] Only much later was the interpretation artificially restricted and direct physical contact demanded between the person of the wrongdoer and the slave or animal killed or injured.[4] At this time there was, for instance, no distinction drawn between *occidere* and *mortis causam praestare*.[5]

When the injury was caused by more than one wrongdoer, the plaintiff could sue each of them in turn for the full amount[6]; but the *actio legis Aquiliae* did not cumulate with a reipersecutory action, say on a contract, and the plaintiff had to choose one of them.[7,8]

INIURIA

The XII Tables had three provisions for assault which later were brought within the scope of the so-called *edictum generale*. For

---

for *culpa*; 9.2.31 (Paul, *10 ad Sab.*) (Quintus Mucius); 9.2.29.4 (Ulpian, *18 ad ed.*) (Alfenus); 9.2.52.1, 2, 4 (Alfenus, *2 dig.*) : cf. Watson, *Obligations*, pp. 236ff.

[1] cf. Daube 'On the meaning of the Term *Damnum*', *Studi Solazzi* (Naples, 1948), pp. 93ff.

[2] Just as in the law of 217 BC on offering sacrifice to Jupiter, *si quis rumpet occidetve insciens, ne fraus esto* cannot be restricted to direct killing or injury, *corpori corpore*, of the sacrificial animal : Livy, 22.10.

[3] Around the middle of the second century BC Brutus gave the action, *quasi rupto*, if a slave woman or mare miscarried after being struck by a punch : D.9.2.27.22.

[4] Appears for Chapter 1 from D.9.2.52.2; for Chapter 3 from D.9.2.39pr; and see also D.9.2.11.4 (Ulpian, *18 ad ed.*); 9.2.29.4 (*idem*); 9.2.31 (Paul, *10 Sab.*) : cf. Watson, *Obligations*, pp. 242ff; 'D.7.1.13.2 (Ulpian, *18 ad Sab.*) : the *Lex Aquilia* and decretal actions', *Iura*, xvii (1966), pp. 174ff; 'Narrow, Rigid and Literal Interpretation in the Later Roman Republic', *T.v.R.*, xxxvii (1969), pp. 351ff at pp. 353ff.

[5] The distinction was verbalized only by Celsus (consul for the second time in AD 129) : D.9.2.7.6 (Ulpian, *18 ad ed.*), though it is in fact older : D.9.2.9 pr (*idem*) (refers to Labeo). In our period the praetor had not yet started to give decretal actions for cases not falling under the *lex*.

[6] Cf. e.g. D.9.2.11.4 (refers to the *veteres*); and for the Empire, e.g. D.9.2.11.2; 9.2.51 (Julian, *86 dig.*).

[7] Emerges most clearly from G.3.216 which shows that the action under Chapter 2 did not cumulate with the *actio mandati* : cf. Watson, *Obligations*, p. 246.   [8] For noxal liability under the statute see infra, p. 159.

membrum ruptum unless the parties reached a financial agreement there was *talio* i.e. the infliction of a similar injury.[1] For *os fractum* the compensation was 300 *asses* if the injured person was a free man, 150 if he were a slave.[2] On account of other assaults (*ceterae iniuriae*) the wrongdoer had to pay 25 *asses*.[3] The line of demarcation between the three provisions is not at all clear[4] but this became of little practical importance with the introduction in the last quarter of the third century BC, probably by the *praetor urbanus*, of an edict and an appropriate form of action. The edict was unusual since the praetor did not declare in it that he would give an action, but simply issued instructions on how to proceed. The approximate wording was : *Qui iniuriarum aget, certum dicat, quid iniuriae factum sit, et taxationem ponat non minorem, quam quanti vadimonium fuerit.*[5] This very wording of the edict makes it plain that the praetor was not altering the substantive law.

The form of action proposed in the Edict began '*Quod...Auli Agerii* (or *Aulo Agerio*) *pugno mala percussa est*'[6] and the condemnation was in the sum of money which seemed *bonum aequum* on account of the assault. The principal work of the praetor was therefore to introduce a flexible system of damages instead of the fixed penalties of the XII Tables – the pecuniary penalties of which

---

[1] The most likely wording is : '*Si membrum rupit, ni cum eo pacit, talio esto*' : cf. Aulus Gellius, *N.A.*, 20.1.14; Festus, *s.v. Talionis*; G.3.223; P.S. 5.4.6; J.4.4.7; Isidorus, *Orig.*, 5.27.24; Cato, *Orig.*, 4.

[2] Cf. *Coll.*, 2.5.5 (Paul, *sing. et tit. de iniuriis*)...*manu* fu*stive si os fregit libero, ccc, si servo, cl poenam subito* se*stertiorum*; G.3.223, 220; P.S. 5.4.6; Cato, *Orig.*, 4; Aulus Gellius, *N.A.*, 20.1.32.

[3] Cf. Aulus Gellius, *N.A.*, 20.1.12 : '*Si iniuriam alteri faxsit, viginti quinque aeris poenae sunto*' [some modern scholars consider that *alteri* was absent from the provision : cf. the authors cited by Simon, 'Begriff und Tatbestand der *Iniuria* im altrömischen Recht', z s s lxxxii (1965), pp. 132 ff at p. 134; he himself retains it]; G.3.223.

[4] Not surprisingly since they fell out of use before 200 BC.

[5] *Coll.*, 2.6.1 (Paul, *sing. sub tit. quemadmodum iniuriarum agatur*); D.47.10.7pr (Ulpian, *57 ad ed.*); Lenel, *Edictum*, pp. 397f; and, most recently, Birks, 'The Early History of *Iniuria*', *T.v.R.*, xxxvii (1969), pp. 163ff at pp. 195f. At some early date, perhaps rather later than this, an edict declared the action was to be heard by *recuperatores* : Aulus Gellius, *N.A.*, 20.1.13, 37; cf. Birks, '*Iniuria*', p. 196.

[6] *Coll.*, 2.6.4. It is this wording which enables us to date the edict before Plautus' *Asinaria*, 371. A *terminus post quem* is provided by Aulus Gellius, *N.A.*, 20.1.13 which demands a date after the reduction of the 10 ounce *as*. For the argument see Watson, 'Praetor's Edict'.

had become absurd as a result of the fall in the value of money[1]–
but this particular innovation would itself end the need to differ-
entiate the kind of assault. The pattern action, as can be seen, was
framed in terms of the minor assaults liable to a penalty of 25 *asses*
under the XII Tables, but serious assaults were not excluded from
the scope of the *edictum*.[2]

In keeping with the suggested scope of the edict the action was
originally given (as under the XII Tables) even where the injury
had not been caused deliberately.[3] Only later was it restricted to
intentional attacks on a man's personality. Likewise it was confined to cases of physical injury, though later juristic interpretation
extended it to cover cases where no blow had been struck.[4] Unlike
the *actio legis Aquiliae*, the *actio iniuriarum* lay primarily for injuries to free men and there was no need for the plaintiff to show
that he had suffered financial loss.

The XII Tables' provisions were not, of course, abolished by
the edict but they would cease to be used, and they, with *omnis illa
duodecim tabularum antiquitas*, were, as Aulus Gellius says,[5] put to
sleep' by the later *lex Aebutia*.[6]

---

[1] Cf. Aulus Gellius, *N.A.*, 20.1.13.
[2] Daube argued that originally only minor assaults were envisaged:
'*Nocere* and *noxa*', CLJ, vii (1939–41), pp. 23ff at pp. 45ff; but see already
Watson, *Obligations*, pp. 248ff (where Daube's view is accepted with hesitation); and now Birks, '*Iniuria*', pp. 202ff. I cannot, however, accept Birks'
opinion (especially at pp. 188ff) as to the original scope of the provisions of
the XII Tables. It seems to me that dissatisfaction with the inability of the
surviving accounts to give a full explanation of the law of the XII Tables has
led him to propose a solution which is supported by none of the sources and
is flatly contradictory to them. It is not surprising that the accounts of Gaius
and Aulus Gellius are not wholly satisfactory since they are writing three
centuries after the XII Tables' provisions became obsolete; but it would be
very strange if they had so completely misunderstood the role of the 25
asses penalty for *iniuriae*. Moreover, the story of Lucius Veratius (Aulus
Gellius, *N.A.*, 20.1.13), whether historically based or not, is very old, as the
use of the word *crumena* with its meaning of 'purse' shows: cf. Watson,
'Praetor's Edict'. But Birks' view demands that the story be invented after
knowledge of the *iniuriae* covered by the 25 *asses* penalty had been lost: cf.
'*Iniuria*', pp. 174ff.
[3] Cf. Birks, '*Iniuria*', p. 203.
[4] For the history of *iniuria* in the later Republic, including the various
edictal provisions, see Watson, *Obligations*, pp. 248ff; 'Praetor's Edict'.
[5] *N.A.*, 16.10.8.
[6] Which dates from sometime in the second century BC: cf. e.g. Kaser,
ZPR, p. 114, and n. 59.

Whether one should consider as falling within private law the XII Tables' clause which punished capitally the singing of defamatory verses is doubtful. That this wrong has to be linked with the later *convicium*,[1] a form of *iniuria*,[2] is clear, but the penalty is so severe that it seems rather to have been regarded as a public offence.[3]

OTHER DELICTS

The XII Tables gave an *actio ex causa depositi* for double damages. This action has at times been thought to be the *actio fiduciae*, or an action for *depositum miserabile* or nothing other than the *actio furti nec manifesti*. But the implausibility of all these views has been shown,[4] and it seems most likely that the XII Tables did establish a specific penal action for deposit, just as it did in the case of the *actio rationibus distrahendis* and the *actio auctoritatis*. This action was not necessarily based on any conception of contract. It can be reasonably presumed that it remained in use until the introduction of the edictal *actio depositi* some considerable time after our period.[5]

When material belonging to another was incorporated into a house or used for supporting vines, the XII Tables did not allow it to be removed, but gave an *actio de tigno iniuncto* for double damages.[6] Whether or not in our period it had to be proved that the material was stolen cannot be determined, but if not the underlying assumption was still that the user was in bad faith.[7] The *actio de*

---

[1] Cf. Cicero, *de re pub.*, 4.10.12 in Augustine, *de Civ. Dei*, 2.9; Cicero, *Tusc. disp.*, 4.2.4; Festus, *s.v. Occentassit*; *P.S.*, 5.4.6; Arnobius, *adv. Gentes*, 4.3.4. The provision should be kept separate from another which spoke of *malum carmen incantare* and concerns witchcraft: cf. in general the references given in FIRA, i, pp. 52f.

[2] The *edictum de convicio* was in existence by the second decade of the first century BC: cf. Watson, 'Praetor's Edict'.

[3] See most recently for the history of *iniuria* in general, von Lübtow, 'Zum römischen Injurienrecht', *Labeo*, xv (1969), pp. 131ff; Raber, *Grundlagen Klassischer Injurienansprüche* (Vienna, Cologne, Graz, 1969).

[4] Cf. e.g. Rotondi, now in *Scritti giuridici*, ii (Milan, 1922), pp. 14f and 16f; Kaser, *Ius*, p. 219 n. 39 and the authors he cites. Recently, Burillo, 'Las formulas de la *actio depositi*', SDHI, xxviii (1962), pp. 233ff at p. 240 has reverted, with hesitation, to the view that the action was the *actio furti nec manifesti*.

[5] Cf. Watson, 'Praetor's Edict'.

[6] Cf. Festus, *s.v. Tignus*; D.47.3.1 (Ulpian, *37 ad ed.*); 6.1.23.6 (Paul, *21 ad ed.*).

[7] Hence the double damages.

tigno inuncto, though no doubt subject to change, was still in existence in the law of Justinian.[1]

The XII Tables also gave an *actio de arboribus succisis* for the wrongful cutting down of another's trees and the penalty was fixed at 25 *asses* for each tree.[2] Eventually, but probably after this period,[3] the praetor gave an *actio arborum furtim caesarum* – with a wider scope and a condemnation in double the plaintiff's interest – which nonetheless was treated as a continuation of the XII Tables' remedy.[4] We know that for this action most Republican jurists interpreted tree as including vines,[5] though in the *legis actio* the plaintiff had naturally to base his ground of action on the statute and claim that his trees – not his vines – had been cut down.[6]

There was also, under the XII Tables, an action for a double penalty against one who dedicated to the gods something whose legal title was disputed[7]; and an action against someone who burnt a house or a heap of grain placed beside a house.[8] In this latter case if the burning was deliberate, the wrongdoer was *vinctus verberatus igni necari*; otherwise he had to pay for the damage caused, or, if he were insolvent, to suffer a lesser beating.

Finally here the XII Tables gave an *actio de pastu* against a person who sent in his animals to feed on the acorns on another's land.[9, 10]

---

[1] Cf. in general, Melillo, *Tignum iunctum* (Naples, 1964); Quadrato, '*Tignum iunctum ne solvito*', *Annali Bari, xxii* (1967), pp. 1ff.

[2] Pliny the Elder, *Hist. nat.*, 17.1.7.

[3] Arguments are (i) the praetorian action did innovate and this is a characteristic of the Edict only at a much later stage; cf. Watson 'Praetor's Edict' : (ii) the 25 *asses* penalty would lose its usefulness with the fall in the value of money, but 25 asses would remain adequate here longer than in the case of *iniuria* where the change to a flexible system of damages dates only from the last quarter of the third century BC.

[4] Cf. e.g. Lenel, *Edictum*, pp. 337; Watson, *Obligations*, pp. 271f.

[5] G.4.11; D.44.7.3pr (Ulpian, *42 ad Sab.*).

[6] G.4.11. Daube's explanation of this text is completely convincing : 'Texts and Interpretation in Roman and Jewish Law', *Jewish Journal of Sociology*, iii (1961), pp. 3ff at pp. 4f.

[7] Still in existence in classical law : D.44.6.3 (Gaius, *6 ad leg. XII Tab.*).

[8] Still available in classical law : appears from D.47.9.9 (Gaius, *4 ad leg. XII Tab.*).

[9] Still possible in classical law : D.19.5.14.3 (Ulpian, *41 ad Sab.*); cf. 10.4.9.1 (Ulpian, *24 ad Sab.*); 50.16.236.1 (Gaius, *4 ad leg. XII Tab.*).

[10] The quasi-delict of a *iudex qui litem suam fecerit* seems to have existed from the beginning of the first century BC : Macrobius, *Sat.*, 3.16.14-16. There is no reason to link this with early criminal penalties against corrupt judges.

NOXAL SURRENDER

When a *filiusfamilias* or a slave committed a delict, the action brought against the *pater* or *dominus* gave him the choice of either paying the amount of the condemnation or of surrendering the wrongdoer to the victim. This was expressly provided for *furtum* by the XII Tables and for *damnum iniuria datum* by the *lex Aquilia*.[1] The provision of the XII Tables,[2] in so far as it has come down to us, read : *Si servus furtum faxit noxiamve no[x]it*. The last two words, whatever their original meaning may have been, were interpreted as giving the right to noxal surrender in all other delicts.[3,4]

The person liable to be sued for a slave's (or *filius'*) wrongdoing was the person who had control of the slave at the time the action was begun even though he had no connection with the slave at the time of the delict.[5]

ACTIO DE PAUPERIE

When a four-footed animal did damage an action was available under a provision of the XII Tables[6] against the animal's owner for the amount of the injury or the surrender of the animal. The relevant clause, it would seem, said nothing about the circumstances of the injury and we know that in the first century BC there was considerable discussion as to the scope of the action. Some degree of 'fault' in the animal seems to have been essential.[7]

---

[1] G.4.76; for the argument see Watson, *Obligations*, pp. 274ff.

[2] XII.2a; D.9.4.2.1 (Ulpian, *18 ad ed.*).

[3] There is no specific evidence for *iniuria* by a slave before the introduction of the edict *de noxali iniuriarum actione* under which the master had the power of handing over the slave to be thrashed : cf. Lenel, *Edictum*, pp. 401f; Daube, '*Nocere*', pp. 48ff.

[4] In classical law the XII Tables' provision was interpreted as meaning that the *dominus* could surrender the slave even if he had allowed the slave to commit the theft when he could have prevented him : but under the *lex Aquilia* the master had this right only if he had been *insciens* : cf. D.9.4.2.1. There is no evidence for our time.

[5] Hence in the sale of a slave the seller guaranteed he was free from noxal liability : cf. supra, p. 136. And see D.6.1 58 (Paul, *3 epit. Alfeni dig.*); D.2.9.1.1 (Ulpian, *7 ad ed.*) (refer to the first century BC); cf. Watson, *Obligations*, pp. 278f.

[6] It seems likely that originally the provision applied only to serious injury to slaves and *pecudes* (and, just possibly, to land) : cf. Watson, 'The original meaning of *pauperies*', to appear in RIDA, xvii (1970).

[7] Cf. D.9.1.1.4, 7 (Ulpian, *18 ad ed.*); 9.1.1.11 (*idem*); 9.2.52.2, 3 (Alfenus, *2 dig.*); Watson, *Obligations*, pp. 280ff (on p. 282 footnotes 1 and 2 should be

A critical modern observer will readily spot gaps in the law of delict around 200 B C. Thus, for instance, no remedy for throwing a man's silver cup into water where it is lost to the owner, but itself suffers no deterioration; none for corrupting the morals of a slave; none for intimidation. The solution is not to extend the scope of the existing actions beyond their natural bounds, but to accept that such gaps are typical of early law. This is clearly seen for instance in the universally acknowledged fact that before the *edictum de dolo* in the first century B C, a person who was fraudulently induced to make a *stipulatio* had no defence to an action brought on the stipulation by the person cheating him.

---

transposed). The aedilician *edictum de feris* is likely to be old but there is no indication as to whether it goes back to our period or not. For it see e.g. Lenel, *Edictum*, pp. 566f.

CHAPTER 14

Actions

This book is concerned with private law and it is not intended to give here more than a mere outline of the forms of action, since a detailed treatment would need a volume of its own.[1] Nor do I want to discuss the effectiveness of Roman justice. Kelly has recently called attention to the fact that the plaintiff's summoning of a defendant to court lacked any satisfactory legal sanction (and social sanctions had restricted value) and that a powerful figure might well resist; and that improper influences, such as bribery and favour, were often used to the advantage of the stronger party.[2]

Two forms of process were in use around 200 BC, the old *legis actiones* and the more recent *formulae*. Some scholars hold that *formulae* were an invention of the peregrine praetor and that before the *lex Aebutia*[3] (of uncertain age but usually thought to date from between 150 and 120 BC), they could not be used in cases where both parties were Roman citizens.[4] Hence, on this view, the consensual contracts which were always based upon *formulae* would in our time be actionable only if at least one of the contracting parties was a peregrine. Still other scholars accept that *formulae* were in use in praetorian actions such as the *bonae fidei*

---

[1] So very much of what we know about early procedure comes from a single source, Gaius' *Institutes*, that it may be felt that even a short account is largely superfluous.

[2] *Roman Litigation* (Oxford, 1966), pp. 1ff : and see the reviews by Kaser, zss, lxxxiv (1967), pp. 510ff; Luzzatto, sdhi, xxxii (1966), pp. 377ff; Crifò, *Latomus*, xxv (1966), pp. 624ff.

[3] The sole sources of our knowledge of the *lex Aebutia* are G.4.30 and Aulus Gellius, *N.A.*, 16.10.8.

[4] E.g. Arangio-Ruiz, *Istituzioni di diritto romano*, 14th edit. (Naples, 1968), pp. 121ff.

iudicia even between citizens, but think that only later were *formulae* allowed in civil law cases.[1] The *lex Aebutia*, suggests Kaser, sanctioned the first intrusion of the formulary procedure into the domain of the *legis actio*, but it was of limited scope and was restricted to allowing the new procedure for *condictio*.[2] But not only would it appear that the *bonae fidei iudicia* were available to citizens before 200 B C, there is also strong evidence in Plautus' *Rudens* that a *formula* was given for a *condictio*.[3] And if in this part of the *ius civile* the formulary system had already made a significant encroachment, the possibility can be by no means excluded that *formulae* were used, side by side with *legis actiones*,[4] in other areas of the *ius civile* for which evidence is lacking.

Both forms of process were in two parts, the first in front of the magistrate usually the praetor (*in iure*), the second in front of the judge selected by the parties (*apud iudicem*). But in other respects the actions were very different. Thus, the form of words typical of the *legis actiones* was spoken by the parties in front of the magistrate, whereas the *formula* was given by the magistrate to regulate the *apud iudicem* stage.

Gaius tells us that there were five forms of *legis actio*; *sacramento, per iudicis postulationem, per condictionem, per manus iniectionem, per pignoris capionem*.[5]

The *legis actio sacramento* was of general application and could be used in all cases where no other procedure had been laid down by statute.[6] Each party challenged the other in an oath for 500 *asses* if the case involved 1,000 *asses* or more, for 50 *asses* in a lesser case, and the action proceeded before the *iudex* on the question of whose *sacramentum* was *iustum*. The party who lost forfeited the amount of the *sacramentum* to the public treasury.[7] The action could be brought either *in rem* or *in personam*, and we have

[1] Cf. e.g. Kaser, Z P R, pp. 109ff.
[2] See now, Z P R, pp. 114f.
[3] Cf. supra, p. 127 and n. 3.
[4] Just as in the time of Cicero both the *legis actio sacramento in rem* and the formulary *vindicatio* were in use : cf. *pro Murena*, 12.26; *in Verrem*, 11, 2.12.31; Watson, *Property*, pp. 96f.
[5] G.4.12.
[6] G.4.13. See in general on the action, Kaser, Z P R, pp. 6off and the references he gives.
[7] G.4.13.

already discussed the form of the action *in rem*.[1] In the *actio in personam*, the plaintiff stated his claim, specifying the reason for it, for instance, *Ope consilioque tuo furtum aio factum esse* (or *aio te ex testamento decem milia mihi dare oportere*). *id postulo aias an neges*.[2] The defendant denied the claim and the plaintiff continued, *quando negas, te sacramento quingenario provoco*, and the defendant replied, *et ego te*.[3]

The *legis actio per iudicis postulationem* could be used only where a statute had authorized this procedure, the XII Tables for a claim on a stipulation and for the division of an inheritance, the *lex Licinnia* for the *actio communi dividundo*.[4] The plaintiff declared : *Ex sponsione te mihi decem milia sestertiorum dare oportere aio. id postulo aias an neges*. The defendant denied the debt and the plaintiff said, *quando tu negas, te praetor iudicem sive arbitrum postulo uti des*.[5]

The *legis actio per condictionem* has already been discussed.[6]

The basic instance of *legis actio per manus iniectionem* was not an action but execution for an unpaid judgement debt,[7] as prescribed by the XII Tables. The successful plaintiff declared : *Quod tu mihi iudicatus* (or *damnatus*) *es sestertium decem milia quandoc non solvisti, ob eam rem ego tibi sestertium decem milium iudicati manum inicio*; and he seized some part of the debtor's body. The debtor was not permitted to release himself and conduct the *legis actio*, but gave a *vindex* who acted for him. A debtor who did not give a *vindex* was led to the creditor's house and put in chains.[8] Subsequent statutes gave *manus iniectio* as if there had been a judgement though there was no prior action; thus, the *lex Publilia* gave it against a person who had not repaid his *sponsor* within 6 months,[9] and the *lex Furia de sponsu* against a creditor who exacted from a *sponsor* more than his rateable share of the debt.[10, 11] The *lex Furia*

---

[1] Supra, pp. 69ff. [2] This appears from G.4.17a, 17b.
[3] See in general, Kaser, ZPR, pp. 64ff and the references he gives.
[4] G.4.17a.
[5] See in general, Kaser, ZPR, pp. 78ff and the references he gives.
[6] Supra, p. 127.
[7] For the procedure *apud iudicem* see in general Kaser, ZPR, pp. 82ff.
[8] G.4.21.
[9] Cf. supra, p. 120.
[10] Cf. supra, pp. 120f.
[11] G.4.22.

testamentaria which probably falls within our period,[1] gave it against a person who took by legacy or *mortis causa* more than 1,000 *asses* (when he was not privileged by the statute to take more) but this time the procedure was in the form known as *pura*, that is, not as if for a judgement debt.[2] In this form the defendant could conduct the *legis actio* on his own behalf.[3]

The *legis actio per pignoris capionem* was a way to distrain for certain debts without going though a court action. It had no application in the field of private law unless it could be used on account of *damnum infectum*.[4] Whether it was a *legis actio* was itself a matter of dispute since the seizure did not occur before the praetor, the presence of the other party was not required, and it could be used on a *dies nefastus* when *legis actiones* were not permitted. But on the other hand the levy of distress was accompanied by a set form of words.[5]

The forms of the *legis actiones* had to be rigidly observed, and any modification of the wording by a party would cost him the case.[6] This inevitably made the law less responsive to social change and the needs of the community,[7] and could cause the desire for a more flexible system.

The new *formulae* did provide this more flexible system, since each *formula* was designed for one particular institution such as *tutela* or *societas*.[8] But this system, too, had its limitations. Thus, to give rise to an action, a situation must fall within the scope of the *formula* prescribed by the praetor; for instance if someone in good

---

[1] Cf. supra, p. 115.

[2] G.4.23, 24. Gaius says, however, that he is not unaware that in the claim under this statute the phrase, *pro iudicato*, is inserted: cf. Watson, *Succession*, pp. 166f. The *legis actio* was for fourfold the amount above 1,000 *asses* which was taken.

[3] See in general on *manus iniectio*, Kaser, ZPR, pp. 94ff.

[4] Cf. supra, p. 76 n. 5.

[5] For *pignoris capio* see G.4.26-9; cf. Kaser, ZPR, pp. 104ff.

[6] G.4.30. There is no evidence for the common view that a slip of the tongue lost a party his case: cf. Daube, 'Texts and Interpretations in Roman and Jewish Law', *Jewish Journal of Sociology*, iii (1961), pp. 3ff at pp. 4f. For the correct interpretation of G.4.11 see Daube, *loc. cit.*

[7] But for the wide scope for interpretation during the period of the *legis actiones* see Daube, 'Texts'.

[8] The *formula* for the *actio tutelae* is given, supra, p. 39; for the *actio aquae pluviae arcendae*, supra, p. 77 n. 6; for the *actio fiduciae*, supra, p. 87; for *condictiones*, supra p. 127; for the *actio pro socio*, supra, pp. 141f.

faith bought a free man who was declared by the seller to be a slave and then the purchaser tried to bring the *actio ex empto* he would lose his case because there was no valid contract of sale. Again, if a plaintiff, no matter how innocently, overclaimed in the *intentio*,[1] he failed in the case and lost his entire right.[2]

Only a Roman citizen could be a party to a *legis actio*,[3] and he had to be *sui iuris*.[4] Women and *impuberes* who were *sui iuris* were competent parties but required *auctoritas tutoris*.[5] *Infantes* were represented by their *tutor*, *furiosi* by their *curator*.[6] Slaves could neither sue nor be sued in a *legis actio* or in an action *per formulam*.

Peregrines could be parties to a formulary action.[7] *Impuberes sui iuris* were competent parties but required *auctoritas tutoris*; so were women, but they needed the authority of their *tutor* only in a *iudicium legitimum*.[8, 9] The *tutor* acted for *infantes*,[10] *curator* for *furiosi*.[11] A *filiusfamilias* could be sued personally, probably only in non-delictal actions[12]; but at this time had no right to sue.[13] When

---

[1] The *intentio* was that part of the *formula* in which the plaintiff set out what he claimed; e.g. *si paret Numerium Negidium Aulo Agerio sestertium decem milia oportere* or *si paret hominem ex iure quiritium Ai Ai esse*. For the *partes formularum* see G.4.39-44; and 4.34-8; 4.115-37. [2] G.4.53-53d.
[3] If there ever was an exception in actions *de repetundis* [cf. Kaser, ZPR, p. 45 for the problem] it arose only later, and so would the exception in respect of cases before the centumviral court; cf. Kaser, *loc. cit.*
[4] But it is perhaps worth mentioning that a *filiusfamilias* could be the defendant in an action *per formulam*, and the only text which suggests even in a general way that a *filius* could not be sued in a *legis actio* is *Schol. Sin.*, 49 which firstly is late and not necessarily of strong authority, and secondly has to be reconstructed to give that sense. But the reconstruction is probably reasonable. [5] *Epit. Ulp.*, 11.24, 27.
[6] D.13.1.2 (Pomponius, *16 ad Sab.*). [7] Cf. G.4.105, 109.
[8] *Epit. Ulp.*, 11.24, 27. It is not clear but it may be that even an *impubes* needed *auctoritas tutoris* only in a *iudicium legitimum*.
[9] A *iudicium legitimum* is a formulary action heard at Rome or within the first milestone, before a single judge, and between parties who are Roman citizens. [10] G.4.82, 99. [11] D.13.1.2.
[12] D.5.1.57 (Ulpian, *41 ad Sab.*); 9.4.33 (Pomponius, *14 (19?) ad Sab.*); 9.4.34 (Julian, *4 ad Urseium Ferocem*); D.44.7.39 (Gaius, *3 ad ed. prov.*). The extent to which actions were given against *filii* is much disputed even for classical law : cf. the references given by Kaser, ZPR, p. 149 n. 19.
[13] Before the end of the Republic an edict gave him a right of action *causa cognita* for an *iniuria* to him when the *paterfamilias* was away and there was no *procurator* to act for the *pater* : cf. Lenel, *Edictum*, pp. 402ff. The provisions of this edict seem to be misstated by Kaser, ZPR, p. 148.

M

her *paterfamilias* brought the *actio rei uxoriae* for the return of dowry which he had given, the *filiafamilias* had to be joined to the action as co-plaintiff,[1] but she was not a competent party in any other action.[2]

In procedure both by *legis actio* and *formula* the parties could have an advocate or orator to plead the case for them. But representation in the Roman sense, that is a person (*cognitor*) who took the actual place of the party he was representing, and who was absolved or condemned, or was given or became liable to the *actio iudicati*, was generally permitted only under the formulary system. Justinian tells us that in the older procedure representation was allowed only *pro populo*, *pro libertate*, *pro tutela* and under the *lex Hostilia* in the *actio furti* on account of a person who was a captive, or absent on State business, or a pupil of such a person.[3]

The development of *interdicta*[4] was in its infancy. These were orders of a magistrate issued on application by a party, and they gave rise to further proceedings if they were disobeyed.

[1] Cf. e.g. D.24.3.66.2 (Javolenus, *6 ex post. Labeonis*).

[2] For the *exceptio legis Laetoriae* see supra, p. 127 n. 3.

[3] J.4.10pr. Generally on representation see Kaser, ZPR, pp. 46f and pp. 152ff. For other questions on procedure the reader is referred in the first instance to the relevant section of Kaser, ZPR.

[4] Cf. G.4.138ff.

Index of Texts

1. Legal Sources

N

2. NON-LEGAL SOURCES

Index of Persons and Subjects